Ecology of the Planted Aquarium

A Practical Manual and Scientific Treatise for the Home Aquarist

by

Diana L Walstad

Echinodorus Publishing, Chapel Hill, North Carolina (U.S.A.)

Ecology of the Planted Aquarium

A Practical Manual and Scientific Treatise for the Home Aquarist

by Diana L. Walstad

Published by:

Echinodorus Publishing
2303 Mt Sinai Rd.
Chapel Hill, NC 27514

Library of Congress Catalog Number 99-72828
Ecology of Aquarium Plants: a practical manual and scientific treatise for the home aquarist / by Diana L. Walstad

Includes table of contents, bibliographical references, and subject index
ISBN 0-9673773-0-7

1. Aquariums (about)
2. Aquariums- handbooks, manuals, etc
3. Aquarium plants
4. Aquatic plants
5. Ecology (in aquariums)

Printed in the United States of America

This book is dedicated to my parents Paul and Marjorie Walstad

Acknowledgements

Below is a list of scientists and professors who have helped me. They have taken the time from their busy schedules to review and comment on parts of the manuscript. Their ideas, comments, and critique have molded and reshaped many of my theories and helped keep the book 'on track'.

- Dave Huebert, Department of Botany, University of Manitoba (Canada)
- Elisabeth Gross, Limnology Institute, University Konstanz (Germany)
- Laura Serrano, Department of Ecology, University of Sevilla (Spain)
- Giovanni Aliotta, Dipartimento di Biologia Vegetale, Universita Degli Studi di Napoli Federico II (Naples, Italy)
- Wolfram Ullrich, Institute of Botany, Technische Hochschule Darmstadt (Germany)
- Dan Weber, NIEHS Marine and Freshwater Biomedical Core Center, University of Wisconsin (Milwaukee)
- David Spencer, Plant Biology Section, Aquatic Weed Control Research Laboratory, University of California (Davis)
- George Bowes, Department of Botany, University of Florida (Gainesville)
- Anthony Paradiso, Cystic Fibrosis Center, University of North Carolina (Chapel Hill)
- Claude E. Boyd, Department of Fisheries and Allied Aquacultures, Auburn University (AL)

I reserve my greatest thanks to Neil Frank and Robert Wetzel, both of whom reviewed the entire manuscript. Neil Frank, editor for the Aquatic Gardeners Association (AGA), reviewed the manuscript not once, but twice. His extensive and insightful comments have greatly contributed to improving the book.

Also, during my 5-year tenure as Technical Advisor for the AGA, I accumulated many Questions and Answers (Q&As). I have included many of those Q&As in this book and would like to thank the AGA members for their permission to use them. The AGA, a non-commercial organization of enthusiastic aquatic gardeners and aquarium hobbyists, has been a continuous source of ideas and inspiration.

To Robert G. Wetzel, Biology Professor and the leading authority on freshwater ecology, I owe special thanks. First, his comprehensive reference work (*Limnology*) provided a solid scientific framework for critical portions of *Ecology of the Planted Aquarium*. Second, his enthusiastic review of that first manuscript draft and subsequent encouragement since then has helped me believe that this book was worth the trouble.

TABLE OF CONTENTS

Chapter I.

INTRODUCTION

Ecology of the Planted Aquarium should appeal to hobbyists who wish to set up a successful planted aquarium plus understand more about its ecology.

Most aquarium plant books simply list/describe plant species or show how to set up a planted aquarium. This book is unique. For it explains the underlying mechanisms of the aquarium ecosystem– how plants affect the ecosystem and how the ecosystem affects the plants. It shows that plants are not just decorative but can also be quite useful in keeping fish healthy and reducing aquarium maintenance.

In addition, my book presents extensive scientific information that hobbyists have never seen. This information often contradicts prevailing ideas in the aquarium hobby– ideas that are often based on antiquated books and hobbyist observations rather than experimental data.

Aquatic plants studied include those from ponds, lakes, wetlands, and oceans. Many of the plants, such as *Vallisneria*, Hornwort, and *Cabomba*, are familiar to aquarium hobbyists. Others such as pondweeds and marine seagrasses may not be. However, aquatic plants, whether from the ocean or a tropical stream, have many of the same basic needs and physiology. Thus, concepts drawn from scientific studies of 'aquatic plants' can often be applied to 'aquarium plants'. In my opinion, any distinction between the two is obscured by the great diversity of species used by both aquarium hobbyists and aquatic botanists.

Although the book is directed toward aquarium keeping, many of the concepts apply equally to ornamental pond keeping. On occasion, I have noted where there might be differences.

In order to make the scientific studies more relevant to hobbyists, I have interspersed the text with typical or actual 'Questions and Answers' (Q & A). These Q & A, plus practical discussions at the end of chapters, show how the scientific information applies to hobbyists' aquariums. The last chapter describes how to keep aquariums that are inexpensive and simple to maintain.

The chapters of this book are grouped around the three goals of the book, which are to discuss: (1) how plants affect the aquarium ecosystems; (2) what factors affect plants; and (3) how the hobbyists can use this information to maintain a successful home aquarium.

A.   Chapters of the Book

1.   Introduction

The introduction briefly describes the purpose and organization of the book and the characteristics of a 'healthy' aquarium.

2.   Plants as Water Purifiers

In Chapter II the toxicity of water contaminants— heavy metals, ammonia, and nitrite— to fish and plants are discussed. I show how plants counteract those toxins to purify the water and protect fish.

3.   Allelopathy

Allelopathy, defined as chemical interactions between organisms, is most likely rampant in home aquariums. I present scientific evidence for allelopathic interactions between aquatic plants, algae, bacteria, invertebrates, and fish. I list specific chemicals isolated from a variety of aquatic plants and then list the organisms these chemicals have been shown to inhibit. Finally, I speculate on how allelopathy affects aquarium keeping.

4.   Bacteria

In Chapter IV, I classify different bacterial processes in terms of their positive and negative impacts on the aquarium. Topics include the generation of plant nutrients, CO_2, and humic substances by heterotrophic bacteria. In addition, I explain how bacterial processes both create and destroy aquarium toxins.

5.   Sources of Plant Nutrients

Chapter V compares three potential sources of plant nutrients in aquariums— fishfood, a soil substrate, and tapwater. I use a model aquarium to quantify the theoretical contribution from each source. I show that fishfood contains all elements that plants require and that soil abundantly supplies most micronutrients. I compare hardwater versus softwater as a nutrient source. In the final analysis, I discuss which of the three sources best provides each nutrient.

6.   Carbon

Carbon is briefly described in terms of alkalinity and water buffering, and then more thoroughly as a plant nutrient. I show that the element carbon often limits the growth of submerged plants both in nature and in aquariums. I describe strategies that aquatic plants use to obtain carbon. Finally, I show how hobbyists can help provide their aquarium plants with more CO_2.

7.   Plant Nutrition and Ecology

Chapter VII describes the fundamentals of aquatic plant nutrition. Thus, the required elements and their chemical (nutrient) form are listed, along with each element's function. Substrate versus water uptake of nutrients is discussed. I show that aquatic plants prefer ammonium over nitrates as their nitrogen source and why this makes biological filtration less critical in aquariums with plants. I discuss how the water chemistry of a plant's natural habitat influences its nutrient requirements.

8.   Substrates

Most hobbyists do not have soil substrates in their aquariums, which may be the main reason they have trouble growing plants. For a better understanding of this critical topic, Chapter VIII discusses the general nature of soils before delving into the even greater complexities of submerged soils. Finally, it describes how hobbyists can use soils in the aquarium effectively.

9.   The Aerial Advantage

In Chapter IX, I discuss the major problems that submerged aquatic plants face and why emergent plants do so much better. For the hobbyist, I describe how to promote aerial growth to optimize the aquarium ecosystem.

10.   Algae Control

Chapter X focuses on a major problem that many aquarium hobbyists have– tanks overrun by algae. Common methods that hobbyists use to counteract algal problems are evaluated. I then thoroughly discuss several additional factors that the hobbyist can use to control algae (the competition between plants and algae, lighting spectra, iron limitation, etc). Using this information, I show how hobbyists can successfully rid their tanks of algae without destroying the ecosystem.

11. Practical Aquarium Setup and Maintenance

In my opinion, planted aquariums are much easier to maintain than those without plants. Plants control alga growth and keep the tank healthy for fish without the drudgery of frequent water changes and gravel cleaning. In Chapter XI, I describe how I set up my planted tanks, which are both inexpensive and easily maintained. I also present my own guidelines as to fish, lighting, substrates, filtration, etc that the hobbyist can use to set up similar tanks.

B.   Is the 'Balanced Aquarium' Dead?

Older aquarium books advocated the "Balanced Aquarium" in which plants and fish 'balanced' each others needs. Intrinsic to the idea of the balanced aquarium was the healthy growth of plants, but many hobbyists found planted aquariums difficult to maintain. Poor plant growth and unrestricted algal growth were persistent problems. Thus over the years, the idea of having a natural, planted aquarium lost its original appeal [1]. Many hobbyists gave up on the idea and dispensed with live plants altogether.

Furthermore, many aquarium hobbyists and retailers have little interest in plants, being primarily interested in keeping and breeding fish. Often the methods they use and recommend are not conducive to growing plants. For example, optimal fishkeeping without plants often depends on enhanced biological filtration, strong aeration, undergravel filters, and frequent tank cleaning. Beginning hobbyists that try to adapt these methods to growing plants in their aquariums often fail.

Other hobbyists, mainly from Europe and within the last 20 years, developed techniques for growing plants in the aquarium that were highly successful. The sophisticated technology they used consistently produced beautiful, planted aquariums, which I will call 'High-tech' aquariums. The end result did, indeed, resemble 'a slice of nature'. Unfortunately, the artificial methods to obtain such an aquarium ignored many of the natural processes of bacteria and plants. The end result– healthy fish and plants– resembled the natural, balanced aquarium, but the means to obtain it were unnatural, expensive, and laborious.[1]

With this book, I would like to resurrect the older version of the natural, planted aquarium but with a much greater understanding of how it works.

C.   Characteristics of a Natural, 'Low-tech' Aquarium

The 'Low-tech' aquariums that I maintain are characterized by a small or moderate number of fish, reduced filtration and cleaning, a large number of healthy growing plants, and diverse microorganisms. Essential to my natural aquarium is moderate lighting, a substrate enriched with ordinary soil, and well-adapted plants. It differs from what most American hobbyists are familiar with– tanks with dim light and gravel substrates.

At the same time, it differs from the High-tech tank in that it takes greater advantage of natural processes. The Low-tech aquarium is easier (and cheaper) to set up and maintain. This is because natural processes are taken full advantage of. For example, bacteria and fish– not artificial CO_2 injection– provide CO_2 to plants. Plants– not trickle filters– remove ammonia from the water and protect fish. Fishfood and soil– not micronutrient fertilizers– provide trace elements to plants.

What are some specific characteristics of Low-tech aquariums?

1.   pH Remains Stable

One criterion to gauge an aquarium's success is a stable pH; acid-generating reactions in the tank are matched by base-generating reactions. Tanks with water that become acidic over time are unbalanced, usually due to excessive

> Q.   I use a pH adjuster to keep the pH at around 7 in my plant tank, because the tank's pH tends to slowly decline. (The plants aren't growing as well as I would like.) Do you think the phosphates in the pH adjuster will encourage algae?
>
> A.   They might, but the bigger problem is that your tank is going acid over time. In many aquariums, nitrification in the filters is the source of the acidity. In 'fish only' tanks it can't be helped, but in planted tanks photosynthesis, not chemicals and water changes, should be able to keep the pH up.
>   The only tanks I've had 'go acid' are those with poor plant growth. (Normally, my planted tanks always show a neutral or alkaline pH.) Base-generating reactions counteract acid-generating reactions. I would work to encourage total plant growth in your tank.

---

[1]High-tech aquariums are sponsored by the two European manufacturers Dupla and Dennerle. The complete systems, which require metal halide lighting, CO_2 injection with automatic pH regulation, trickle filters, daily plant fertilization, and substrate heating cables [2,3], are quite expensive. For example, two hobbyists [4] report that the set-up for their 90 gal 'Super Show Tank' based on the Dupla system cost more than $3,500.

nitrification in the filter. **Table I-1** lists the biological and physical processes that affect the pH in aquariums.

2.   Low Maintenance

The hallmark of a Low-tech aquarium is that it is easily maintained. Aquariums seem to do well without hobbyist adjustment, maintenance, and cleaning. For example, my own aquariums often go for six months or more without water changes. Fish get fed well, so that plants do not need to be fertilized artificially. The only routine maintenance is replacing evaporated water and pruning excess plant growth. Tanks that are unbalanced need constant-cleaning and adjustment.

Table I-1. Major Processes that Affect Aquarium pH.

Acid-Generating Processes (pH goes down)	Base-Generating Processes (pH goes up)
Respiration of fish	Photosynthesis by plants and algae
Nitrification by filter bacteria	Denitrification by bacteria
Bacterial metabolism (e.g. decomposition of organic matter)	Water and air mixing (loss of CO_2)

3.   Fish Behavior is Normal

Normal fish behavior is a good indicator of a healthy, balanced ecosystem. In tanks, this means that vigorous fish like Rainbows and cichlids should be thrashing over food at meals. Male guppies should be actively courting female guppies.

Abnormal fish behavior (not eating) or an inability to reproduce often indicates contaminated water. For example, otherwise vigorous fish will stop eating when water nitrite levels get too high.

D.   How Plants Benefit Aquariums

Below are the benefits that plants– given a chance– play in the aquarium:

1.   Protect fish by removing ammonia. Plants readily take up ammonia, which is toxic, even though there may be adequate nitrogen in the substrate or plentiful nitrates in the water. This is because aquatic plants have a decided and overriding preference for ammonia (see pages 107-108).

2.   Protect fish by removing metals from the water. Heavy metals may or may not directly kill fish, but they can inhibit reproduction and suppress normal appetite, such that the fish eventually succumb to disease. Plants rapidly take up large quantities of 'heavy metals' like lead, cadmium, copper, and zinc from the water. Also, plant decomposition produces humic substances, which bind and detoxify metals (see pages 14-16).

3.   Control algae. Good plant growth seems to inhibit algae, whether in nature or aquariums. How plants do this is not certain. However, plants produce and release a wide variety of allelochemicals that are mildly toxic to algae (see pages 41-43). Plants also help remove iron from the water, a nutrient that probably controls algal growth in many aquariums (see pages 167-170).

4.   Stabilize the pH. Photosynthesis is a major acid-consuming reaction. Thus, vigorous plant growth keeps the water from becoming acidic over time.

5.   Increase biological activity within the tank. Most microorganisms (bacteria, protozoa, fungi, algae, etc) do not live freely in the water but live attached to surfaces. Plants, especially the roots of floating plants provide an ideal home for numerous microorganisms (see page 153), many of which recycle nutrients and stabilize the aquarium ecosystem.

6.   Oxygenate the water. Actually, the air probably provides more oxygen consistently to fish than plant photosynthesis. And while it is true that plants also consume oxygen (plants 'breathe' just as humans do), healthy plants give off far more oxygen via photosynthesis than they consume by respiration. Even when plants are not photosynthesizing, such as at night, they probably remove less oxygen than one would expect. This is because they prefer to use the oxygen stored in their tissues rather than take up oxygen from the water.[2]

Q.   My Black Moor has been sick for the last two weeks. It seems to be losing its scales and has white stringy stuff on its body. Its body is now gray-colored, instead of its original dark brown color. I keep the Moor in a small 2 gal tank with no plants, but it has a small box filter and I do 10-20% water changes every week.

I have another tank, a 10 gal with heavy plant growth with many red swordtails (including babies) that are doing fine. Should I try antibiotics?

A.   Poor aquarium conditions may have lowered your fish's immunity to natural bacteria. Antibiotics might cure the immediate infection, but won't help much to counteract the underlying problem-- a toxic substrate, contaminated water, etc. I would either clean the tank or transfer the Black Moor to the planted tank.

Results: I put the Moor into the 10-gal tank. Within 2 weeks his problems cleared up. He is now eating all the snails in the tank!

7.   Remove CO_2 from the water. Excess CO_2– as much as oxygen depletion– can cause respiratory distress in fish (fish gasping at the surface). Normally, plants would be expected to remove all CO_2 from the water during daylight hours.

8.   Prevent substrates from becoming toxic. In my experience, a substrate that supports good plant growth doesn't become toxic, and it rarely (if ever) needs to be vacuumed. Plant roots keep it healthy (see page 135-136).

---

[2]During photosynthesis, oxygen accumulates rapidly within the plant lacunae, which are huge gas storage areas making up about 70% of the plant's interior. This internal oxygen is used for the plant's respiration both day and night [5].

E. Promoting Plant Growth in the Aquarium

Many hobbyists would like to keep plants in their aquariums, but repeated failures or the expense of the 'High-tech' systems has discouraged them. Thus, the rest of the book addresses the factors that affect plant growth in the aquarium. They are:

1. Nutrients. Tapwater, a soil substrate, and fishfood can easily provide all nutrients required by aquarium plants (see Ch V 'Sources of Plant Nutrients'). CO_2 probably limits plant growth in most aquariums.

2. Algae Control. Plants cannot grow if algae smother them. Practical strategies, both short-term and long-term, for the control of algae are discussed in Ch XI 'Algae Control'.

4. Fertile substrates. Theoretically, aquatic plants can get all nutrients from the water, so what's wrong with a gravel substrate? However, in practice, gravel substrates do not work very well. Plants need a fertile substrate to grow well and compete with algae. (See Ch VIII 'Substrates'.)

5. Bacteria. Bacteria break down organic matter into CO_2 and other nutrients that plants can use. Bacteria also modify substrate toxins. Bacteria have been given their own chapter (Ch IV 'Bacteria'), but their complex and interesting role in aquarium ecology is discussed throughout the book.

6. Aerial (Emergent) Growth. Aquatic plants that have access to air grow much better than fully submerged plants (Ch IX 'The Aerial Advantage'). By combining aerial growth with submerged plants in the same aquarium, the hobbyist greatly increases an aquarium's chances for success.

7. Light. Adequate light is essential for growing plants effectively in the aquarium. In Ch XI, I discuss using window light and fluorescent light in the home aquarium.

8. Plant Species. Different plant species may respond differently to individual tank conditions, such as lighting, substrate, water chemistry, CO_2, and even other plants. If the species can't adjust, plant growth will be poor and the tank will be unsuccessful. Hobbyists that plant a wide variety of plant species increase an aquarium's chances for success.

REFERENCES

1. Atz JW. 1952. The balanced aquarium myth. In: Axelrod HR (Ed.). Tropical Fish as a Hobby. McGraw-Hill (New York), pp 215-227.
2. Horst K and Kipper HE. 1986. The Optimum Aquarium. AD aquadocumenta Verlag GmbH (Bielefeld, West-Germany).
3. Dennerle L and Lilge H. *System for a Problem-Free Aquarium* (catalog published by Dennerle GmbH, Germany).
4. Booth G and Booth K. 1993. Some assembly required (Pt 8). The Aquatic Gardener 6(4): 109-116.
5. Wetzel RG. 1983. Limnology (Second Ed.). Saunders College Publishing (Philadelphia, PA), p. 529.

8

Chapter II.

PLANTS AS WATER PURIFIERS

Aquatic plants protect fish from toxic ammonia, nitrite, and heavy metals. Intrinsic to the idea of plants as water purifiers are three facts:

1.   Aquatic plants readily take up heavy metals
2.   Humic substances from decomposed plant tissue detoxify heavy metals
3.   Aquatic plants readily take up ammonia and nitrites

A.   Heavy Metals

'Heavy metals' are toxic to all organisms, whether they are required micronutrients (zinc, copper, iron, manganese, nickel) or environmental pollutants (aluminum, lead, mercury, cadmium, etc).[1] **Table II-1**, which ranks several heavy metals according to their molar toxicity to various organisms, shows that mercury and copper are the most toxic of heavy metals.

Table II-1. Toxicity of Various Heavy Metals to Organisms [3].	
Organism	High Toxicity $\Rightarrow$ Low Toxicity
Algae	Hg > Cu > Cd > Fe > Cr > Zn > Co > Mn
Fungi	Hg > Cu > Cd > Cr > Ni > Pb > Co > Zn > Fe
Fish	Hg > Cu > Pb > Cd > Al > Zn > Ni > Cr > Co > Mn
Flowering Plants	Hg > Pb > Cu > Cd > Cr > Ni > Zn
Abbreviations: Al = aluminum; Cd = cadmium; Co = cobalt; Cr = chromium; Cu = copper; Fe = iron; Hg = mercury; Mn = manganese; Pb = lead; and Zn = zinc.	

1.   Metals in Our Water Supplies

Which heavy metals in tapwater might be a problem for our fish? If human water standards were the same as fish standards, water good enough for human drinking water would be good enough for fish. However, this is not the case, especially for zinc and copper. First, safe

---

[1]'Heavy' metals are also classified chemically as 'Borderline' and 'Class B' metals. In contrast, calcium and magnesium are 'Class A' metals and are generally not toxic [1,2].

levels for fish are much lower than those for humans (**Table II-2**). For example, fish require that Cu levels be 65 times lower (0.02 ppm versus 1.3 ppm) and Zn levels be 50 times lower (0.1 ppm versus 5.0 ppm). Second, Cu and Zn are not considered to be toxic to humans; their standards are set for aesthetic reasons (taste, porcelain staining, etc) and are not federally enforced. This means that drinking water could conceivably contain enough copper and/or zinc to harm fish.

Table II-2. Some Heavy Metal Standards for Humans and Fish [4,5].

Metal	Humans (ppm)	Fish (ppm)
Cadmium	0.005	0.01
Chromium	0.1	0.05
Copper	1.3	0.02
Lead	0.015	0.1
Mercury	0.002	0.01
Zinc	5.0	0.1

Q. I am concerned with your conclusion regarding the extent of metal contamination in aquariums. It is unlikely that most municipal water systems would contain enough metals to seriously harm aquatic life; the only other source of metal contamination is from pipes. The danger in tapwater is the chlorine, which must be removed.

A. I'm not convinced. Hobbyists blithely add copper to their tanks to control algae and parasites with no idea of how toxic copper can be. Both zinc and copper could be in drinking water at levels that could be toxic to fish. My own well water has enough zinc, apparently from metal leaching from the well-head and metal storage tank, to create problems in my aquariums. A few hobbyists have reported problems from excessive copper in municipal tapwater. Other hobbyists might not even recognize problems from metal toxicity. (Sick fish and plant melt-downs are so easily attributed to other causes.)

Metal toxicity has rarely been discussed in the aquarium literature. This interesting topic, which is related to micronutrient nutrition in plants, fish physiology, and decompositional processes in aquariums, in my opinion, deserves some attention.

Municipal water treatment procedures such as coagulation-flocculation and lime softening help remove Zn and Cu. Thus, metal contamination of city water would seem unlikely. However, high copper levels have been reported in certain areas. For example, several Connecticut towns (Bridgeport, Hawkstone, Norfolk, etc) in 1997 reported 'high-risk' areas with Cu levels ranging from 0.14 to 1.1 ppm. And one hobbyists from Massachusettes has reported aquarium problems arising from Cu levels in the city water that fluctuate from 0.5 to as high as 2 ppm.

Ground water, especially water from private wells, could also contain harmful

Q. Surely, if the water is safe for humans to drink, it must be okay for the fish?

A. As humans we don't live and breathe in the water, so our dosage is small. Furthermore, much of the metals that enter our digestive tract would be inactivated by binding to organic matter (partially digested food).

In contrast, fish are continuously exposed to whatever metals are in the water. Heavy metals 'sneak in' through pathways designed for nutrient uptake, particularly calcium. Thus, in metal-contaminated water, the fish will contain high levels of metals-- and be injured accordingly.

levels of zinc and copper. Indeed, one survey [6] of U.S. ground water shows huge variations in both Cu (0.01 to 2.8 ppm) and Zn (0.1 to 240 ppm). Additional heavy metal contamination of drinking water may come from the leaching of metal pipes, heating coils, and storage tanks.

2.   Mechanisms of Heavy Metal Toxicity

Many metals are toxic, because they capriciously bind to organic molecules within organisms. For example, mercury binds to the sulphydryl groups (-SH) found on virtually all proteins, thereby inactivating the proteins and their cellular functions.

Iron toxicity occurs in plants as well as humans (e.g., hemophiliac patients overloaded with iron from continuous blood transfusions [7,8]). The toxicity occurs when cellular oxidation of iron (Fe^{2+}) produces highly reactive oxygen radicals, which can kill cells by destroying DNA, membrane lipids, and proteins.

However, the most common mechanism of metal toxicity is when a foreign metal displaces another metal from its specific binding site on organic molecules. For example, nickel can displace zinc from its proper binding site on the enzyme carbonic anhydrase thereby inactivating the enzyme [1]. (Many enzymes require the attachment of a specific metal in order to function.)

Heavy metal substitution for calcium is often an underlying factor in metal toxicity. All cell membranes have a phospholipid bilayer that is stabilized by Ca. Intruding heavy metals can displace the desired Ca and disrupt cell membrane structure and function [1]. And calcium's unique role as a secondary messenger in cells insures that many functions of almost any organism are susceptible to metal toxicity [9,10].

3.   Metal Toxicity in Fish

While high levels of heavy metals can cause gross tissue damage and death in fish [11], the most common effects (behavioral changes and reproductive failure) are from minor contamination. Behavioral changes result when heavy metals disrupt the release of neurotransmitters and hormones from producing cells [12].

Fish had problems capturing live daphnia following a 4 week exposure to lead (**Table II-3**). Control (untreated) fish reacted to the daphnia much further away than Pb-exposed fish. Also, lead accumulated in the brains of Pb-exposed fish.

Low levels of heavy metals may affect normal fish behavior such as schooling, feeding, swimming, and successful spawning. For example, copper was shown to significantly reduce the

Table II-3. Effect of Lead (Pb) on Feeding Behavior in Minnows [17].

Variable	Controls (no lead)	Lead Exposure	
		0.5 mg/l	1.0 mg/l
Reaction distance (cm)	2.7	1.9	1.7
Miscues during feeding (number of)	9.0	50	49
Time to consume 20 daphnia (min)	1.4	6.2	5.5
Pb in fish brain (mg/l)	Not detected	0.45	0.82

swimming performance of rainbow trout [13]. Continuous exposure to aluminum decreased the appetite and growth rate of young trout [14]. Lead had no effect on the growth of young male trout, but it profoundly affected sperm production [15]. The smell receptors of salmon, which are critical to the upstream spawning migration of this fish, were shown to be impaired by Cu [16].

Fish are guided by their own unique circadian rhythms, which are controlled by neurotransmitter levels within specific regions of the fish brain. By disrupting neurotransmitter function, heavy metals can affect the natural circadian rhythm of fish [12]. For example, when sea catfish were exposed to 0.1 ppm copper, they lost their normal circadian rhythm and became hyperactive (**Fig. II-1**). That is, treated catfish were more active both day and night, whereas untreated (control) catfish were much less active during the day, especially in the afternoon.

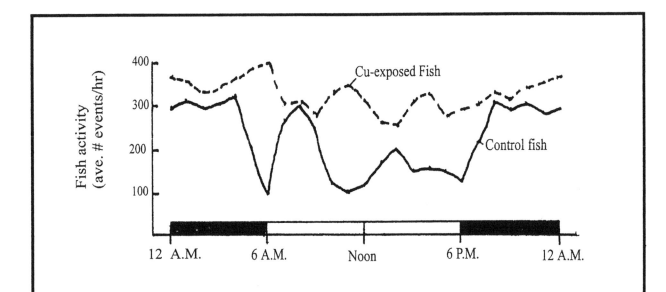

Figure II-1. Diel Activity of Sea Catfish as Affected by Copper. Sea catfish were exposed to 0.1 mg/l of Cu for 3 days and then monitored for activity over a 24 h measurement period. Activity was determined when fish tripped a photodiode as they moved between compartments. (Fig. 1 from Steele [18] redrawn and used with kind permission from Kluwer Academic Publishers.)

Fish are most sensitive to heavy metals during their developmental stages. Thus, while a particular metal concentration might be safe for adult fish, it might injure fish during a critical phase of development. For example, the yolk sac membrane (chorion) was very fragile and easily ruptured in embryos exposed to just 0.3 ppm of zinc [19].

Table II-4 shows standards for seven heavy metals on various freshwater fish. These standards, which are based on the sensitivity of developing fish, are much more stringent than the general standards listed earlier in Table II-2.

4.   Metal Toxicity in Plants

Plants afflicted with metal toxicity exhibit various symptoms that might be interpreted incorrectly as nutrient deficiencies. Symptoms of aluminum toxicity for *Vallisneria* are premature browning and senescence of leaf tips [22]. Excesses of copper, manganese, and zinc may induce iron deficiency and chlorosis [23].

Iron toxicity has been studied in at least two aquatic plant species. Thus, investigators [24] reported a 75% growth reduction in the pondweed *Potamogeton pectinatus* as a consequence of adding iron (1.2 mg $FeCl_3$/g) to the substrate. The leaves turned brown, and the roots became pale or red brown and did not reach the bottom of the pots in which they were planted. *Hydrilla verticillata*, exposed to well water containing 1.2 ppm Fe, became covered with a rusty brown color and began to decay [25].

Q. I added iron (as $FeCl_3$) to my tank to reduce phosphates in the water. (Phosphate reacts with iron to form insoluble iron phosphate.) Six days afterwards, the phosphate concentration had decreased from 0.6 ppm to 0.1 ppm, but I began to see phosphate deficiency in some of my plants. It started with the slower growing plants. For example, the *Cryptocoryne* had brown spots on their leaves, which expanded until the whole leaf was affected. Fast-growing plants species seemed unaffected by the P deficiency, which surprised me, as these plants usually require more nutrients.

A. I think you're confusing phosphate deficiency with iron toxicity. Phosphate levels of 0.1 ppm in the water are more than sufficient for plant growth. The brown spotting of the leaves suggests iron toxicity. The browning is due to iron deposits in the leaves, as the plant tries to store the excessive iron coming in.

The fact that your faster growing plants did not show the 'deficiency' supports my contention that the problem is metal toxicity not nutrient deficiency. Metal toxicity in plants can be overcome by rapid growth. Faster growing plants 'dilute out' the problem; metal concentrations within the tissues decreases with new growth. Slow-growing plants are at a disadvantage; the metal concentration within the plant builds up to injurious levels.

Table II-4. Heavy Metal Standards for Sensitive Life Stages of Fish [19].

Metal	Fish	Metal's Effect on:	Maximum Acceptable Concentration (ppm or mg/l)
Cadmium	Flagfish	Spawning	0.004- 0.008
"	Flagfish	Juvenile mortality	0.003- 0.017
Copper	Brook Trout	Juvenile mortality	0.010- 0.017
Chromium	Brook Trout	Juvenile mortality	0.20- 0.35
Lead	Brook Trout	Juvenile deformity	0.058- 0.12
Mercury	Fathead Minnow	Juvenile growth	< 0.00026
Nickel	Fathead Minnow	Egg hatching	0.38- 0.73
Zinc	Flagfish	Growth	0.026- 1.2
"	Fathead Minnow	Egg fragility	0.078- 0.15

5. Factors that Moderate Metal Toxicity

Because metal toxicity is so often affected by other factors, it is very difficult to say that a particular metal concentration is toxic. It may or may not be depending on water hardness, pH, organic matter, and the target species. In general, metal toxicity is reduced when metals are bound to organic matter, soil particles, or carbonate ions. These bound metals are less likely to be absorbed by plants and fish.

a)   Water hardness and pH

In general, metal toxicity is a much greater problem in soft, acidic water. Many scientific studies were prompted by environmentalist's concerns over the acidification of natural lakes by acid rain. As lakes acidifies to pHs below 5.5, heavy metals like aluminum, copper and zinc are released from the sediment into the water.

Experiments show that water hardness (see page 86) by itself influences metal toxicity. Thus, trout exposed to 1.5 ppm of aluminum had a 45% mortality in softwater but only 10% in hardwater [14]. Daphnia exposed to 0.13 mg/l of zinc survived less than 10 days in softwater but over 50 days in medium hardwater [26].

Copper toxicity to fish may be lowered significantly (up to 90%) in hardwater, due solely to the competition between copper (Cu^{2+}) and calcium (Ca^{2+}) for fish uptake [27][2]. Investigators [9] showed that if they increased water calcium from 4.4 to 43 ppm, heavy metal uptake (and toxicity) in mussels was greatly reduced. Ca was found to be much more important than Mg in preventing metal uptake. The investigators hypothesized that calcium's competition with heavy metals for uptake via the calcium channels of cells was the main mechanism for hardwater's protective effect.

pH mildly influences metal toxicity, with neutral pH providing the most protection. Thus, copper was twice as toxic to rainbow trout when the pH was lowered from pH 7.2 to pH 5.4 [27]. Aluminum is especially influenced by pH; it is only toxic at extremely acidic pH (< 5.5) or alkaline pH (>8) [14]. In general, metals will be more toxic in soft, acidic water and less toxic in hard, alkaline water.

> **Q.**   I'm using an aluminum reflector that may drip some aluminum condensate into the water. Should I be concerned about aluminum toxicity?
>
> **A.**   No. If your aquarium water is between pH 6.0 and 8.0, aluminum is not toxic.

b)   Dissolved Organic Carbon

Although water hardness and pH can individually reduce metal toxicity, organic carbon confers the greatest protection by far [14]. Thus, for metal toxicity in flagfish, investigators [31] showed that organic carbon provided 27 times more protection than water hardness.

---

[2] Fish get the majority of their calcium by absorbing it from the water through their skin and gills, not from digesting fishfood in the gut [28,29]. Both carp and trout readily extract calcium from water containing 5-20 ppm Ca [30].

Dissolved organic carbon (DOC) is found in lakes and rivers at fairly high concentrations, ranging from 1 to 30 mg/l (average is 6 mg/l) [32]. Although it can color the water, DOC is often invisible except for the soapy foam it forms in flowing stream waters (and aquarium protein skimmers).

Metals readily bind to DOC. Every mg of DOC has the capacity to bind 1 µeq of metal [33].[3] Bound metals are not readily taken up, and therefore, are much less toxic than soluble metals [34].[4] Examples of DOC that bind metals are: amino acids (glycine, alanine, etc), sugars (malate, citrate, etc), polypeptides, proteins, and humic substances.[5] For example, **Fig. II-2** shows how 3 organic compounds (glycine and two humic compounds) bind copper (Cu).

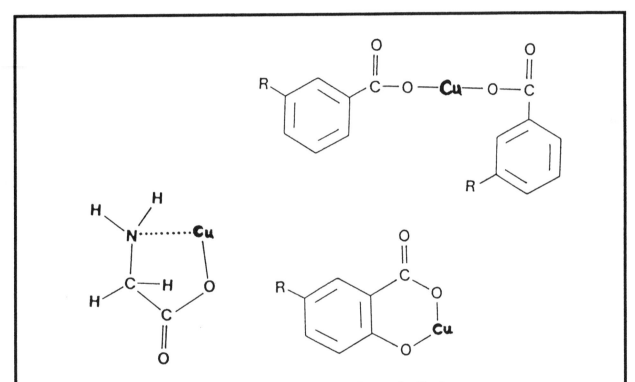

Fig. II-2. Examples of Copper (Cu) Binding to Organic Carbon. Figs. 11.28 and 11.29 from Thurman [33] used with kind permission from Kluwer Academic Publishers.

Humic substances bind to heavy metals more tightly than calcium [9]. This means that humic substances will alleviate metal toxicity, even if the water is hard and contains much Ca.

---

[3]For an explanation of µeq (microequivalent), see 'mg/l v. molarity v. equivalents' on page 187.
[4]Not all metals bound to organic matter are less toxic. If the organic matter is hydrophobic (i.e., lipid soluble), it may act like an 'ionophore' in that it will actually carry the metal through the lipid bilayer into the cell. For example, mercury binding to methyl groups greatly increases its toxicity [2].
[5] Humic substances are random, nonspecific compounds resulting from the bacterial decomposition of plant matter (see page 61).

Several studies have shown that either DOC (or its humic acid component) decrease metal toxicity. For example, when natural DOC was removed from lake water by charcoal filtration, copper toxicity (4 day LC50) to minnows increased over ten-fold [36]. In another study, most daphnia were killed within 24 to 48 hr by 0.015 ppm copper, but when 1.5 ppm humic acid was added, they survived at least 40 days [37]. Rainbow trout continuously exposed for 16 days to 0.1 ppm of soluble aluminum had no deaths and grew about 40% faster in the presence of humic acid [14].

Investigators [31] studied DOC's effect on toxic mixtures of aluminum, zinc, and copper towards flagfish in soft, acidic waters. (Note: these particular metals often increase when lakes acidify.) Fish mortality from the metal mixture was reduced 2 to 15 fold by lakewater DOC. The investigators concluded that young flagfish probably couldn't survive in acidified, softwater containing less than 2.2 mg/l of total organic carbon.

Metal binding to DOC (or its humic

Q. The yellow color of 'aged aquarium water' represent a polluted, unhealthy condition for fish. Therefore, the water in aquariums should be changed frequently?

A. Not necessarily. In an established aquarium containing plants, the yellowish color of 'aged aquarium water' is from humic substances not from raw animal waste. Humic substances are formed from decomposed plant matter.

Hobbyists have debated the value of this old, yellowish water for years, with some saying that 'aged aquarium water' represents an unhealthy environment for fish. In the case of heavy metals, scientific evidence suggests otherwise. The color is due to humic substances, which bind and chelate heavy metals and reduce their toxicity to fish. And even if the aquarium water is not colored, humic substances will probably be there.

Humic substances are natural water purifiers that provide an important mechanism by which plants protect fish from metal toxicity.

---

substance component) prevents metals from being taken up by organisms. This is true for plants as well as fish. One investigator showed that the water hyacinth didn't take up copper (Cu) when humic acid was present (**Table II-5**). The plant removed 94 % of the copper from a 1 mg/l solution of copper with no humic acid. Some of this copper (0.94 mg) was found in the plant's tissue. In the solution with humic acid though, copper was not removed from the water and no copper was found in the plants. This is because the copper was bound to the humic acids and could not be taken up by the water hyacinth.

Table II-5. Effect of Humic Acid on Copper Uptake by Water Hyacinth [38]. Plants were grown in 4 liters of nutrient media containing copper (Cu) for 1-2 weeks with or without 20 ppm of humic acid.

Treatment	Cu added (mg/l)	Cu Remaining in Solution (mg/l)	Cu Accumulation in Plants (total mg)
Control (no humic acid)	1	0.063	0.94
Plus Humic Acid	1	1	0

c) Artificial Chelators

Artificial chelators bind tightly to heavy metals. Unlike DOC, they bind metals in a one-to-one molar ratio, with a well-known order of priority [39]. For example, every molecule of EDTA was shown to bind one copper molecule in a highly predictable manner [38].

Table II-6 shows the stability constants for the formation of some EDTA metal complexes. They are listed in order of increasing 'binding tightness', with ferric iron the most tightly bound and magnesium the least tightly bound. Fortunately, EDTA binds much more tightly to heavy metals like Zn and Fe than Ca and Mg. For example, EDTA binds to Zn 790,000 times more tightly than it does to Ca.[6]

Metals can switch places on the EDTA molecule [41]. (That is, Ca can be 'bumped off' the EDTA molecule by Zn, because Zn binds more tightly to EDTA than Ca.). Thus, even though EDTA does bind to Ca and Mg, it will still alleviate metal toxicity in hardwater.

Table II-6. Stability of Metal-EDTA Complexes [40]. (Note: Although not listed here, the copper-EDTA complex has about the same stability as the zinc-EDTA complex [41].)

Reaction	Log K
$Mg^{2+} + EDTA^{4-} \Rightarrow MgEDTA^{2-}$	9.99
$Ca^{2+} + EDTA^{4-} \Rightarrow CaEDTA^{2-}$	11.9
$Mn^{2+} + EDTA^{4-} \Rightarrow MnEDTA^{2-}$	15.3
$Zn^{2+} + EDTA^{4-} \Rightarrow ZnEDTA^{2-}$	17.8
$Fe^{3+} + EDTA^{4-} \Rightarrow FeEDTA^{-}$	27.0

Q. Will chelated iron fertilizer (Fe-EDTA) reduce metal toxicity to fish?

A. No. This is because the EDTA is already bound to a metal, in this case iron (Fe). Since iron is the metal that binds most tightly to EDTA, metals like zinc or copper are not going to exchange for the iron in the Fe-EDTA. Only if you add pure EDTA will zinc, copper, and other toxic metals be removed. (Commercial water conditioners for aquariums often contain EDTA.)

Q. I don't understand. Many plant-growers use chelated iron as a fertilizer. If iron binds so tightly to EDTA, how can chelated iron provide iron to plants?

A. Iron is slowly released (as Fe^{2+}) from FeEDTA in the presence of light (see page 167). This process, which also applies to DOC-bound iron, provides iron to plants.

d) Variation between Species

Species variation in response to metal toxicity is genetically fixed; species that are more sensitive to metal toxicity don't easily become 'resistant' when exposed to heavy metals. For example, one strain of terrestrial grass eventually adapted to lead-contaminated soil, but it took about 100 years [42].

One way plants protect themselves is by producing their own metal chelators [43]. For example, an aluminum-resistant strain of wheat was found to release more of the chelator malate

---

[6]Calculations: Log K of zinc (17.8) minus Log K of calcium (11.9) = 5.9. Antilog of 5.9 (e.g. $10^{5.9}$) is 790,000.

from its root tips than an aluminum-sensitive strain when exposed to increasing amounts of Al [44].

Plant and fish species that developed in hard alkaline waters during their evolution had little exposure to heavy metals. As a consequence, these organisms have not developed the physiological mechanisms that would protect them from metal toxicity.

e)   Other Factors

Growth, by itself, may reduce or eliminate metal toxicity by simply 'diluting out' the metal's concentration within the organism's tissue. For example, the aluminum and iron toxicity that hinders *Vallisneria americana's* growth in acidic lakes could be eliminated by stimulating the plant's growth with CO_2 fertilization [45], which decreased the aluminum concentration from 2,000 ppm to 693 ppm.

Soil particles readily bind heavy metals (see pages 125-127). Investigators [46] analyzing heavy metal association with soil particles in two South Carolina streams found that lead (Pb) was strongly associated with the larger soil particles, especially clay.

> **Comment.** For a long time, I had trouble keeping Rainbows and Tanganyikan cichlids. I would do a water change, and these fish would inexplicably die, while the Tetras were unaffected. I had very poor luck raising fry of most sorts in my water. In addition, I had trouble keeping 'beginner' plants like *Vallisneria*, Hornwort, and *Sagittaria*, but had no problem with *Cryptocoryne*. Later I learned that my city water sometimes contained as much as 2 ppm of copper.
>
> **Reply.** The fish and plants injured by the copper in your tapwater originate from hardwater. They would be expected to more sensitive to heavy metals than the Tetras and *Cryptocoryne*, which originate from soft, acidic waters.

6. Metal Uptake by Plants

Aquatic plants readily take up heavy metals. For example, both leaves and roots of *Elodea nuttallii* rapidly took up copper and zinc (**Figure II-3**). Metal uptake by roots was especially rapid. Thus, within 2 hours, roots exposed to 3.2 ppm zinc had accumulated over 1,000 mg/kg of zinc, while leaves had accumulated about 300 mg/kg.

Metal uptake is passive in that accumulation seems to increase in direct proportion to the metal concentration of the bathing solution [49]. Also, metal uptake has little to do with nutrient requirements of the plant. *Hydrilla verticillata* did not become iron-saturated until water levels of chelated iron reached 6 mg/l and its tissues contained over 21,000 mg/kg iron [50]. [Note: the critical concentration for iron is only 60 mg/kg (see pages 104-105).] Furthermore, the waterhyacinth, which is particularly resistant to metal toxicity, was shown to remove virtually all Cu from concentrated copper solutions (1 and 10 mg/l) within 1 to 3 weeks without any apparent harm to the plants [38].

Table II-7, documenting work with the duckweed *Spirodela polyrhiza*, correlates inhibitory metal concentrations with how much metal is found in the plant's tissue. For plants grown in solutions containing 3.7 mg/l Pb, growth is inhibited 50% and the plant tissue will contain over 6,700 ppm lead.

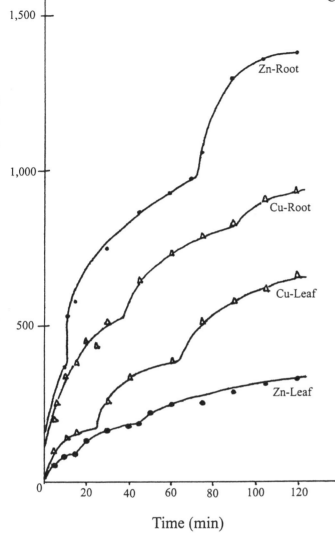

Metal Concentration (mg/kg)

1,500

1,000

Zn-Root

Cu-Root

Cu-Leaf

500

Zn-Leaf

0

20   40   60   80   100   120

Time (min)

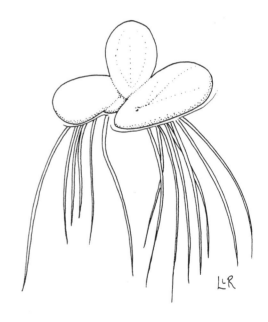

Figure II-3. Cu and Zn Uptake by Leaves and Roots of *Elodea nuttallii.* Leaf or root sections were exposed to Cu or Zn (3.2 ppm) and then analyzed for metal accumulation in terms of dry wt. (Fig. 1 from Marquenie-van der Werff [48] redrawn and used with permission of Urban & Fischer Verlag Niederiassung Jena.)

Table II-7. Metal Uptake by *Spirodela polyrhiza* [51]. The metal concentration in the growth media and in the plants associated with 50% growth inhibition (EC$_{50}$) was calculated after exposing 10 plants to 5-6 different metal concentrations for 4 days.

Metal	Metal Concentration Correlated with Growth Inhibition	
	In Media (mg/l)	In Plant Tissue (mg/kg)
Cadmium	0.089	773
Cobalt	0.14	590
Chromium	0.37	156
Copper	0.11	502
Nickle	0.11	1,290
Lead	3.7	6,730
Zinc	0.93	3,510

Giant duckweed (*Spirodela polyrhiza*). *S. polyrhiza*, like many other aquatic plants, can rapidly remove large quantities of heavy metals from contaminated water (see **Table II-7**). Plants are about 3 times bigger than ordinary duckweed (*Lemna minor*). Plant drawing from the IFAS [52].

20

B.   Ammonia

Ammonia is one of the most important and common pollutants of aquariums. Fish and bacteria excrete ammonia as a waste product of their metabolism. Ammonia (NH_3), which is toxic, exists in equilibrium with non-toxic ammonium (NH_4^+) in the following reaction:

$$NH_3 + H_2O \Leftrightarrow NH_4OH \Leftrightarrow NH_4^+ + OH^-$$

The percentage of ammonia in a solution with a given N concentration changes dramatically with pH. Typically, there is a 10 fold increase in ammonia for every 1 unit increase in pH as NH_4^+ converts to NH_3 in the above equilibrium reaction. For example, if the pH increases from 7.0 to 8.0, the % of N that is NH_3 increases from about 0.33% to 3.3%, while the % of N that is NH_4^+ correspondingly falls from 99.7% to 96.7% [53]. Thus, the higher the pH the greater the NH_3 concentration and the toxicity of a given concentration of inorganic nitrogen.

1.   Ammonia Toxicity in Fish

Fish differ in susceptibility to ammonia. For example, lethal ammonia concentrations for rainbow trout were found to range from 0.2 to 1.1 mg/l of NH_3, while those for the less vulnerable channel catfish were between 1.8 to 3.8 mg/l of NH_3 [54].

Chronic ammonia toxicity impairs reproduction (e.g., delays spawning and reduces egg viability). Long-term (1 wk to 3 mo.) exposure to ammonia concentrations as low as 0.002 to 0.15 mg/l of NH_3 can suppress appetite and inhibit growth of young fish [54]. Other symptoms may be ragged fins or deformities in young fish such as missing gill covers, or the fish may simply become increasingly susceptible to disease.

Recommendations for safe ammonia levels vary. Water quality experts recommend that ammonia (NH_3) levels be kept below 0.01 mg/l in natural freshwaters to avoid chronic effects [55]. Aquarium hobbyists, who measure total ammonia (NH_3 plus NH_4^+) with their test kits, should keep total ammonia below 0.02 mg/l for their freshwater fish [56].

2.   Ammonia Toxicity in Plants

Ammonia can reduce growth or kill plants [57]. Aquatic plants vary in their ability to tolerate ammonia– even within the same genus. For example, *Elodea canadensis* showed a slight (~20 %) reduction in photosynthesis when exposed for 7 days at pH 8.4 to 3.2 mg/l NH_4^+.[7] In contrast, both *Elodea nuttallii* and *E. ernstae* were either unaffected or stimulated by 9.6 mg/l NH_4^+ [58].

Other studies show that *Potamogeton densus* growth was inhibited by 5.0 mg/l NH_4^+, while *Stratiotes aloides* showed decay and destruction of plant tissue when exposed for 10 weeks to only 0.9 mg/l NH_4^+ [59]. High concentrations (2.6 to 26 mg/l NH_4^+) did not inhibit *Salvinia molesta*, and in some instances, stimulated growth [60].

---

[7]At pH 8.4 about 15% of this ammonium (NH_4) would be in the form of ammonia (NH_3) [56].

Thus, it appears that sensitive species of aquatic plants would be harmed by about 1 mg/l NH_4^+. However, less sensitive aquatic plants, particularly those adapted to nutrient-rich waters, would not be harmed by concentrations as high as 26 mg/l NH_4^+.

Plants rapidly detoxify ammonia [61]. As NH_3 enters the cell by simple diffusion across the membrane, it may combine with a hydrogen ion (H^+) and convert to non-toxic ammonium (NH_4^+) [62]. This NH_4^+ can be stored in cell vacuoles. Indeed, the vacuoles of *Nitella clavata* were found to contain over 2,400 mg/l NH_4^+ [64].

Another method plant use to detoxify ammonia is to immediately use the ammonia to synthesize proteins. Toxic NH_3 is combined with stored carbohydrates to form ordinary amino acids (see page 111). Thus, plants that grow well can tolerate more ammonia, because they have more carbohydrates to combine with ammonia.

Q. Is there any evidence that plants in the aquarium take up ammonia (NH_3)?

A. There is no definitive evidence that ammonia itself is actively taken up by plants. However, ammonia diffuses freely across the cell membranes of all organisms (animals, plants, bacteria, fish, etc) while ammonium does not [62]. This situation may be analogous to CO_2 and bicarbonate. NH_3 and CO_2, which are gases without an electrical charge, diffuse freely into plant cells. In contrast, bicarbonate (HCO_3^-) and ammonium (NH_4^+) both have electrical charges and cannot diffuse freely into the cell; their uptake requires energy and materials (membrane transporters, enzymes, etc), and therefore, makes them less likely to be taken up by plants.

Indeed, the toxicity of small, uncharged molecules like NH_3, HNO_2, CO_2, and H_2S may be due, in part, to the fact that cells often can't keep these molecules out and/or regulate their uptake. Thus, all organisms are vulnerable to these molecules if their concentrations are high enough.

---

3. Ammonia Uptake by Aquatic Plants

Most aquatic plants studied, when presented with a choice between ammonium and nitrates as their nitrogen source, take up ammonium exclusively. Only when ammonium is unavailable, do plants take up nitrates (see pages 107-108).

C. Nitrites

Problems with nitrites (NO_2^-) are less discussed in the aquarium hobby than those with ammonia. However, nitrites can sometimes be a problem in freshwater aquariums.

Because several bacterial processes produce nitrites (see pages 65-66), instances of nitrite accumulation are not uncommon. Nitrite levels as high as 100 mg/l NO_2^- have been reported in contaminated natural waters [54]. [8]

---

[8]Nitrite is often quantified as nitrite nitrogen (i.e., NO_2^-N). Because NO_2^- is 30% N, 100 mg/l of NO_2^- is equivalent to 30 mg/l of NO_2^-N.

1.   Nitrite Toxicity

Oxygen is transported within blood by hemoglobin molecules. Nitrite converts hemoglobin to methemoglobin, which is a brown-colored molecule that cannot bind oxygen. Fish hemoglobin may convert to methemoglobin when the water contains only 0.05 mg/l of nitrites [54].

Nitrites affect different fish species differently. Thus, lethal concentrations range from 0.1 to 0.4 mg/l NO_2^--N for Rainbow trout to 1.6 mg/l for Mosquito fish and 10 mg/l for Channel catfish [54]. These are 3 day LC50s, which means that half of the fish were killed within 3 days. As with all toxins lower concentrations may not kill the fish outright, but they may stress the fish such that eventually they succumb to disease or other problems. For example, Steelhead trout exposed to low NO_2^--N concentrations (0.015 to 0.060 mg/l) for 6 months showed temporary but not permanent gill damage [54].

Nitrite is more toxic at low pH, because nitrite (NO_2^-) converts to nitrous acid (HNO_2), which is the toxic form of nitrite [65]. Also, nitrite's toxicity declines sharply with increasing salt (NaCl) concentration, because Cl^- competes directly with NO_2^- for absorption by fish gills [66]. Thus, nitrite toxicity in Rainbow trout exposed to 12 mg/l NO_2^--N was reduced 96% by simply increasing the Cl^- concentration from 1 to 41 mg/l [54]. Not surprisingly, nitrite is not toxic in saltwater [67] where the Cl^- concentration is 19,000 mg/l [34].

Experimental work with the Rainbow trout [66], a fish particularly sensitive to nitrite, suggests that hobbyists should keep nitrite levels below 0.01 mg/l NO_2^--N.

Nitrite is much less toxic to plants than fish. For example, investigators used media containing 14 to 56 mg/l NO_2^--N for their studies with nitrite uptake and assimilation in duckweed [68,69]. The relative non-toxicity of nitrites to plants is supported by work with terrestrial plants, such as one study showing that wheat seedlings were only slightly inhibited when nitrite concentrations reached 70 mg/l [70].

> **Q.**   Why do brown streaks develop in goldfish when the weather turns cold?
>
> **A.**   Brown streaking in fins suggests nitrite poisoning. During the summer when algae and plants grow well, your fish were probably fine. In the winter, though, plant and algal growth slows, so that there is less nitrogen removal from the water. Also, in cold weather nitrification is often incomplete and nitrites tend to accumulate (see pages 65-66).
>   I would immediately change the water and remove debris. I would also add 1 teaspoon of ordinary table salt to each 10 gal of pond water. (The standard treatment for nitrite poisoning is to add NaCl at the rate of 20 mg/l for every 1 mg/l NO_2^--N [63].) You may want to monitor nitrite levels in your pond, especially during the winter months.

2.   Nitrite Uptake by Plants

Although plants definitely can use nitrite as a nitrogen source, the pertinent question for aquarium hobbyists is– Do aquatic plants remove the toxic nitrite in preference to the non-toxic nitrate? No definitive answer to this question in the scientific literature is currently available. But when the duckweed *Spirodela oligorrhiza* was grown in media containing nitrate and nitrite, it clearly took up nitrite in preference to nitrate (**Fig. II-4**).

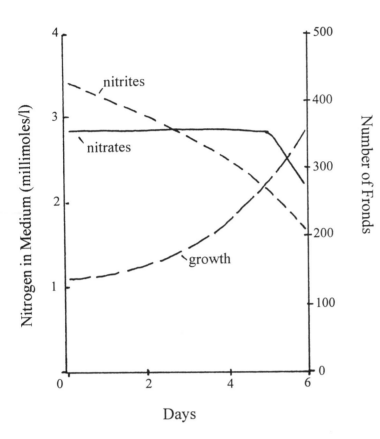

Figure II-4. Nitrite (NO$_2^-$) and Nitrate (NO$_3^-$) Uptake by *Spirodela oligorrhiza*. Plants that had been grown with ammonium as their sole N source were transferred to medium containing both nitrite and nitrate. Plants were grown under sterile conditions. (Thus, the above changes in nitrite and nitrate levels could not have been due to bacterial processes.) Fig. 4 from Ferguson [68] redrawn and used with permission of Springer-Verlag GmbH & Co. KG.

When the same investigator grew *Spirodela oligorrhiza* in media containing ammonium and nitrite, it removed both ions at approximately the same rate. These results suggest that aquatic plants might remove both ammonium and nitrite equally in preference to nitrates. However, the results with *Spirodela oligorrhiza* can probably not be generalized to other aquatic plants. This is because nitrite uptake and assimilation into proteins requires specific transporters and enzymes, whereas ammonium uptake does not [70]. For example, the enzyme nitrite reductase required for the duckweed *Lemna minor* to use nitrite must be induced [69]. This induction can be blocked by ammonium suggesting that *L. minor* is one aquatic plant species that does not use nitrite if ammonium is available. In general, nitrite and nitrate are less desirable N sources than ammonium.

D.   Using Aquatic Plants in Wastewater Treatment

Q.   If aquatic plants are so good at removing toxic metals and ammonia from water, why aren't they used more for wastewater treatment?

A.   The problem is that water purification by aquatic plants requires large areas for pond sites, year-round tropical temperatures, and the continuous (and often costly) harvesting of plants [71].

The waterhyacinth is commonly used for wastewater treatment because of its fast growth rate. **Table II-8** shows the performance of some wastewater treatment systems using the waterhyacinth. Plants were particularly effective at the Coral Springs facility where total nitrogen was reduced from 22.4 mg/l to 1.0 mg/l.

Table II-8. Effect of Waterhyacinth on the Water Quality of Wastewater [72]. BOD (Biological Oxygen Demand) is a measure of water quality. The more organic matter in the water, the more oxygen will be required or 'demanded' by bacteria to digest it. Unpolluted waters have a lower BOD than polluted waters.

Location	BOD (mg/l)		Total N (mg/l)		Total P (mg/l)	
	Influent	Effluent	Influent	Effluent	Influent	Effluent
National Space Tech. Lab, MS	110	7	12	3.4	3.7	1.6
Williamson Creek, TX	46	6	7.7	3.3	7	5.7
Coral Springs, FL	13	3	22.4	1.0	11	3.6

Waterhyacinth (*Eichhornia crassipes*). *E. crassipes* is one of the many floating plants that have been used in wastewater treatment. Its high growth rate, which makes it a major nuisance by blocking navigational water ways, also makes it highly effective in removing water contaminants. While the waterhyacinth is too large for most aquariums, other floating plants more suited to aquariums (duckweed, water lettuce, water sprite, etc) share the waterhyacinth's enormous capacity to remove water contaminants. This is because all floating plants have the 'aerial advantage' (See Ch. IX). (Plant drawing from IFAS [52].)

The duckweed *Lemna gibba* was also found to be highly effective in removing ammonia from fish effluent, particularly when the water was circulated (**Fig II-5**). Ammonia levels in stagnant water rose during the first 20 h in both the plant-free pond and the one covered with a mat of duckweed. When the water was circulated, however, ammonia declined 90% within 48 h in the duckweed pond. In contrast, in the plant-free pond ammonia levels remained constant for the first 48 h after which there was a gradual decrease due to bacterial activity.

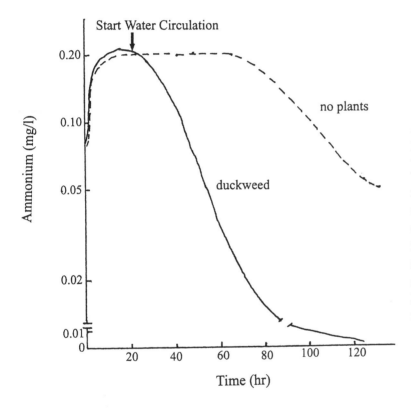

Figure II-5. Ammonia Levels in Fish Effluent in Ponds with or without Duckweed. The fish effluent was taken from a large tank containing *Tilipia* fish and similar concentrations of nitrates and ammonium (0.08 mM of each). In terms of mg/l, this would be 5.0 mg/l of NO_3 and 1.4 mg/l of NH_4. (Redrawn from Porath [73] and used with permission from Elsevier Science.)

E.   Plants and Toxic Compounds in Aquariums

My own well water contains a small, probably harmless level of copper (0.05 ppm) but enough zinc (0.8 ppm) to sometimes cause problems in my aquariums. For example, when I did a large water change in one of my tanks with raw tapwater, the shrimp became agitated, scurrying here and there. I rescued two of the shrimp by immediately putting them into another tank, but the third shrimp, which I was unable to catch, died by the next morning. Also, some of the guppies became diseased within the next few days.

Plants are also affected. The Amazon Swordplants in my aquariums are slightly pale and contain very high levels of zinc. If I put *Egeria densa* into pure tapwater, plants quickly turn brown and decay. (I observed these same symptoms in an experiment where I grew the plant in nutrient media containing 1 ppm zinc.) When I grew *Alternanthera* in subsoil with a high manganese concentration, growth slowed and the leaves became crinkled and misshapen.

Some aquarium water conditioners contain the metal chelator EDTA, which is quite effective in counteracting metal toxicity. For example, I was able to neutralize zinc toxicity to *Egeria densa* completely by adding a very small molar excess of EDTA.[10] One investigator [74] routinely added 5 mg/l of EDTA to prevent toxicity to the guppies used for experiments.

Although water conditioners containing EDTA provide short-term protection, plants provide long-term protection. I calculated that my plants take up about 13% of the zinc from the aquarium water each month.[11] Although this removal seems small and hardly adequate, the plants are specifically taking up only the toxic form of zinc (Zn^{2+}).

Finally, it is not just live plants that take up metals from the water and protect fish. Dead plant matter decomposes and eventually becomes humic substances, which bind and detoxify metals. Humic substances often give color to the water, but even if the water is colorless, humic substances may still be present.[12] Aquarium plants– whether living or dead– protect fish from metal toxicity.

Q. What factors would affect metal toxicity in aquariums?

A. Below are some of the measures that aquarium hobbyists often use that would be expected to **reduce** metal toxicity to fish:

- Using R.O. (reverse osmosis) or deionized water for water changes
- Using water conditioners that contain metal chelators like EDTA
- Using peat filtration– peat binds metal ions in exchange for H^+
- Using 'Black Water Extract'– its humic acids would bind metals
- Increasing water hardness– calcium protects organisms from metals
- Fostering good plant growth and routinely pruning excess plant growth.
- Allowing DOC to accumulate

Cleaning measures that could **increase** metal toxicity are:

- water changes– removes protective DOC, and if the tapwater is contaminated, each water change is, in essence, a fresh dose of metals
- protein skimming– removes DOC
- charcoal filtration– removes DOC

---

[10] I neutralized the 2.0 ppm zinc (3.0×10^{-5} M) with 2.5×10^{-5} M EDTA.

[11] I remove about 20 g. (0.020 kg) of plants (dry wt) from my 50 gal (~ 200 l.) aquarium each month. The zinc concentration in these plants is 1,000 mg/kg, so the zinc removed from the tank each month is 0.020 kg X 1,000 mg/kg or about 20 mg. If the zinc concentration in 200 l of tapwater is 0.8 mg/l, then the tank begins with a total of 160 mg of zinc, because 200 l X 0.8 mg/l = 160 mg zinc. Thus, plant pruning removes 20 mg (~13%) of the starting 160 mg total zinc in the water.

[12] Using an ordinary spectrophotometer, I checked the light absorption of water samples from several of my tanks. All samples showed little absorption of visible light but strong absorption of UV light. For example, colorless water from one of my tanks showed no absorption above 400 nm wavelength, but at 225 nm the optical density (O.D.) was 1.9, and at 200 nm the O.D. was 3.7. (Quartz cuvettes used for the analysis had a 1 cm pathlength.) This strong UV light absorption is characteristic of humic substances [75].

In aquariums both fish and bacteria continuously release ammonium as they metabolize food and organic matter. Fortunately for hobbyists, most aquatic plants (and algae) vastly prefer ammonium over nitrates as their nitrogen source. This means that plants continuously sift the water for ammonium and its toxic component ammonia. Thus, I've never had problems with ammonia in my planted aquariums.

Hobbyists can protect fish from toxins by hard work, e.g. frequent water changes, gravel vacuuming, and enhanced filtration. However, given a chance, plants can purify the water naturally and effortlessly for the aquarium hobbyist. In my opinion, the ability of plants to purify aquarium water and protect fish has been woefully-underestimated.

Comment from Fish Breeder. I thought you might like to hear about my experience using plants in my breeding tanks. For 7 years I have been breeding and selling Angelfish wholesale to the aquarium stores in the local area. I sell about 2,400 per month, so I always have at least 100 tanks stocked with 100 to 500 fry of different ages.

For many years I've used homemade canister filters and do 50% water changes twice a week. If I don't change the water, the fish quickly (within a week) begin to show what I call 'ammonia burn'. That is, their long pectoral fins look ragged and chewed off. Sometimes the gill covers are missing or the fish have 'gill burn'.

A couple of years ago, by chance, I started adding Hornwort to some of the tanks. I've found that the fish in the Hornwort tanks need less care and water changes than in tanks without Hornwort. That is, the fish seem to have less tendency to get 'ammonia burn'.

Because I'm happy with the results of keeping plants in the tanks, I've installed additional lighting in my fish room and have started adding trays of planted Val to other tanks.

Hornwort or coontail (*Ceratophyllum demersum*). *C. demersum* is a rootless submerged plant that is common in nature, but it is also well-adapted to aquariums. One successful fish breeder reported that the young fish showed less problems with gill and fin deformities when tanks contained Hornwort. Drawing from IFAS [52].

REFERENCES

1. Nieboer E and Richardson DHS. 1980. The replacement of the nondescript term 'heavy metals' by a biologically and chemically significant classification of metal ions. Environ. Pollut. 1: 3-26.

2. Roesijadi G and Robinson WE. 1994. Metal regulation in aquatic animals: mechanisms of uptake, accumulation, and release. In: Malins DC and Ostrander GK (eds.). Aquatic Toxicology. Lewis Publishers (Boca Raton LA), pp 387-420.

3. Sposito G. 1986. Distribution of potentially hazardous trace metals. In: Sigel H (ed), Metal Ions in Biological Systems (Vol 20). Concepts on Metal Ion Toxicity, pp 1-20.

4. van der Leeden F, Troise FL, and Todd DK. 1990. The Water Encyclopedia, Second Ed., Lewis Publishers (Boca Raton LA), p. 433, 472.

5. information provided in 1995 by the Orange Water and Sewer Authority (Carrboro NC, USA).

6. van der Leeden (1990), p. 430, 445, 483.

7. Bienfait HF and van der Mark F. 1983. Phytoferritin and its role in iron metaboloism. In: Robb DA and Pierpoint WS (eds.). Metals and Micronutrients: Uptake and Utilization by Plants. Academic Press (New York), pp. 111-123.

8. Halliwell B and Gutteridge MC. 1984. Oxygen toxicity, oxygen radicals, transition metals and disease. Biochem. J. 219: 1-14.

9. Markich SJ and Jeffree RA. 1994. Absorption of divalent trace metals as analogues of calcium by Australian freshwater bivalves: an explanation of how water hardness reduces metal toxicity. Aquat. Toxicol. 29: 257-290.

10. Pineros M and Tester M. 1997. Calcium channels in higher plant cells: selectivity, regulation and pharmacology. J. Exp. Bot. 48: 551-577.

11. Leland HV and Kuwabara. 1985. Trace metals. In: Rand GM and Petrocelli SM (Eds.), Fundamentals of Aquatic Toxicology. Hemisphere Publishing Corp. (Washington, D.C.), pp. 374-415.

12. Weber DN and Spieler RE. 1994. Behavioral mechanisms of metal toxicity in fishes. In: Malins DC and Ostrander GK (eds.). Aquatic Toxicology. Lewis Publishers (Boca Raton LA), pp 421-467.

13. Waiwood KG and Beamish. 1978. Effects of copper, pH and hardness on the critical swimming performance of rainbow trout (*Salmo gairdneri* Richardson). Water Res. 12: 611-619.

14. Gundersen DT, Bustaman S, Seim WK, and Curtis LR. 1994. pH, hardness, and humic acid influence aluminum toxicity to rainbow trout (*Oncorhynchus mykiss*) in weakly alkaline waters. Can. J. Fish. Aquat. Sci. 51: 1345-1355.

15. Ruby SM, Jaroslawski P, and Hull R. 1993. Lead and cyanide toxicity in sexually maturing rainbow trout, *Oncorhynchus mykiss* during spermatogenisis. Aquat. Toxicol. 26: 225-238.

16. Bjerselius R, Winberg S, Winberg Y, and Zeipel K. 1993. Ca^{2+} protects olfactory receptor function against Cu(II) toxicity in Atlantic salmon. Aquat. Toxicol. 25: 125-138.

17. Weber DN, Russo A, Seale DB, and Spieler RE. 1991. Waterborne lead affects feeding abilities and neurotransmitter levels of juvenile fathead minnows (*Pimephales promelas*). Aquat. Toxicol. 21: 71-80.

18. Steele CW. 1989. Effects of sublethal exposure to copper on diel activity of sea catfish, *Arius felis*. Hydrobiologia 178: 135-141.

19. McKim JM. 1985. Early life stage toxicity texts. In: Rand GM and Petrocelli SM (Eds.), Fundamentals of Aquatic Toxicology. Hemisphere Publishing Corp. (Washington, D.C.), pp. 58-95.

20. Rogge RW and Drewes CD. 1993. Assessing sublethal neurotoxicity effects in the freshwater oligochaete, *Lumbriculus variegatus*. Aquat. Toxicol. 26: 73-90.

21. Kraak MHS, Wink YA, Stuijfzand SC, Buckert-de Jong MC, de Groot CJ, and Admiraal W. 1994. Chronic ecotoxicity of Zn and Pb to the zebra mussel *Dreissena polymorpha*. Aquat. Toxicol. 30: 77-89.

22. Grise D, Titus JE, and Wagner DJ. 1986. Environmental pH influences growth and tissue chemistry of the submersed macrophyte *Vallisneria americana*. Can. J. Bot. 64: 306-310.

23. Wild A and Jones LHP. 1988. Mineral nutrition of crop plants. In: Wild A (ed.) Russell's Soil Conditions and Plant Growth (11th Edition). John Wiley & Sons (NY), pp. 69-113.

24. van Wijck C, de Groot C-J, and Grillas P. 1992. The effect of anaerobic sediment on the growth of *Potamogeton pectinatus* L.: the role of organic matter, sulphide and ferrous iron. Aquat. Bot. 44: 31-49.

25. Cooley TN, Dooris PM, and Martin DF. 1980. Aeration as a tool to improve water quality and reduce the growth of *Hydrilla*. Water Res. 14: 485-489.

26. Winner RW and Gauss JD. 1986. Relationship between chronic toxicity and bioaccumulation of copper, cadmium and zinc as affected by water hardness and humic acid. Aquat. Toxicol. 8: 149-161.

27. Pagenkopf GK. 1986. Metal ion speciation and toxicity in aquatic systems. In: Sigel H (ed), Metal Ions in Biological Systems (Vol 20). Concepts on Metal Ion Toxicity, pp 101-118.

28. Flik G, van der Velden JA, Dechering KJ, Verbost PM, Schoenmakers TJM, Kolar ZI, and Wendelaar Bonga SE. 1993. Ca^{2+} and Mg^{2+} transport in gills and gut of tilapia, *Oreochromis mossambicus*: A review. J. Exp. Zool. 265: 356-365.

29. Perry SF and Wood CM. 1985. Kinetics of branchial calcium uptake in the rainbow trout: Effects of acclimation to various external calcium levels. J. Exp. Biol. 116: 411-433.

30. Hilton JW. 1989. The interaction of vitamins, minerals and diet composition in the diet of fish. Aquaculture 79: 223-244.

31. Hutchinson NJ and Sprague JB. 1987. Reduced lethality of Al, Zn and Cu mixtures to American flagfish by complexation with humic substances in acidified soft waters. Environ. Toxicol. Chem. 6: 755-765.

32. Wetzel RG. 1983. Limnology (Second Ed.). Saunders College Publishing (Philadelphia, PA), p 668.

33. Thurman EM. 1985. Organic Geochemistry of Natural Waters. Martinus Nijhoff/Dr W. Junk (Boston), 410, 412.

34. Bowen HJM. 1979. Environmental Chemistry of the Elements. Academic Press (New York).

35. Thurman 1985, p. 105.

36. Welsh PG, Skidmore JF, Spry DJ, Dixon DG, Hodson PV, Hutchinson NJ, and Hickie BE. 1993. Effect of pH and dissolved organic carbon on the toxicity of copper to larval fathead minnow (*Pimephales promelas*) in natural lake waters of low alkalinity. Can. J. Fish. Aquat. Sci. 50: 1356-1362.

37. Winner RW. 1985. Bioaccumulation and toxicity of copper as affected by interactions between humic acid and water hardness. Water Res. 19: 449-455.

38. Nor YM and Cheng HH. 1986. Chemical speciation and bioavailability of copper: Uptake and accumulation by *Eichornia*. Environ. Toxicol. Chem. 5: 941-947.

39. Sprague JB. 1985. Factors that modify toxicity. In: Rand GM and Petrocelli SM (Eds.), Fundamentals of Aquatic Toxicology. Hemisphere Publishing Corp. (Washington, D.C.), p. 153.

40. Brand LE, Sunda WG, and Guillard RRL. 1983. Limitation of marine phytoplankton reproductive rates by zinc, managanese, and iron. Limnol. Oceanogr. 28: 1182-1198.

41. Reddy CN and Patrick WH. 1977. Effect of redox potential on the stability of zinc and copper chelates in flooded soils. Soil Sci. Soc. Am. J. 41: 729-732.

42. Raven PH, Evert RF, and Eichhorn SE. 1992. Biology of Plants (5th Ed.), Worth Publishers (NY), p. 156.

43. Ernst WHO, Verkleij JAC, and Schat H. 1992. Metal tolerance in plants (Review). Acta Bot. Neerl. 41: 229-248

44. Huang JW, Pellet DM, Papernik LA, and Kochian LV. 1996. Aluminum interactions with voltage-dependent calcium transport in plasma membrane vesicles isolated from roots of aluminum-sensitive and -resistant wheat cultivars. Plant Physiol. 110: 561-569.

45. Titus JE, Feldman RS, and Grise D. 1990. Submersed macrophyte growth at low pH. 1. CO_2 enrichment effects with fertile sediment. Oecologia 84: 307-313.

46. Giesy Jr, JP and Briese LA. 1978. Trace metal transport by particulates and organic carbon in two South Carolina streams. Verh. Int. Ver. Limnol. 20: 1401-1417.

47. Charpentier S, Garnier J, and Flaugnatti R. 1987. Toxicity and bioaccumulation of cadmium in experimental cultures of duckweed, *Lemna polyrrhiza* L. Bull. Environ. Contam. Toxicol. 38: 1055-1061.

48. Marquenie-van der Werff M and Ernst WHO. 1979. Kinetics of copper and zinc uptake by leaves and roots of an aquatic plant, *Elodea nuttallii*. Z. Pflanzenphysiol. Bd. 92: 1-10.

49. Nakada M, Fukaya K, Takeshita S, and Wada Y. 1979. The accumulation of heavy metals in the submerged plant (*Elodea nuttallii*). Bull. Environ. Contam. Toxicol. 22: 21-27.

50. Basiouny FM, Garrard LA and Haller WT. 1977. Absorption of iron and growth of *Hydrilla verticillata* (L.F.) Royle. Aquat. Bot. 3: 349-356.

51. Gaur JP, Noraho N, and Chauhan YS. 1994. Relationship between heavy metal accumulation and toxicity in *Spirodela polyrhiza* (L.) Schleid. and *Azolla pinnata* R. Br. Aquat. Bot. 49: 183-192.

52. Aquatic plant line drawings are the copyright property of the University of Florida Center for Aquatic Plants (Gainesville). Used with permission.

53. Wetzel 1983, p. 233.

54. Russo RC. 1985. Ammonia, nitrite, and nitrate. In: Rand GM and Petrocelli SM (Eds.), Fundamentals of Aquatic Toxicology. Hemisphere Publishing Corp. (Washington, D.C.), pp. 455-471.

55. Van der Leeden 1990, p. 467.

56. Frank, Neil (1992), Ammonia toxicity to freshwater fish. The effects of pH and temperature. The Aquatic Gardener 5(6): 172-174.

57. Bennett AC. Toxic effects of aqueous ammonia, copper, zinc, lead, boron, and manganese on root growth. In: Carson EW (ed.). The Plant Root and Its Environment. Univ. Press of Virginia (Charlottesville VA), pp. 670-683.

58. Dendene MA, Rolland T, Tremolieres M, and Carbiener R. 1993. Effect of ammonium ions on the net photosynthesis of three species of *Elodea*. Aquat. Bot. 46: 301-315.

59. Santamaria L, Dias C, and Hootsmans MJM. 1994. The influence of ammonia on the growth and photosynthesis of *Ruppia drepanensis* Tineo from Donana National Park (SW Spain). Hydrobiologia 275-276: 219-231.

60. Cary PR and Weerts PGJ. 1983. Growth of *Salvinia molesta* as affected by water temperature and nutrition. 1. Effects of nitrogen level and nitrogen compounds. Aquat. Bot. 16: 163-172.

61. Givan CV. 1979. Metabolic detoxification of ammonia in tissues of higher plants. Phytochemistry 18: 375-382.

62. Kleiner D. 1981. The transport of NH_3 and NH_4^+ across biological membranes. Biochim. Biophys. Acta 639: 41-52.

63. Sperling A. 1995. Managing the characteristics of water to support pond life (Part 2). Pondscapes 8 (1): 34-36.

64. Barr CE, Koh MS and Ryan TE. 1974. NH_3 efflux as a means for measuring H^+ extrusion in *Nitella*. In: Zimmermann U and Dainty J (eds.). Membrane Transport in Plants. Springer-Verlag (New York), pp. 180-185.

65. Anthonisen AC, Loehr RC, Prakasam TBS, and Srinath EG. 1976. Inhibition of nitrification by ammonia and nitrous acid. J. Water Pollut. Control Fed. 48: 835-852.

66. Palackova J and Adamek Z. 1994. The use of methaemoglobin concentration to measure sublethal effects in fish. In: Muller R and Lloyd R (eds), Sublethal and Chronic Effects of Pollutants on Freshwater Fish, Fishing News Books (Blackwell Science Ltd; Cambridge MA).

67. Spotte S. 1979. Fish and Invertebrate Culture. Second Ed. Wiley-Interscience Publications (New York), p. 116.

68. Ferguson AR and Bollard EG. 1969. Nitrogen metabolism of *Spirodela oligorrhiza* 1. Utilization of ammonium, nitrate and nitrite. Planta 88: 344-352.

69. Stewart GR. 1972. The regulation of nitrite reductase level in *Lemna minor* L. J. Exp. Bot. 23: 171-183.

70. Zsoldos F, Haunold E, Vashegyi A, and Herger P. 1993. Nitrite in the root zone and its effects on ion uptake and growth of wheat seedlings. Physiol. Plant. 89: 626-631.

71. Reddy KR and Sutton DL. 1984. Water hyacinths for water quality improvement and biomass production (Reviews and Analyses). J. Environ. Qual. 13: 1-8.

72. Reed SC, Middlebrooks EJ, and Crites RW. 1988. Natural Systems for Waste Management and Treatment. McGraw-Hill Book Co (New York), p. 132.

73. Porath D and Pollock J. 1982. Ammonia stripping by duckweed and its feasibility in circulating aquaculture. Aquat. Bot. 13: 125-131.

74. Fitzgerald GP. 1969. Some factors in the competition or antagonism among bacteria, algae, and aquatic weeds. J. Phycol. 5: 351-359.

75. Graneli W, Lindell M, and Tranvik L. 1996. Photo-oxidative production of dissolved inorganic carbon in lakes of different humic content. Limnol. Oceanogr. 41: 698-706.

Chapter III.

ALLELOPATHY

Q.   In my 55 gal tank with garden soil and good lighting I'm getting good growth of some plants but not others. The five *Anubias nana* and four *Echinodorus cordifolius* seem really at home. However, the *Hygrophila polysperma* and the *Hottonia inflata* are not doing well. The Hygro's leaves are curled and starting to shed, while the *Hottonia* has developed a brown layer on some of the leaves.

I wonder if the temperature has any bearing on the brown I'm getting on the *Hottonia*? One book says the temperature range for this plant is 64-73 °F. (I keep the tank at 77° F.)

A.   I wouldn't be too concerned about plant species that aren't doing well in your tank, provided that others are thriving. It's true that a plant species may not do well, because conditions aren't right for it. Thus, your *Hottonia* may like cooler water and your *Hygrophila* may need more CO_2 than the other plants.

However, the other plants in your tank may be secreting chemicals ('allelochemicals') that inhibit the *Hygrophila* and the *Hottonia*. Allelopathy between plants may explain many instances of a particular plant species not doing well in a particular home aquarium. For example, Amazon swordplants, *Anubias nana*, *Limnophila*, and some *Cryptocoryne* thrive together in my 50 gal. However, I have not been able to grow any *Vallisneria* in this tank. Yet *Vallisneria* thrives in other tanks. I accept allelopathy between plant species as natural and inevitable.

Theoretically, allelopathy is the production and release of chemicals ('allelochemicals') by organisms into their environment that act on other organisms. Although some animals do produce defensive chemicals, allelochemicals are typically produced by plants and other non-motile organisms, and the most likely effect on other organisms is inhibition. For unlike animals, plants are not protected by their size, speed, and strength. Basically, plants must use chemical defense to protect themselves from disease and consumption by herbivorous animals [1,2].

It seems that plants have made a major investment in chemical defense. For allelochemicals are not waste products, because plants produce them at considerable energy cost. Plants actively divert the essential amino acids phenylalanine and tyrosine from protein synthesis to the

34

phenylpropanoid metabolic pathway (**Fig III-1**) to produce phenolic acids, tannins, flavonoids, stilbenes, and lignins. Many of these compounds are allelopathic. The chemical structures of three common phenolic allelochemicals are shown in **Fig. III-2**. Gallic acid and caffeic acid are phenolic acids, while quercetin is a flavonoid.

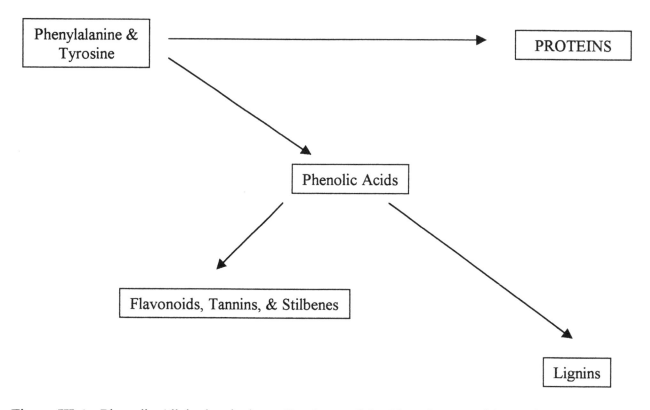

Figure III-1. Phenolic Allelochemicals are Products of the Phenylpropanoid Metabolic Pathway.

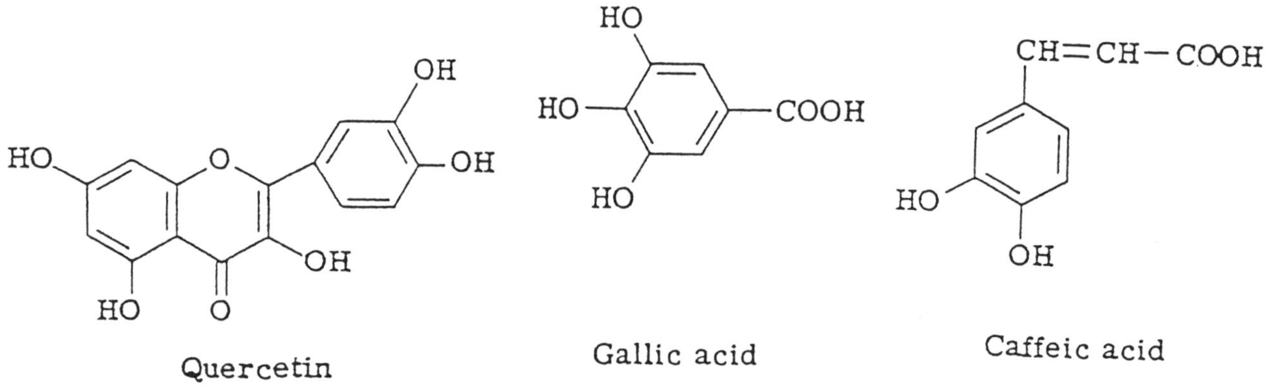

Figure III-2. Chemical Structure of Several Phenolic Allelochemicals.

Because allelochemicals could inhibit the producing plant if they are not stored and handled properly, allelochemicals require more effort than just their production. But the total cost of allelochemicals may be worth the price. Consider that a 10% metabolic investment by the plant in allelochemicals may prevent a 90% loss to herbivore grazing.

Allelopathy in the aquatic environment would be expected to have many random secondary effects. Although the primary action is between the allelochemical producer and the target organism, most allelochemicals are water-soluble, and thus, could influence other organisms in the surrounding water. In a closed environment such as the aquarium where allelochemicals could accumulate, allelopathic effects would be further increased.

A. Allelopathy in Aquatic Plants

Aquatic plants contain a variety of allelochemicals whose primary function[1] is to protect the plant from being eaten by fish and insects or being destroyed by disease. In general, aquatic plants are considered to be more resistant to disease and herbivory than terrestrial plants [6].

Allelopathic behavior has been reported in 97 species of aquatic plants [7]. Indeed, when investigators tested extracts from 17 different aquatic plant species, all 17 extracts inhibited either duckweed or lettuce seedlings (**Table III-1**). Included in the two studies were common aquarium plants like *Cabomba*, Hornwort, and *Vallisneria*. The most inhibitory plant by far was the yellow water lily *Nuphar lutea*; which caused death (not just inhibition) in both duckweed and lettuce seedlings.

Allelochemicals isolated from aquatic plants (**Table III-2**) have been shown to inhibit a variety of organisms (**Table III-3**).

Q. I can't seem to get infusoria to grow. I put a jar on the windowsill with fish mulm for nutrients, some snails, and Java moss. Even though the jar gets sunlight and the moss is growing well, I can't seem to get the green water that I need for infusoria.

A. I think that green water algae is going to have a tough time competing with a healthy aquatic plant in a small volume of water. That water is probably loaded with all kinds of allelochemicals that are preventing alga and infusoria growth. You need to remove the Java moss if you want to grow infusoria.

I think hobbyists see allelopathy as some kind of isolated, strange event, such as a possible reason for not keeping *Vallisneria* and *Sagittaria* in the same tank. The truth, though, is that allelopathy is pervasive throughout the plant kingdom. It is only recently that we (as humans) are recognizing how plants use chemicals to compete and protect themselves. I would assume that all aquatic plants, including Java moss, actively produce and secrete allelochemicals into the water.

---

[1]Allelochemicals may have other functions. For example, the two flavonoids apigenin and luteolin are allelopathic (see table on page 38), but they may also provide protection from harmful UV radiation for the aerial growth of some aquatic plants [3]. And caffeic and chlorogenic acids apparently act as chelators for root uptake of iron by some terrestrial plants [4,5].

Table III-1. Toxicity of Aquatic Plant Extracts.[2]

AQUATIC PLANT	% INHIBITION OF:	
	Lettuce	Duckweed
Brasenia schreberi (water shield)	70 %	60 %
Cabomba carolina (cabomba)	50	60
Ceratophyllum demersum (hornwort)	60	30
Eleocharis acicularis (hair grass, spikerush)	100	50
Eleocharis obtusa (hair grass, spikerush)	100	10
Hydrilla verticillata (hydrilla)	50	30
Juncus repens (rush)	70	40
Limnobium spongia (frog's bit)	60	40
Myriophyllum aquaticum (parrotfeather)	40	70
Myriophyllum spicatum (Eurasian watermilfoil)	50	50
Najas guadalupensis (water nymph)	60	50
Nuphar lutea (yellow water lily)- tops	Death	Death
Nuphar lutea (yellow water lily)- roots	Death	Death
Nymphaea odorata (white water lily)- tops	60	80
Nymphaea odorata (white water lily)- roots	80	60
Nymphoides cordata (floating hearts)	60	40
Potamogeton foliosus (a pondweed)	50	40
Sparganium americanum (bur-reed)	50	30
Vallisneria americana (Val, tapegrass*)*	70	20

[2]Elakovich and Wooten [8,9]. Percent inhibition of lettuce seedlings represents the root length for lettuce seedlings grown in petri plates containing plant extracts as compared to controls (those grown in petri plates without plant extracts). Inhibition of duckweed represents the number of new fronds in nutrient media with plant extracts as opposed to the controls (duckweed without plant extracts). Except for the water lilies, plant extracts were prepared from whole plants. Two hundred grams of fresh plant matter from each species was chopped and thoroughly mixed with 200 ml of distilled water and refrigerated for 1-3 days. The extracts were filter-sterilized and then diluted (1:5) with the growth media of the lettuce and duckweed plants. The duckweed bioassay was run under sterile conditions with bacteria-free duckweed.

Table III-2. Allelochemicals found in Aquatic Plants.

PLANT SPECIES	ALLELOCHEMICAL and REFERENCE
Acorus gramineus	caff, F, pC, S [11]; *a*-asarone and 3 other polyphenols [12]
Aponogeton krauseanus	Km, pOHB, Qu [11]
Bacopa monniera	nicotine [11]
Ceratophyllum demersum	caff, cg, Cy, F, S [11]; sulfur [13]
Eichhornia crassipes	cg, pC, protocatechuic acid, V [14]
Eleocharis coloraodoensis	dihydroactinidiolide, F, Lu, pC [15]
Eleocharis microcarpa	33 oxygenated fatty acids [16]
Elodea callitrichoides	cg, Cy [11]
Elodea canadensis	caff, cg, Cy, Qu [11]
Elodea crispa	caff, cg [11]
Elodea densa	caff, cg, Cy, Qu [11]
Hottonia palustris	Qu [11]
Lemna minor	cg, isoorientin, S, vitexin [11]
Myriophyllum aquaticum	cyanogenic compounds [17]
Myriophyllum brasiliense	G, tellimagrandin II, Qu [18]
Myriophyllum proserpinacoides	E, Cy, cyanogenic compounds, Qu [11]
Myriophyllum spicatum	caff, cinn, E, F, G, pC, protocatachuic, S, Sy, tannic acid [19]; tellima-grandin II [20]
Myriophyllum verticillatum	3 phenylpropanes, 2 oxygenated fatty acids [21]
Nuphar lutea	6,6' dihydroxythiobinupharidine [22]
Nymphaea capensis	caff, cy, E, F, Km, pC, Qu, S, tannins [11]
Pistia stratiotes	caff, cy [11]; *a*-asarone, 2 fatty acids, linolenic acid, a sterol [23]
Posidonia oceanica	caff, F, G, pC, pOHB, pC, protocatechuic, V [24]; F, pOHB, pC, S [25]
Potamogeton species	Ap, isoorientin, Lu [3]
Potamogeton crispus	Ap, Lu [3]; rutin [11]
Sagittaria variabilis	caff, Cy, F, Km, Qu, S [11]
Spartina alterniflora	F, pC [26]
Stratiotes aloides	caff, Cy, rutin [11]
Thalassia testudinum	caff, F, G, protocatechuic, pC, pOHB, V [24]
Typha latifolia	3 sterols and 3 fatty acids inhibitory to algae [27]
Ultricularia vulgaris	Cy [11]
Vallisneria americana	F, G, pC, V [28]
Vallisneria spiralis	caff, pC [11]
Zostera nana	caff, pC, tannins [11]
Zostera marina	caff, F, G, pC, pOHB, protocatechuic, V [29,24]; Ap, Lu [30]

FULL NAMES of compounds are shown in Table III-3.

Table III-3. Allelopathy of Compounds found in Aquatic Plants.[3]

ALLELOPATHIC COMPOUND	ORGANISM (or organ) SHOWN TO BE INHIBITED BY
a-asarone	algae and cyanobacteria [23,31]
apigenin (Ap)	mitochondria [32]; aphids [33]
caffeic acid (caff)	many organisms [34]; enzyme [35]; cyanobacteria [21]; marine slime mould [29]
chlorogenic acid (cg)	many organisms [34]; aphids [33]; fungus [14]
t-cinnamic acid (cinn)	many organisms [34]
cyanidin (Cy)	many organisms [34]
cyanogenic compounds	many organisms [1]
dihydroactinidiolide	radish and watercress seedlings [15]
6,6' dihydroxythiobinupharidine	lettuce seedlings [22]
ellagic acid (E)	many organisms [34]; enzyme [35]; nitrifying bacteria [36]
ferulic acid (F)	cyanobacteria [36]; nitrifying bacteria [37]; enzyme [35]; lettuce seedlings [38]; watercress seedlings [15]; snail [26]
gallic acid (G)	nitrifying bacteria [36]; enzyme [35]; *Hydrilla* tubers [39]; cyano-bacteria [21,18]
isoorientin	bacteria (*Nitrosomonas*) [40]
kaempferol (Km)	many organisms [41]; mitochondria [32]
linoleic acid	algae and cyanobacteria [23]
luteolin (Lu)	radish and watercress seedlings [15]; aphids [33]
nicotine	aphids [1]; duckweed, bacteria, lettuce seedlings [42]
oxygenated fatty acids: *P. stratiotes* *M. verticillatum* *E. microcarpa*	algae and cyanobacteria [23] algae [21] algae [16]
p-coumaric acid (pC)	many organisms; [34]; cyanobacteria [21,36]; nitrifying bacteria [37]; lettuce seedlings [38]; enzyme [35]; radish and watercress seedlings [15]; fungus [14]
p-hydroxybenzoic acid (pOHB)	many organisms [34]; *Hydrilla* tubers [39]; enzyme [35]; lettuce seedlings [38]; aphids [33]; herb seedlings [43]; nitrifying bacteria [37]
phenylpropanes: *M. verticillatum* *A. gramineus*	cyanobacteria [21] algae and cyanobacteria [12]
protocatechuic acid	fungus [14]
quercetin (Qu)	many organisms [34]; aphids [33]; cyanobacteria [18]
rutin	aphids [33]

[3]Abbreviations follow well-known allelopathic phenols. Caff, cinn, E, F, G, *p*C, *p*OHB, protocatechuic, S, Sy, and V are simple phenolic acids and phenylpropanes, while Ap, Cy, Km, Lu and Qu are flavonoids. Linoleic is a C_{18} fatty acid. The newly isolated and identified phenylpropanes, oxygenated fatty acids, sterols, and tannins are described in the references.

sinapic acid (S)	cyanobacteria [21]
sterols: *P. stratiotes* *T. latifolia*	algae [23] algae [27]
sulfur	algae [13]
syringic acid (Sy)	lettuce seedlings [38]; herb seedlings [43]; nitrifying bacteria [37]
tellimagrandin II	cyanobacteria [18]; enzyme [20]
tannic acid	many organisms [1]; nitrifying bacteria [36]
vanillic acid (V)	cyanobacterium [36]; nitrifying bacteria [37]; *Hydrilla* tubers [39]; lettuce seedlings [38]; herb seedlings [43]; fungus [14]
vitexin	aphids [33]

1. Phenolics as Allelochemicals in Aquatic Plants

It is natural that phenolics (rather than alkaloids, etc) play a prominent role in aquatic plant allelopathy.[4] This is because phenolics are part of the plant's phenylpropanoid metabolism for synthesizing lignins, which give structural support to terrestrial plants and trees allowing them to stand upright. During evolution when land plants moved into the water to become aquatic plants, they lost their need for lignins, because water buoyancy provided the needed structural support. Thus, the lignin content was gradually reduced.[5] Most submerged aquatic plants now contain little if any of the unneeded lignins, but they still contain the phenolic precursors of lignins [45,46].

The fact that the phenolic precursors of lignins mildly inhibit a variety of organisms was fortuitous for aquatic plants. Because the phenylpropanoid pathway was already in place, aquatic plants didn't have to create a completely new metabolic pathway to make allelochemicals. Over the course of evolution, spontaneous mutations almost surely occurred that increased the inhibitory properties of phenolics already being produced. Indeed, one investigator [31] showed how simple chemical alterations of common phenolic acids could dramatically affect their inhibition of algae.

The higher the aquatic plant's phenolic content, the less chance it will be consumed [47,48]. Plants containing more than 6% phenolics are considered to be indigestible and of little food value to herbivores. (Agricultural forage crops, which are developed for palatability, contain less than 2-3% phenolics.) The phenolic content of aquatic plants averages about 6% ranging from a low of 0.8% for *Elodea densa* to a high of 15% for *Cabomba caroliniana* [45].

---

[4]Alkaloids like nicotine, digitoxin, strychnine, morphine, and curare are well-known allelochemicals of terrestrial plants [1]. Water lilies have been found to contain a variety of alkaloids [17]. However, alkaloids in other aquatic plants are apparently scarce; fifteen species of submerged plants were found to contain less than 0.06% alkaloids [44].

[5]McClure [11] provides phylogenetic evidence for the gradual reduction of lignin that occured along with aquatic plant evolution. Vanillin and syringaldehyde are specific phenol precursors of lignin. The more primitive species of the Lemnaceae (e.g. *Spirodela intermedia*, *S. polyrhiza*, and *S. oligorhiza*) contain these phenols, whereas the more evolved species of Lemnaceae (e.g. *Lemna minor*, *L. gibba*, and *L. trisulca*) do not.

Phenolics may also affect allelopathy between aquatic plants. For example, plant species (*Nymphaea odorata*, *Brasenia schreberi*, and *Cabomba caroliniana*) that contain the highest levels of phenolics [45,46] were found to inhibit duckweed the most [8].

Phenolics inhibit diverse organisms, because they indiscriminately inactivate proteins [49]. The leather tanning industry is based on the ability of plant polyphenols like tannins to inactivate and polymerize proteins in the curing process of animal skins [50]. In the live plant, these same tannins deter insect feeding by damaging proteins in the insect's gut.

Phenolic acids may be found in very high concentrations in specialized 'phenol cells'. In the waterhyacinth, phenol cells are mainly interspersed with ordinary cells in the subepidermal tissue of both leaf surfaces [51]. The phenolic acids in these cells are found in very high concentrations– about 1,000 ppm– and consist of chlorogenic, protocatechuic, vanillic, and *p*-coumaric acids [14]. Phenol cells are believed to play a role in waterhyacinth resistance to the fungus responsible for 'leaf-spotting' disease [52].

2. Allelochemical Release from the Plant

Do allelochemicals ever actually leave the aquatic plant? If they remain tightly bound within the plant, their impact on the aquarium environment– algae, bacteria, or other plants– would be limited.

Terrestrial plants frequently release allelochemicals into their surroundings [36]. For example, the roots of young papaya trees were found to secrete the allelochemical benzyl isothiocyanate at the rate of 2 µg/tree/day [53]. The soft chaparral shrub releases from its leaves a variety of water-soluble phenolic acids that are the same as those found in aquatic plants. Rainwater washes these compounds off the leaves and into the soil where they prevent the germination and growth of competitive herbs [43].

Aquatic plants probably release large amounts of allelochemicals, for they are leaky when they're alive and even more so when they're dead. The annual release of dissolved organic carbon (DOC) by submersed aquatic plants is believed to be about 4% of total carbon fixed when alive and 40% when dead [54]. [Bacteria convert much of this DOC to humic substances (see page 61).] Furthermore, aquatic plants continuously turn over their leaves, replacing older, decaying leaves with new leaves. For example, the water lily *Nymphaea odorata* growing in the Southern USA reportedly had 7 full leaf turnovers per year. Along with this abundant biomass turnover is the enhanced potential for allelochemical release into the water [55].

Indeed, allelochemicals have been found in the culture media of aquatic plants. When duckweed is grown in sterile culture media, 'cinnamic acids are quickly detected in the medium and, after several days, flavonoids are found' [11]. And *Myriophyllum brasiliense* reportedly released a small amount of its allelopathic polyphenols into the culture media [18]. Phenolic acid release from *Myriophyllum spicatum* within 10 days was 2-4 mg/g dry plant matter [20]. Several allelochemicals from *Eleocharis microcarpa* were found in the pond water it was growing in [16].

Although much of the DOC released by aquatic plants is quickly metabolized by bacteria, there is always a portion that resists decomposition. For example, much of the DOC released by *Scripus subterminalis* was metabolized by bacteria within 3 days, but about 5 to 10% was left untouched at 40 days [56]. This long-lasting DOC would include phenolic compounds (both synthesized allelochemicals and humic substances), because they are by nature resistant to bacterial degradation. (Decomposition rates of different components of plant residues after one year were found to be 99% for sugar, 90% for hemicellulose, 75% for cellulose, 50% for lignin, 25% for waxes and only 10% for phenolic compounds [57].)

3. The Subtle Nature of Aquatic Plant Allelopathy

Most plant allelochemicals are only mildly inhibitory; thus, allelopathy is difficult for scientists to prove.

'The probability is very high that the allelopathy of plants results from the combined effect of many, mildly potent chemicals. This lack of specificity and potency can be aesthetically dissatisfying and difficult for scientists to prove. Thus, scientists continue to search for more definite evidence of specific and highly potent phytotoxins, although in reality the inhibitory quality of plants may lie in the combined actions of a large number of individually inadequate toxic compounds .' [43]

Indeed, an allelochemical may inhibit more when combined with other allelochemicals than when tested alone (i.e., the 'synergistic effect') [59]. For example, two not-too-potent phenolics (gallic acid and caffeic acid) inhibited blue-green algae 6 times more strongly when they were mixed together than when they were tested alone [21]. This is an important finding, because the low potency of many phenolic allelochemicals suggests that they might have little or no effect outside the laboratory. However, if there are a lot of allelochemicals (as there are) and they are acting synergistically, then allelopathy is possible.

Allelopathy in aquatic plants is not dramatic. It is subtle. However, all aquatic plants continuously produce a large number and variety of defensive compounds that mildly inhibit all organisms. It is likely that these allelochemicals might have subtle and unrecognized effects on the plants, bacteria, algae, and invertebrates in aquatic ecosystems.

4. Aquatic Plants versus Algae

Aquatic botanists have observed that lake areas with heavy plant growth often have reduced algal growth [20]. Granted that some of this apparent inhibition may be due to plant competition with algae for light and nutrients. However, some inhibition may be due to specific plant-produced allelochemicals. Other inhibition may be due to humic substances, which can inhibit organisms [61]. Humic substances, which are phenolic compounds, are derived from the decomposition (rather than the synthesis) of plant phenolics (see page 61).

One investigator [62] tracked algal growth as a function of phenolics (mainly humic substances) in 6 Spanish ponds over a two year period. Because of seasonal floods, phenolics in the ponds varied in concentration from 4 to 26 mg/l. When concentrations were at or above 10 mg/l and nutrient levels were low, algal growth was lessened. In an investigation using phenolic extracts from *Myriophyllum spicatum* [19], a 10 mg/l concentration of phenolics moderately inhibited algae and cyanobacteria.

Although phenolic allelochemicals and non-specific humic acids may help control algal growth, other compound types are probably involved in aquatic plant allelopathy. *Chara globularis* ('skunk-weed') produces two sulfur-containing compounds, a dithiolane and a trithiane, which were found to strongly inhibit algal photosynthesis [13]. In another study, 33 of the 43 different oxygenated fatty acids found in the pondwater containing the spikerush *Eleocharis microcarpa* inhibited blue-green algae *in vitro* [16].

Table III-4 shows the inhibition of various algae by allelochemicals of the emergent plant *Typha latifolia*. The activity of plant allelochemicals was compared to the algaecide copper sulfate. Two species of blue-green algae (*Anabaena flosaquae* and *Synecococcus leopoliensis*) were quite sensitive to both the crude plant extract and the sterol.

Table III-4. Inhibition of Algae by *Typha latifolia* Compared to Copper Sulfate [27]. 'Plant Extract' is an ethyl ether extract. Sterol 'C' is stigmast-4-ene-3, 6-dione. The bioassay was done on petri dishs containing nutrient agar inoculated with exponentially growing algae. Acetone solutions containing known quantities of chemicals were dried on filter disks, which were then added to the petri dishs. The plates were incubated in the light until alga growth became visible. Growth inhibition was manifested as clear zones around the filter disks.

Algal Species	Plant Extract (0.5 mg)	Sterol 'C' (0.7 µmol)	Copper Sulfate (0.5 µmol)
Anabaena flosaquae	++	++	++
Aulosira terrestre	-	-	++
Chlamydomonas sphagnophila	-	-	-
Chlorella emersonii	+	+	+++
Chlorella vulgaris	+	+	+++
Closterium acerosum	+	-	-
Coccomyxa elongata	+	-	-
Euglena gracilis	-	-	-
Muriella aurantiaca	+	+	-
Navicula pelliculosa	+	-	+
Nostoc commune	-	-	+
Phormidium autumnale	++	-	+
Porphyridium aerugineum	+	-	-
Porphyrosiphon notarisii	++	-	+
Scytonema hofmanni	++	-	+
Selenastrum capricornutum	+	-	-
Stichococcus bacillaris	+	-	-
Synecococcus leopoliensis	++	+++	++

Symbols: - is no inhibition of algal growth; + is a 7-14 mm diameter of inhibition; ++ is 15-23 mm diameter of inhibition; and +++ is a 23 mm diameter of inhibition.

Although most allelochemicals of aquatic plants only mildly inhibit algae, some are more potent inhibitors. While studying nutrient uptake from polluted waters, investigators [18] suspected that *Myriophyllum brasiliense* was secreting inhibitory substances against the nearby blue-green algae. Using careful extraction methods, they were able to isolate from the plant 2 very potent polyphenols, Tellimagrandin II and 1-desgalloyleugeniin.

Myriophyllum spicatum's success in dominating North American lakes may be due to its phenolics. The plant's phenolic compounds were shown to completely inhibit blue-green algae at a concentration of 10 mg/l; green algae was inhibited by 20 mg/l [19]. Tellimagrandin II, which was first discovered in the terrestrial perennial *Tellima grandiflora* and subsequently in other members of the order Rosales [63], was found in high concentrations in *M. spicatum* [20]. The investigator calculated that if *M. spicatum* released only 1% of its Tellimagrandin II, the release would be enough to severely affect both ephiphytic (attached to plant) and planktonic (suspended) algae [64].

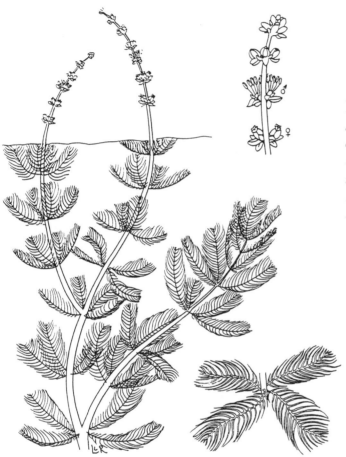

Eurasian water milfoil (*Myriophyllum spicatum*). *M. spicatum* appears to produce allelochemicals against a variety of different organisms (duckweed, blue-green algae, mosquito larva, and the aquatic plant *Najas marina*). It releases a fairly potent allelochemical (Tellimagrandin II) that may protect it from algae. (Plant drawing from IFAS [65].)

Recently, a group of investigators has systematically screened several aquatic plants for allelochemicals against algae. Seven different phenolic acids were isolated from *Acorus gramineus*, including some that inhibited several species of algae and cyanobacteria with a toxicity comparable to copper sulfate [12]. The investigators also found assorted allelochemicals– sterols, polyprenols, fatty acids, and *a*-asarone– in *Pistia stratiotes* [23]. The most inhibitory compound was the phenolic acid *a*-asarone, which inhibited 14 of the 19 algal species tested [31].

Although the above studies show that plants contain small quantities of potent algal inhibitors like *a*-asarone and Tellimagrandin II, many aquatic plants may not produce these compounds in quantities sufficient to control algal growth in nature (or in our aquariums). The bulk of aquatic plant allelopathy probably lies with the sheer quantity (~6% of plant dry weight) of total miscellaneous phenolic acids.

5. Aquatic Plants versus Bacteria and Invertebrates

Because allelochemicals are often non-specific inhibitors, aquatic plants may inhibit bacteria. For example, extracts of *Brasenia schreberi* were tested against 9 species of bacteria, both gram-negative and gram-positive; all 9 species were inhibited by various fractions of the plant extract [66]. Extracts of the water lily *Nymphaea tuberosa* showed high antimicrobial activity against several species of bacteria [67]. The allelochemicals responsible for the inhibition were identified as tannic acid, gallic acid, and ethyl gallate, all common phenolics found in many aquatic plants. Moreover, several studies show that allelochemicals produced by aquatic plants inhibit cyanobacteria ('blue-green algae'). (This infers that other bacteria might be inhibited as well.)

Aquatic plants apparently release chemicals into the water that repel invertebrates. Thus, daphnia moved away from *Elodea*, *Myriophyllum*, and *Nitella* in experimental tanks more than they did in control tanks with plastic plants [68]. Another investigator [69] showed that extracts of *Myriophyllum spicatum* inhibited midges and mosquito larva. Allelopathy may explain what biologists have observed in nature– reduced populations of mosquitoes, midges, and daphnia in stagnant lake areas of heavy plant growth.

Snails avoid eating healthy leaves of aquatic plants, but will consume dead or diseased ones [70,71]. For example, when periwinkle snails were offered a choice between freshly collected leaves of the saltwater *Spartina alterniflora*, they preferred dead (but intact) leaves over healthy leaves about three to one. The

Q. *Vallisneria gigantea* has proved a great challenge for me, although it is supposed to be a relatively easy plant to grow. After an initial flush of growth, with luxuriant scrolling of leaves over the surface of the tank, the plants seem to always decline.

Another problem I have experienced is with mystery snails. While the snails have been observed occasionally munching on the newest growth of *H. polysperma*, little lasting damage occurs. *V. gigantea* seems to be a favorite food. The snails will make it their exclusive food until it is virtually all consumed. The same snails placed in a tank with *V. spiralis* revert to an exclusive algae diet. Why consume *V. gigantea* and not *V. spiralis*? No other plants in the 75 gal tank are attacked like this. Have other aquatic gardeners had this experience? Are there other plants with which mystery snails cannot be trusted?

A. Your question about *Vallisneria gigantea* and mystery snails is most interesting.

Although I have no practical information about mystery snails consuming plants, everything I have read in the scientific literature suggests that most species of snails benefit plants, cleaning the leaves and consuming only dead or dying plants. [All healthy aquatic plants contain protective chemicals (allelochemicals) that repel snails and other herbivores, but once the plant tissue begins to disintegrate, these repellent chemicals leach out. Only then do the snails feed on the plant.] Since you have described a problem with *V. gigantea* dying, possibly the snails are merely consuming a dying plant and leaving the healthy *V. spiralis* alone?.

lower ferulic acid content in the dead leaves was believed to account for the difference in preference [26]. (Ferulic acid, an allelopathic phenolic acid, would leak out as the leaves died and make them less inhibitory.)

6. Chemical Warfare between Aquatic Plants

Aquatic plants often grow better alone than when paired with another species [67]. Besides protecting themselves from being eaten, aquatic plants also synthesize allelochemicals that make them more competitive in their immediate environment. That is, they can poison neighboring plants and take over the territory.

a.) Allelopathy in the Substrate

Allelochemical release into the substrate has been proven conclusively for the dwarf spikerush (*Eleocharis coloradoensis*). This tiny plant, which in nature could eliminate heavy stands of large pondweeds, was suspected of secreting allelochemicals into the substrate.

In a series of experiments, investigators [72] first showed that the pondweeds *Potamogeton nodosus* and especially *P. pectinatus* did not multiply well when their tubers were planted in soil containing the dwarf spikerush. However, because the plants were growing together in the same aquaria, the reduced growth of the pondweeds could have been due to competition for nutrients or possible modifications of water quality by the spikerush.

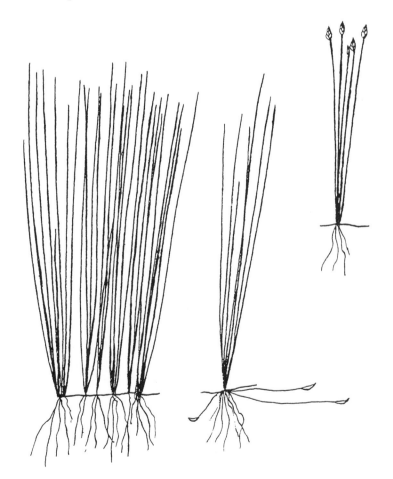

Dwarf spikerush *Eleocharis coloradoensis* (a hairgrass). This small (2"-3"), turf-forming plant found in the western USA is apparently able to compete well with much larger plants by releasing poisons into the substrate. Although allelopathy has been suspected and probably occurrs in other *Eleocharis*, it has been proven definitively for *E. coloradoensis*. Drawing from Hotchkiss 1967 [76].

So the same investigators proceeded on to a more definitive experiment where the plants were grown in separate aquaria. Dwarf spikerush were planted and grown for 3 months in one set of containers, while the pondweeds were planted in separate, lower-level containers. A plastic hose at the bottom connected the containers. Water, driven by gravity, slowly percolated down through the soil where the spikerush was growing and passed up through the soil of the pond-weed cultures. The control for this experiment was the same set-up without the spikerush. The leachate from the spikerush soil reduced growth in the pondweeds to less than half; chlorosis was also apparent in the treated plants. The investigators were also careful to show that the nutrient content of the spikerush leachate was similar to the bare soil leachate, indicating that nutrient deficiencies were not responsible for the poor growth of the pondweeds.

However, even these experiments did not conclusively prove that the spikerush was allelopathic. Bacteria and other microbes in the root area can enhance or degrade allelochemicals secreted by plant roots. Soil humus and clay can absorb allelochemicals and lessen their inhibition [73,74]. All these factors could affect allelopathic activity in sediments and soils. Only if the spikerush remained inhibitory in the absence of bacteria and soil particles, could the inhibition be attributed directly to spikerush allelochemicals. When later investigators [75] cultured *Eleocharis coloradoensis* in sand and nutrient media under sterile conditions, the root exudates were still inhibitory (i.e., against *P. pectinatus* and *Hydrilla vercillata*). These final experiments provide definitive evidence that the spikerush releases inhibitory allelochemicals into the substrate.

Although the dwarf spikerush contains several known inhibitory compounds, its allelopathy is believed to be due mainly to dihydroactinidiolide [15].

b.) Allelopathy in the Water

Allelopathy also occurs in the overlying water and can be quite specific. For example, investigators [77] planted twenty *Najas* alone or paired with 20 plants of another species in large (200 liter) containers containing a sandy loam soil. The three other species that *Najas* was paired with were *Potamogeton lucens*, *Scirpus litoralis*, or *Myriophyllum spicatum*. During the 2 month growth period, *Najas* was given enough room so that plants were not restricted by either space or nutrients. The results showed that *Najas* grew just as well with *P. lucens* and *S. litoralis* as it did alone. However, *Najas* growth was reduced in half when it was grown with *M. spicatum*.

In a separate experiment, water from pure *M. spicatum* cultures was added each week to containers with *Najas*. Growth of *Najas* over the summer in *M. spicatum* water was less than 1/3 of its growth in ordinary tap water. Again, investigators were careful to show that nutrient depletion was not the cause of the *Najas'* poor growth. *M. spicatum* was also shown to be inhibited by *Najas*. The results could explain why *Najas marina* and *Myriophyllum spicatum* do not usually grow together in native water bodies (of Israel).

Apparently, *Hydrilla* and *Ceratophyllum* sometimes do not grow well together in nature. Investigators [78] sought to find a reason why just a few shoots of *Hydrilla* entering Indian ponds and reservoirs could quickly and totally eliminate stands of *Ceratophyllum*. So *Ceratophyllum demersum* and *C. muricatum* were grown either alone or with *Hydrilla verticillata* in cement tanks containing garden soil. Plants were separated by wire netting so that the plants were not in direct competition; they just shared the same water. The results were dramatic. Initially both *Hydrilla* and the *Ceratophyllum* species grew well together, but after 30 days, the *Ceratophyllum* turned pale and gradually decayed. After 70 days, the *Ceratophyllum* had died, while *Hydrilla* had grown well in all available space. Control plants (*Ceratophyllum demersum* and *C. muricatum* grown without exposure to *Hydrilla*) were healthy and grew well.

7. Defensive Chemicals Induced by Infection

Although all plants contain a large variety of phenolic acids, some phenolic acids may also be induced by infection [79]. For example, the slime mould *Labyrinthula zosterae* devastated North Atlantic seagrass beds of *Zostera marina* in the 1930s. When investigators [80] purposely infected this plant species with the slime mould, the plant's phenolic acid production was stimulated, especially near the infection site (**Fig. III-3**). At 2 cm from the slime mold lesion, the phenolic acid concentration was about 0.2 mg/kg dry wt, but at 8 cm away the phenolic acid concentration decreased by almost half to about 0.1 mg/kg. Caffeic acid, in particular, was shown to increase about 5-fold in infected leaves, thereby reaching inhibitory concentrations [29].

Marine eelgrass (*Zostera marina*). *Z. marina*, the most widely distributed sea grass in America, forms large underwater meadows. When *Z. marina* was deliberately infected with a pathogenic slime mold, plants synthesized more protective phenolic acids around the infection site. Plant drawing from Hellquist [81].

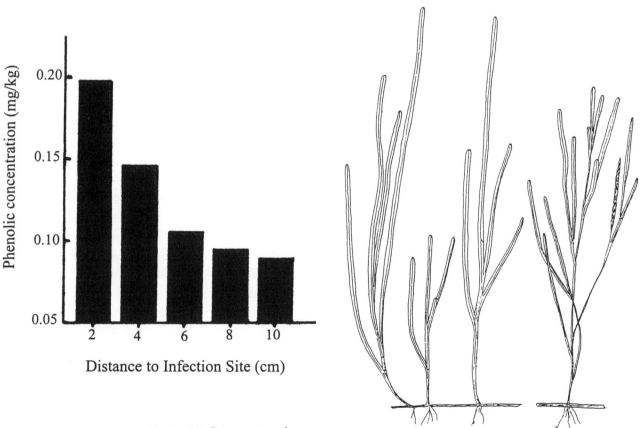

Figure III-3. Phenolic Acid Concentrations near the Infection Site of *Zostera marina* Leaves. Phenolic concentration is based on dry weight. (Fig. 3 from Vergeer [80] redrawn and used with permission from Elsevier Science.)

Plants threatened by algae may increase their defensive phenolic acids. A large parasitic algae (*Caulerpa taxifolia*), accidentally introduced into the Mediterranean Sea in 1984, has invaded large seagrass meadows of *Posidonia oceanica* along the French coast. Algae attach to the plant's rhizome and subsequently damage or kill the plant. Investigators [82] showed that the leaf area occupied by phenol cells was 43% in threatened plants, almost twice that of plants from sediment areas that had not been invaded. In a separate study, the phenolic acids (especially ferulic acid) in threatened plants (641 µg/g dry wt) was almost twice that of plants from non-invaded areas (391 µg/g dry wt) [25].

8. Auto-inhibition

Allelopathic auto-inhibition, in which a plant inhibits its own species, has been reported in a variety of native plants and agricultural plants [1]. For example, the allelochemical amygdalin (a cyanogenic glycoside) was found in the bark of peach tree roots. Bacteria in the soil break down the non-inhibitory amygdalin into a cyanide that strongly inhibits young peach trees [83].

Auto-inhibition has also been reported for several species of algae [84] and emergent aquatic plants [67]. For example, soil extracts from the reed *Phragmites karka* strongly inhibited seed germination in this species.

But why would plants release compounds that inhibit their own species? One investigator [73] explains that auto-inhibition may help plants regulate their own population density. Frequently, auto-inhibition involves toxicity to seeds and seedlings but not adult plants. While auto-inhibition limits the number of plants, especially under stressful conditions, it does not destroy the species. Therefore, auto-inhibition may be an adaptive strategy than enhances species survival.

> **Q.** My plants have everything. Lighting is strong, the substrate is an ideal mixture of soil, sand, and vermiculite. I use CO_2 injection, micronutrient fertilizers, and add pieces of pond fertilizer plugs to the substrate each month. I get excellent plant growth and no algae. However, after about a year there's a decline in plant vigor and the increasing presence of algae. Is it because the substrate becomes increasingly anaerobic?
>
> **A.** Possibly, but an anaerobic substrate is probably a secondary effect. The primary problem is that the plants have stopped growing for some reason. The substrate degradation you're seeing could be due to allelopathy.
>
> Many plant species release allelochemicals that either inhibit other plants or themselves ('auto-inhibition'). The aquarium substrate with its solid bottom is particularly conducive to the gradual buildup of allelochemicals. Moreover, in your tank with the CO_2 injection and rapid plant growth, allelochemicals may build up faster in the substrate than they can be decomposed by bacteria or bind to soil particles. The accumulation of auto-inhibitory allelochemicals may be one reason why your substrate gave out.

B. Allelopathy in Algae

Algae produce their own allelochemicals, some probably designed to compete with other algae, others to deter algae-eating protozoa and other herbivores. The intended target organism is often difficult to determine, because secondary effects abound in aquatic ecosystems. One investigator [85] expressed the frustration of trying to study algal allelopathy in the aquatic environment: "Allelochemistry is so pervasive in aquatic systems that in our laboratory, even when we specifically try to avoid it, we find it wherever we look. Our greatest problem is sorting it out."

Another investigator [86] routinely used the filamentous algae *Pithophora* to keep his aquariums free of other algae, especially 'green-water' algae. Eventually, he set up 4 experimental aquariums containing guppies with and without the *Pithophora* algae. Even though the aquariums had continuous lighting, aquariums containing *Pithophora* remained clear for all 4 weeks, whereas the water in the aquariums without *Pithophora* became green in 7 days. The growth of the green- water algae seemed to have nothing to do with nitrate and phosphate levels in the water (**Table III-5**).

Table III-5. Effect of *Pithophora* Algae on 'Green Water' Algae [86].

Tank Treatment	Water Color	Phosphates (mg/l P)		Nitrates (mg/l N)	
		Initial	Final	Initial	Final
None	Green	2.0	1.1	5.5	1.9
None	Green	0.05	0	1.6	7.5
Pithophora algae	Clear	0.9	1.4	2.4	14.0
Pithophora algae	Clear	0.04	0.07	0.8	1.4

Algae are leaky vessels; they release about every substance they make, including allelochemicals [87]. One investigator [85] surveyed over 200 different pairings of algal species from a Connecticut lake for possible allelopathy. ('Pairings' consisted of exposing one algal species to heat-treated filtrates from another algal species.) Over two-thirds of the 200 pairings were allelopathic, in that the filtrate either inhibited or stimulated the tested species. Moreover, the investigator found that the lab results matched the sequence of algal blooms in the lake itself. That is, alga species dominating the lake during one season secreted substances into the water that inhibited their predecessors and stimulated their successors.

Algae may be able to inhibit competitors not just by releasing allelochemicals into the water but by transferring the allelochemicals directly into their targets. Thus, one investigator [64] grew a blue-green algae that produced the lipophilic allelochemical Fischerellin A in the presence of tiny beads that had a lipophilic surface. This lipophilic (fat-soluble) surface would experimentally mimic the cell surface of competing blue-green algae. Interestingly, no Fischerellin A was detected in the water; rather the allelochemical was found attached to the beads suggesting that the algae probably transfers the allelochemical directly to target organisms.

Do algae produce allelochemicals that affect plants? Apparently they do. Allelopathic terpenoids of the macroalgae *Caulerpa taxifolia* have been cited as one reason this algae has been able to decimate underwater meadows of the aquatic plant *Posidonia oceanica* [82]. And the water hyacinth became chlorotic, grew poorly, and eventually died when introduced into cement tanks containing a mixture of various common algae [88].

50

When investigators [89] exposed *Zannichellia peltata* to filtered water from blue-green algae, the plant's growth was significantly inhibited (about 25% after 1 month). However, culture water from the plants did not affect the algae (mostly *Anabaena*). The investigators concluded that allelochemicals released by blue-green algae may play a role in algal take-overs of this particular species in some polluted waters.

When duckweed was grown with individual algal species isolated from wastewater, 7 of the 9 species induced chlorosis in the duckweed [90]. Under certain conditions, three algal species could actually kill the duckweed. Interestingly, when duckweed was tested against combinations of algal species, the results were unpredictable. For example, two algal species that strongly inhibited duckweed when tested individually against duckweed, actually stimulated the duckweed when both were grown together with duckweed.

In contrast to the subtle nature of aquatic plant allelopathy, algal allelopathy can be quite dramatic [92,93]. About 1% of algal species release extremely toxic allelochemicals, some of the most lethal

Zannichellia peltata. *Z. peltata*, a brackish water plant from southern Europe, was found to be susceptible to the allelochemicals of blue-green algae. (Drawing from van Vierssen [90] and used with permission of Elsevier Science.)

biological toxins known. Oceanic 'red tides' of certain dinoflagellate algae can cover hundreds of square miles and wreak havoc on marine life. Not only do they kill fish, but they can also cause 'shell-fish poisoning' in man– respiratory paralysis and death within 12 hours [94].

The toxins secreted by certain dinoflagellates and blue-green algae include potent neuro-toxins and hepatoxins [95]. Blue-green algae in livestock drinking water are responsible for some cattle death each year. After the algae are ingested, they die in the animal's digestive tract and release their toxins [96].

C. Allelopathy in the Aquarium

Often strange things happen in planted aquariums for which there appears to be no rational explanation. I wrote this chapter, because I realized that nutrients, water chemistry, and light could not be the only factors controlling the aquarium ecology.

For example, tanks with heavy plant growth often seem to have very little algae. All of my tanks have adequate light, often with many hours of direct sunlight. Nitrate and phosphate levels greatly exceed algal requirements. The fact that algae does not do well despite intense light and high nutrient levels, suggests that allelochemicals released by the plants might help control algal growth.

Plant allelochemicals are relatively harmless and would not be expected to injure fish in the aquarium. However, the allelochemicals of some algal species can be highly toxic. Thus, I once watched what happened to some fish (*Lamprologus leleupi*) when I innocently scraped off a heavy algal film from the aquarium glass. Within hours, the fish were literally jumping out of the tank and could only be saved by putting them into completely new water. (Other fish species in the tank were wholly unaffected.) I suspect that the alga was a toxic species, and that upon its death, it released an allelochemical that was neurotoxic to the *L. leleupi*, but not the other fish. (That algal toxins affect certain fish species more than others has been described [93].)

Several years after this one incident, I received a large, late-night shipment of fancy, show-quality guppies. Not having time to set up a separate tank and knowing the guppies were from healthy stock, I divided up the guppies and added some to three well-established tanks. The show guppies in two

> **Q.** Do you see any advantage in setting up a 'High-tech' aquarium?
>
> **A.** Yes, and it is because allelopathy is reduced in these tanks. Generally, high-tech systems advocate frequent water changes. Also, many tanks have substrate heating cables, which induce water circulation into and out of the substrate. In essence, the substrate is continuously 'washed' so that the allelochemicals are brought into the overlying water where they can either be metabolized or diluted out.
>
> Thus, allelochemicals are prevented from accumulating in both the water and substrate in high-tech systems. Auto-inhibition is lessened and strongly allelopathic plants are prevented from dominating other species. Generally, a much wider variety of plant species can thrive within the same tank. Thus, hobbyists with 'High-tech' aquaria can indulge in aquascaping and carefully controlled planting schemes.

of the tanks behaved strangely, dive-bombing into objects and swimming erratically. I thought it was their fright from the late-night handling, but the next day these guppies were dead. Meanwhile, common 'feeder' guppies and their babies in these same two tanks were completely unaffected. I might have attributed the cause to some defect in the show guppies, except that the third set of show guppies in my 50 gal 'Rainbow' tank appeared wholly normal. After much thought, I attributed the difference to algal allelopathy. This is because the two problem tanks contained small amounts of green mat algae whereas the 'Rainbow' tank had a light dusting of 'fuzz' algae on the glass, but none of the green mat algae. I believe that one or more species of the green mat algae (see page 164) was secreting a neurotoxin to which the show guppies, but not the common guppies, were exquisitely sensitive.

Also, allelopathy between plants may explain less dramatic, but more common phenomena I have observed in my aquariums. Some plant species in my tanks dwindle away with time for no apparent reason. Because all my tanks contain high nutrient levels and adequate light, I believe that some species are slowly poisoned by the allelochemicals released by other species.

I've made a few changes in my aquariums since I became aware of allelopathy. I like to keep prized plant species in their own pots, so that the plant's roots are protected from substrate allelochemicals from neighboring plants. I keep plants that I particularly like in their own tanks.

For example, I have set aside separate tanks for *Cryptocoryne*, *Vallisneria*, and Swordplants. I'm not too dismayed when a newly introduced plant species doesn't do well in an established tank. Above all, I don't expect to keep a wide variety of plants in a single tank.

Although allelopathy in the aquarium includes negative interactions between organisms, I generally accept allelopathy as being a natural part of their competition. Moreover, allelochemicals probably keep algae under control and help protect fish from bacterial disease. Aquariums, because of their small water volume and contained substrate, lend themselves to allelopathic interactions between organisms. A variety of allelochemicals released by plants, bacteria, and algae accumulate and produce many unexpected (and unintended) effects. I believe that allelopathy is rampant in the home aquarium.

REFERENCES

1. Whittaker RH and Feeny PP. 1971. Allelochemics: Chemical interactions between species. Science 171: 757-770.
2. Berenbaum MR. 1995. The chemistry of defense: Theory and practice. Proc. Nat. Acad. Sci. 92: 2-8.
3. Les DH and Sheridan DJ. 1990. Biochemical heterophylly and flavonoid evolution in North American *Potamogeton* (Potamogetonaceae). Am. J. Bot. 77: 453-465.
4. Hether NH, Olsen RA, and Jackson LL. 1984. Chemical identification of iron reductants exuded by plant roots. J. Plant Nutr. 7: 667-676.
5. Hopkins WG. 1995. Introduction to Plant Physiology. John Wiley (NY), pp 75-76.
6. Wetzel RG. 1983. Limnology (Second Ed.). Saunders College Publishing (Philadelphia, PA), p. 543.
7. Elakovich SD and Wooten JW. 1995. Allelopathic, herbaceous, vascular hydrophytes. In: Inderjit, Dakshini KMM, and Einhellig FA (eds), Allelopathy: Organisms, Processes, and Applications. ACS Symposium Series 582 (Washington D.C), pp. 58-73.
8. Elakovich SD and Wooten JW. 1989. Allelopathic Aquatic Plants for Aquatic Plant Management; A Feasibility Study. Environmental Laboratory, Univ. of Southern Miss. (Hattiesburg, MS). 40 pp. (AD A217 441)
9. Elakovich SD and Wooten JW. 1991. Allelopathic potential of *Nuphar lutea* (L.) Sibth. & Sm. (Nymphaeaceae). J. Chem. Ecol. 17: 707-714.
10. Preston CD and Croft JM. 1997. Aquatic Plants in Britain and Ireland. B.H. & A. Harley Ltd (Essex, England).
11. McClure JW. 1970. Secondary constituents of aquatic angiosperms. In: Harborne JB (ed), Phytochemical Phylogeny. Academic Press (NY), pp 233-268.
12. Della Greca MD, Monaco P, Previtera L, Aliotta G, Pinto G, and Pollio A. 1989. Allelochemical activity of phenylpropanes from *Acorus gramineus*. Phytochemistry 28: 2319-2321.
13. Wium-Andersen S and Houen G. 1983. Elemental sulphur, a possible allelopathic compound from *Ceratophyllum demersum*. Phytochemistry 22: 2613.
14. Martyn RD and Cody YS. 1983b. Isolation of phenol cells from waterhyacinth leaves and possible effect on the growth of foliar pathogens. J. Aquat. Plant Manage. 21: 58-61.
15. Stevens KL and Merrill GB. 1981. Dihydroactinidiolide– a potent growth inhibitor from *Eleocharis coloradoensis* (spikerush). Experientia 37: 1133.
16. van Aller RT, Pessoney GF, Rogers VA, Watkins EJ, and Leggett HG. 1985. Oxygenated fatty acids: A class of allelochemicals from aquatic plants. In: Thompson AC. (Ed.). The Chemistry of Allelopathy, ACS Symposium Series 268, pp 387-400.

17. Hutchinson GE. 1975. A Treatise on Limnology. Vol III. John Wiley & Sons (NY), p. 368.

18. Saito K, Matsumoto M, Sekine T, Murakoshi I, Morisaki N, and Iwasaki S. 1989. Inhibitory substances from *Myriophyllum brasiliense* on growth of blue-green algae. J. Nat. Prod. 52: 1221-1226.

19. Planas D, Sarhan F, Dube L, Godmaire H, and Cadieux C. 1981. Ecological significance of phenolic compounds of *Myriophyllum spicatum*. Verh. Int. Ver. Limnol. 21: 1492-1496.

20. Gross EM, Meyer H, and Schilling G. 1996. Release and ecological impact of algicidal hydrolysable polyphenols in *Myriophyllum spicatum*. Phytochemistry 41: 133-138.

21. Aliotta G, Molinaro A, Monaco P, Pinto G, and Previtera L. 1992. Three biologically active phenylpropanoid glucosides from *Myriophyllum verticillatum*. Phytochemistry 31: 109-111.

22. Elakovich SD and Yang J. 1996. Structures and allelopathic effects of *Nuphar* alkaloids: Nupharolutine and 6,6'-dihydroxythiobinupharidine. J. Chem. Ecol. 22: 2209- 2219.

23. Aliotta G, Monaco P, Pinto G, Pollio A, and Previtera L. 1991. Potential allelochemicals from *Pistia stratiotes* L. J. Chem. Ecol. 17: 2223-2234.

24. Zapata O and McMillan C. 1979. Phenolic acids in seagrasses. Aquat. Bot. 7: 307-317.

25. Cuny P, Serve L, Jupin H, and Boudouresque CF. 1995. Water soluble phenolic compounds of the marine phanerogam *Posidonia oceanica* in a Mediterranean area colonized by the introduced chlorphyte *Caulerpa taxifolia*. Aquat. Bot. 52: 237-242.

26. Barlocher F and Newell SY. 1994. Phenolics and proteins affecting palatability of *Spartina* leaves to the gastropod *Littoraria irrorata*. Mar. Ecol. 15: 65-75.

27. Aliotta G, Della Greca MD, Monaco P, Pinto G, Pollio A, and Previtera L. 1990. In vitro algal growth inhibition by phytotoxins of *Typha latifolia* L. J. Chem. Ecol. 16: 2637-2646.

28. Cheng TS and Riemer DN. 1989. Characterization of allelochemicals in American eelgrass. J. Aquat. Plant Manage. 27: 84-89.

29. Vergeer LHT, and Develi A. 1997. Phenolic acids in healthy and infected leaves of *Zostera marina* and their growth-limiting properties towards *Labyrinthula zosterae*. Aquat. Bot. 58: 65-72.

30. Harborne JB. 1975. Flavonoid sulphates: A new class of sulphur compounds in higher plants. Phytochemistry 14: 1147-1155.

31. Della Greca MD, Monaco P, Pollio A, and Previtera L. 1992. Structure-activity relationships of phenylpropanoids as growth inhibitors of the green alga *Selenastrum capricornutum*. Phytochemistry 31: 4119-4123.

32. Stenlid G. 1970. Flavonoids as inhibitors of the formation of adenosine triphosphate in plant mitochondria. Phytochemistry 9: 2251-2256.

33. Dreyer DL and Jones KC. 1981. Feeding deterrency of flavonoids and related phenolics towards *Schizaphis graminum* and *Myzus persicae*: Aphid feeding deterrents in wheat. Phytochemistry 20: 2489-2493.

34. Rice EL. 1984. Allelopathy (Second Edition), Academic Press (NY), pp. 272-279.

35. Wetzel RG. 1993. Humic compounds from wetlands: Complexation, inactivation, and reactivation of surface-bound and extracellular enzymes. Verh. Int. Ver. Limnol. 25: 122-128.

36. Rice EL. 1992. Allelopathic effects on nitrogen cycling. In: Rizvi SJH and Rizvi V, Allelopathy, Basic and Applied Aspects, Chapman and Hall (NY), pp 31-58.

37. Jobidon R. 1992. Allelopathy in Quebec forestry– case studies in natural and managed ecosystems. In: Rizvi SJH and Rizvi V, Allelopathy, Basic and Applied Aspects, Chapman and Hall (NY), pp 341-356.

38. McPherson JK, Chou CH, and Muller CH. 1971. Allelopathic constituents of the chaparral shrub *Adenostoma fasciculatum*. Phytochemistry 10: 2925-2933.

39. Sutton DL. 1986. Influence of allelopathic chemicals on sprouting of Hydrilla tubers. J. Aquat. Plant Manage. 24: 88-90.

40. Rice EL and Pancholy SK. 1974. Inhibition of nitrification by climax ecosystems. III. Inhibitors other than tannins. Am.. J. Bot. 61: 1095-1103.

41. Rice 1984, p. 333.

42. Wink M and Twardowski T. 1992. Allelochemical properties of alkaloids. Effects on plants, bacteria and protein biosynthesis. In: Rizvi SJH and Rizvi V, Allelopathy, Basic and Applied Aspects, Chapman and Hall (NY), pp. 129-150.

43. Muller CH and Chou CH. 1972. Phytotoxins: An ecological phase of phytochemistry. In: Harborne JB (ed), Phytochemical Ecology, Academic Press (NY), pp 201-216.

44. Ostrofsky ML and Zettler ER. 1986. Chemical defences in aquatic plants. J. Ecol. 74: 279-287.

45. Boyd CE. 1968. Fresh-water plants: a potential source of protein. Econ. Bot. 22: 359-368.

46. Kerfoot WC. 1989. Glucosinolates and phenolics in aquatic macrophytes: implications for allelopathy studies and suggested practical uses for metabolic blocking agents. Proceedings of 23rd Annual Meeting, Aquatic Plant Control Research Program. (Environmental Laboratory, U.S. Army Engineer Waterways Experiment Station (Vicksburg, MS), pp178-187.

47. Lodge DM. 1991. Herbivory of freshwater macrophytes. Aquat. Bot. 41: 195-224.

48. Center TD and Wright AD. 1991. Age and phytochemical composition of waterhyacinth (Pontederiaceae) leaves determine their acceptability to *Neochetina eichhorniae* (Coleopetera: Curculionidae). Environ. Entomol. 20: 323-334.

49. Baziramakenga R, Leroux GD, and Simard RR. 1995. Effects of benzoic and cinnamic acids on membrane permeability of soybean roots. J. Chem. Ecol. 21: 1271-1285.

50. Haslam E. 1989. Plant Polyphenols. Vegetable Tannins Revisited. Cambridge Univ. Press (NY), pp 1-13.

51. Martyn RD, Samuelson DA, and Freeman TE. 1983a. Phenol-storing cells in waterhyacinth leaves. J. Aquat. Plant Manage. 21: 49-53.

52. Martyn RD, Samuelson DA, and Freeman TE. 1983c. Electron microscopy of the penetration and colonization of waterhyacinth by *Acremonium zonatum*. J. Aquat. Plant Manage. 21: 53-58.

53. Tang C-S. 1986. Continuous trapping techniques for the study of allelochemicals from higher plants. In: Putnam AR and Tang C-S (Eds.), The Science of Allelopathy, John Wiley & Sons (NY).

54. Hough RA and Wetzel RG. 1975. The release of dissolved organic carbon from submersed aquatic macrophytes: Diel, seasonal, and community relationships. Verh. Int. Ver. Limnol. 19: 939-948.

55. Wetzel RG, personal communication (1996).

56. Otsuki A and Wetzel RG. 1974. Release of dissolved organic matter by autolysis of a submersed macrophyte, *Scirpus subterminalis*. Limnol. Oceanog. 19: 842-845.

57. Boyd, CE. 1995. Bottom Soils, Sediment, and Pond Aquaculture. Chapman & Hall (New York), p. 169.

58. Thurman EM. 1985. Organic Geochemistry of Natural Waters. Martinus Nijhoff/Dr W. Junk (Boston), pp. 114-115.

59. Rice 1984, pp. 356-361.

60. Wetzel RG. 1983. Limnology (Second Ed.). Saunders College Publishing (Philadelphia, PA), p. 553.

61. Kim B and Wetzel RG. 1993. The effect of dissolved humic substances on the alkaline phosphatase and the growth of microalgae. Verh. Int. Ver. Limnol. 25: 129-132.

62. Serrano L and Guisande C. 1990. Effects of polyphenolic compounds on phytoplankton. Verh. Int. Ver. Limnol. 24: 282-288.

63. Haslam (1989), p. 132.

64. Gross EM. 1999. Allelopathy in benthic and littoral areas: Case studies on allelochemicals from benthic cyanobacteria and submersed macrophytes. In: Dakshini, Inderjit, and Foy (eds), Principles and Practices in Plant Ecology: Allelochemical Interactions, pp. 179-199.

65. Aquatic plant line drawings are the copyright property of the University of Florida Center for Aquatic Plants (Gainesville). Used with permission.

66. Elakovich SD and Wooten JW. 1987. An examination of the phytotoxicity of the water shield, *Brasenia schreberi*. J. Chem. Ecol. 13: 1935-1941.

67. Gopal B and Goel U. 1993. Competition and allelopathy in aquatic plant communities. Bot. Rev. 59: 155-210.

68. Pennak RW. 1973. Some evidence for aquatic macrophytes as repellents for a limnetic species of Daphnia. Int. Revue ges. Hydrobiol. 58: 569-576.

69. Dhillon MS, Mulla MS and Hwang Y. 1982. Allelochemics produced by the hydrophyte *Myriophyllum spicatum* affecting mosquitos and midges. J. Chem. Ecol. 8: 517-526.

70. Newman RM. 1991. Herbivory and detritivory on freshwater macrophytes by invertebrates: a review. J. N. Am. Benthol. Soc. 10: 89-114.

71. Rogers KKH and Breen CM. 1983. An investigation of macrophyte, epiphyte and grazer interactions. In: Wetzel RG (ed). Periphyton of Freshwater Ecosystems. Dr. W. Junk Publishers (Boston), pp 217-226.

72. Frank PA and Dechoretz N. 1980. Allelopathy in dwarf spikerush (*Eleocharis coloradoensis*). Weed Sci. 28: 499-505.

73. Chou C-H. 1987. Allelopathy in subtropical vegetation and soils in Taiwan. In: Waller GR (ed), ACS Symposium Series 330 (Washington DC), pp 102-117.

74. Dao TH. 1987. Sorption and mineralization of plant phenolic acids in soil. In: Waller GR (ed), ACS Symposium Series 330 (Washington DC), pp 358-370.

75. Ashton FM, Di Tomaso JM, and Anderson LWJ. 1985. Spikerush (*Eleocharis* spp.): A source of allelopathics for the control of undesirable aquatic plants. In: Thompson AC. (Ed.). The Chemistry of Allelopathy, ACS Symposium Series 268, pp 401-414.

76. Hotchkiss N. 1967. Underwater and Floating-leaved Plants of the United States and Canada. Bureau of Sport Fisheries and Wildlife (Washington D.C.). Resource Publication 44.

77. Agami M and Waisel Y. 1985. Inter-relationships between *Najas marina* L. and three other species of aquatic macrophytes. Hydrobiologia 126: 169-173.

78. Kulshreshtha M and Gopal B. 1983. Allelopathic influence of *Hydrilla verticillata* (L.F.) Royle on the distribution of *Ceratophyllum* species. Aquat. Bot. 17: 207-209.

79. Nicholson RL and Hammerschmidt R. 1992. Phenolic compounds and their role in disease resistance. Annu. Rev. Phytopathol. 30: 369-389.

80. Vergeer LHT, Aarts TL, and de Groot JD. 1995. The 'wasting disease' and the effect of abiotic factors (light intensity, temperature, salinity) and infection with *Labyrinthula zosterae* on the phenolic content of *Zostera marina* shoots. Aquat. Bot. 52: 35-44.

81. Hellquist CB and Crow GE. 1980. Aquatic Vascular Plants of New England. Part 1. Zosteraceae, Potamogetonaceae, Zannichelliaceae, Najadaceae. NH Agric. Exp. Sta. Bull No. 515.

82. de Villele X and Verlaque M. 1995. Changes and degradation in a *Posidonia oceanica* bed invaded by the introduced tropical alga *Caulerpa taxifolia* in the North Western Mediterranean. Bot. Mar. 38: 79-87.

83. Putnam AR and Weston LA. 1986. Adverse impacts of allelopathy in agricultural systems. In: Putnam AR and Tang C-S (eds). The Science of Allelopathy. John Wiley and Sons (NY), pp 43-56.

84. Rice 1984, p. 199.

85. Keating KI. 1987. Exploring allelochemistry in aquatic systems. In: Waller GR (ed), ACS Symposium Series 330 (Washington DC), pp 136-146.

86. Fitzgerald GP. 1969. Some factors in the competition or antagonism among bacteria, algae, and aquatic weeds. J. Phycol. 5: 351-359.

87. Rice 1984, Ch 6.

88. Sharma KP. 1985. Allelopathic influence of algae on the growth of *Eichhornia crassipes* (Mart.) Solms. Aquat. Bot. 22: 71-78.

89. van Vierssen W and Prins TC. 1985. On the relationship between the growth of algae and aquatic macrophytes in brackish water. Aquat. Bot. 21: 165-179.

90. van Vierssen W and van Wijk RJ. 1982. On the identity and autecology of *Zannichellia peltata* Bertol. in western Europe. Aquat. Bot. 13: 367-383.

91. Szabo S, Braun M, Balazsy S, and Reisinger O. 1998. Influences of nine algal species isolated from duckweed-covered sewage miniponds on *Lemna gibba* L. Aquat. Bot. 60: 189-195.

92. Anderson DM. 1994. Red tides. Sci. Am., August 1994.

93. Barker R. 1997. And the Waters Turned to Blood. Simon & Schuster (NY), 346 pp.

94. Lee RE. 1989. Phycology (Second Edition). Cambridge University Press (NY), p. 358.

95. Carmichael WW. 1994. The toxins of cyanobacteria. Sci. Am., Jan 1994.

96. Lee 1989, p. 81.

Chapter IV.

BACTERIA

The bacteria of natural waters include multitudinous unnamed species. All bacteria are aquatic in that they feed and reproduce in water [1]. (Even the bacteria in dry terrestrial soils live within the soil's pore water.) However, few bacteria live freely suspended in water; most live attached to surfaces– rocks, sediment, plants, etc– within the water. Thus, there may be 100,000 more bacteria in the sediment than in the overlying water [2]. Often these bacteria don't live as individual cells or in pure colonies, but rather they live in biofilms– complex associations with other bacteria, algae, and protozoa.

Bacteria that are important in aquariums can be compared with other organisms by the chemicals they use for their metabolic processes (**Table IV-1**). Animals and heterotrophic bacteria use organic compounds for energy, while chemoautotrophic bacteria use inorganic chemicals. Most organisms use oxygen to accept electrons for respiration.[1]

Organisms	**Energy Source**	**Carbon Source**	**Electron Acceptor** (for respiration)
Man, Animals, and Fish	Organic cpds	Organic cpds	oxygen
Plants	Light	CO_2 and HCO_3^-	oxygen
Chemoautotrophic Bacteria	Inorganic cpds	CO_2 and HCO_3^-	oxygen
Heterotrophic Bacteria:			
Aerobes	Organic cpds	Organic cpds	oxygen
Anaerobes	Organic cpds	Organic cpds	NO_3^-, NO_2^-, Mn^{4+}, Fe^{3+}, SO_4^{2-}, organic cpds

Table IV-1. Organisms Classified by Chemicals Required to Sustain Life.

ABBREVIATIONS: CO_2 = carbon dioxide; cpds = compounds; HCO_3^- = bicarbonate; Fe = iron; Mn = manganese; NO_2^- = nitrite; NO_3^- = nitrate; SO_4^{2-} = sulfate

---

[1] Oxygen provides much more energy than other electron acceptors. For example, aerobic bacteria gain 26.5 kcal/mole of energy using oxygen as compared to the 18 and 3.4 kcal/mole that anaerobic bacteria gain when using nitrates and sulfates (respectively) [25].

The metabolic processes of bacteria also result in the conversion of one chemical to another. Some of the chemical conversions important to aquariums are shown in **Table IV-2**. For example, in the bacterial process of nitrification, ammonium is converted to nitrate.

Process	Input	Output
Nitrification	NH_4^+	NO_3^-
H_2S oxidation	H_2S	SO_4^{2-}
Methane oxidation	CH_4	CO_2
Aerobic decomposition	organic cpds	CO_2, NH_3, PO_4^{2-}, H_2S, etc
Anaerobic decomposition	organic cpds	organic acids, ethanol, NH_3, PO_4^{2-}, H_2S, etc
*Denitrification	NO_3^-	N_2O, N_2
*Nitrate respiration	NO_3^-	NO_2^-
*Manganese reduction	Mn^{4+}, Mn^{3+}	Mn^{2+} (soluble manganese)
*Iron reduction	Fe^{3+}	Fe^{2+} (soluble iron)
*Sulfate reduction	SO_4^{2-}	H_2S
*Fermentation	organic cpds	organic acids, alcohols, CO_2
*Methanogenisis	acetic acid, CO_2, H_2	CO_2, CH_4

Table IV-2. Input and Output of Chemicals during Bacterial Metabolism.

*Forms of anaerobic decomposition by heterotrophic bacteria.
ABBREVIATIONS: CH_4 = methane; H_2S = hydrogen sulfide; N_2 = nitrogen gas; NH_4^+ = ammonium; NH_3 = ammonia; N_2O = nitrous oxide; PO_4^{2-} = phosphate. See also Table IV-I.

All metabolism, including decomposition of organic matter, generates electrons. For example, the sugar glucose provides four electrons when bacteria break it down to pyruvic acid:

$$C_6H_{12}O_6 \Rightarrow 2\ CH_3COCOOH\ +\ 4\ H^+\ +\ 4\ electrons$$

Every electron generated by metabolism requires an electron acceptor. Otherwise metabolism (and life) stops.

Anaerobic metabolism differs from aerobic metabolism in that oxygen is not the electron acceptor. Under anaerobic conditions, bacteria must find other, less desirable compounds. Instead of oxygen, bacteria use nitrates, manganese, iron, sulfates, etc. Thus, when bacteria use sulfates to accept electrons, sulfates are converted to hydrogen sulfide.

A. Bacteria Processes

1. Decomposition by Heterotrophic Bacteria

The decomposition of organic matter by ordinary (i.e., heterotrophic) bacteria is important to planted aquariums. Organic matter contains all the elements that plants require, but the elements are 'locked up' in large organic compounds. Heterotrophic bacteria convert organic matter, whether in the form of fishfood, plant debris, dead bacteria, etc, into the nutrients that plants can use (see pages 80-82). Some of the conversions that occur are:

Organic Matter	⇒	Inorganic Compounds (Plant Nutrients)
organic N	⇒	ammonia + CO_2
organic P	⇒	phosphates + CO_2
organic S	⇒	sulfides + CO_2

Because organic matter invariably contains carbon, CO_2 is always released during decomposition. Moreover, other elements, not just N, P, S, and C, are converted from their organic forms to plant nutrients by heterotrophic bacteria.

Organic matter that heterotrophic bacteria feed on comes in two physical forms– particulate organic carbon (POC) and dissolved organic carbon (DOC). POC, which includes fish feces and fibrous plant matter, is harder for bacteria to digest than the much smaller DOC. (Here is where fungi and snails are useful, because they reduce particle size, thereby speeding up the decomposition process [3,4].

Ironically, DOC, which we can't see, is usually a much larger reservoir of carbon in natural systems [5], plus it is the form of organic matter from which plant nutrients will be most rapidly released. The average DOC concentration for the world's rivers is 5.8 mg/l, while the average for 500 Wisconsin lakes is 15.2 mg/l. (For all natural waters the range is 1-30 mg/l [5].)

Almost all DOC and debris in aquariums is in various stages of decay, but the rate of nutrient release may vary considerably. (Heterotrophic bacteria have their own preferences in terms of what constitutes desirable food and a suitable environment.) DOC includes proteins, organic phosphates, and simple sugars, which are metabolized rapidly, probably within hours at the warm temperatures and neutral pH of most aquariums. The less-digestible portion of DOC, such as humic substances, may take months or longer for bacteria to digest.[2] Finally, complete digestion of POC in the anaerobic substrate environment may be impossible, resulting in the gradual accumulation of sediment humus ('fish mulm').

Bacteria understandably divert part (20-60%) of the nutrients released by decomposition to synthesize their own cellular material [8]. However, these bacteria also die and decompose themselves. Indeed, in lake water over a 20 day period, four separate and sequential bacteria populations were associated with reed decomposition [9]. There may be several of these 'recyclings' before a nutrient is finally taken up by plants.

Aerobic decomposition, which requires oxygen, is much faster than anaerobic decomposition. Thus, air/water mixing and plant photosynthesis stimulate decomposition by adding oxygen to the water.

Most bacteria require a neutral pH, such that pH can have a major impact on decomposition. For example, swamps containing *Sphagnum* ('peat') mosses are often very acidic (pH 3 to

---

[2] While some DOC is not easily digested by bacteria, it is quite susceptible to decomposition by light (i.e., photo-oxidation). Thus, DOC photo-oxidation in several unpolluted Swedish lakes released 0.086 to 0.41 mg of C/l/day as compared to 0.1 to 0.27 mg of C/l/day for bacterial metabolism [16]. Metals like iron, manganese and copper act as catalysts for DOC photo-oxidation (see page 167).

4.5), because the plants themselves are acidic [6]. Bacterial activity and decomposition slow considerably in this acidic environment. Organic matter accumulates, because bacteria are not converting it to gases such as methane, CO_2, and hydrogen. The end result is that a *Sphagnum* swamp gradually fills in with the undigested organic matter.

In the final analysis, decomposition in an ecosystem is a summation of many separate, on-going metabolic processes. Thus, in lakes as well as in the established aquarium, decomposition and the release of plant nutrients is typically a steady, stable, and continuous process.

a) Decomposition in the Sediment as a CO_2 Source

The decomposition of sediment organic matter by heterotrophic bacteria releases CO_2 and methane into the water. Almost all lakes have more CO_2 than what would result solely from their equilibration with atmospheric CO_2 [10]. Much of this CO_2 surplus comes from decomposition in the sediments.

CO_2 release by sediments depends on the amount and type of organic matter it contains. For example, investigators [11] compared the decomposition rates of different types of organic matter mixed with lake sediment. Sediment containing a 5% addition of fresh aquatic plant matter generated large amounts of CO_2 (1,000 μg/g dry sediment/day). In contrast, sediment containing a 5% addition of dead oak tree leaves gave off CO_2 much less rapidly (150 μg/g/day).[3] Chemical analysis confirmed that the fresh aquatic plant matter was richer in nutrients than the dead tree leaves. Bacteria activity was greater on the richer organic matter, so that CO_2 was more rapidly released.

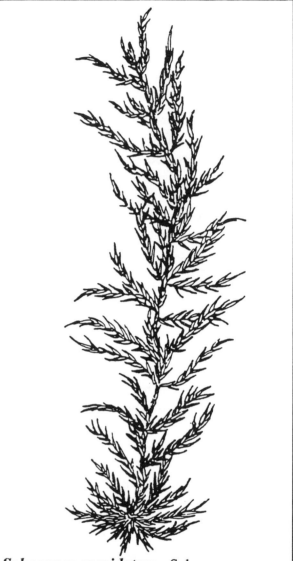

Sphagnum cuspidatum. Sphagnum mosses, here represented by *S. cuspidatum*, form dense, spongy mats in swamps and bogs. *S. cuspidatum*, a species with long (5"-16") feather-like stems, often grows fully submerged. These mosses are inherently acidic and the main ingredient of 'peat'. Some hobbyists use peat in aquarium filters to naturally soften and acidify the water. (Ca and Mg exchange for acidic protons on the peat's numerous binding sites.) Drawing from Watson [7] and reprinted with the permission of Cambridge University Press.

---

[3]Methane was also released from the two experimental sediments, 310 μg/g/day for the sediment spiked with aquatic plant matter, and 15 μg/g/day for the sediment spiked with dead oak tree leaves.

b) Production of Humic Substances (HS)

The recycling of organic matter into CO_2 and nutrients that plants can use is not decomposition's only benefit. Incomplete decomposition of plant matter results in humic substances, which accumulate both in the water and substrate [12].

Humic substances (HS) are non-specific molecules or particles originating from the random decomposition of plant material, especially lignin, by non-specific bacteria. Often HS are phenolic in their chemical nature, because they retain some of the phenolic groups of the original lignin. Exactly, how bacteria form HS from a 'chemical soup' of proteins, polyphenols, and other plant material is still a mystery. However, it may involve the polymerization of phenols (after their oxidation to quinones) with proteins [13]. Because HS formation inevitably involves bacterial oxidation of the plant molecules to obtain energy, HS carry multiple carboxylic acid groups. Even at neutral pH the carboxylic acid groups are negatively charged (R-COO⁻). Multiple negative charges increase the water solubility of HS. They also bind positively charged ions, such as iron (Fe^{3+}) and manganese (Mn^{4+}). After the metals are bound, they can be released into the water in a light-induced process that simultaneously reduces (chemically) the metal and oxidizes the organic matter (see pages 167-169).

Humic substances, which sometimes add color to natural waters, make up about 50% of the DOC in natural freshwaters (**Fig. IV-1**).

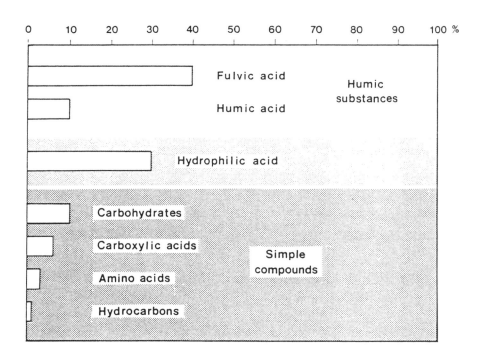

Figure IV-1. DOC Composition in an 'Average' River'. Fulvic, humic, and hydrophilic acids are all humic substances, which have a similar molecular weight (~1,000 to 2,000); they differ mainly in their solubility, with humic acids the least soluble and the hydrophilic acids the most soluble. 'Simple compounds' include amino acids, phospholipids, peptides, etc whose chemical structure and origins are well-known. Fig. 4.1 from Thurman [35] used with kind permission from Kluwer Academic Publishers.

The humic substances found in the aquatic environment are different than those found in the terrestrial environment. Aquatic HS tend to have less phenolic groups, less color, and are more water-soluble than soil HS [12,15]. Sometimes they can only be detected by their strong absorption of UV light [16].

Humic substances benefit aquariums in two major ways. First, they help keep micronutrients in solution and available to plants. (Without HS, many metals, especially iron and manganese, would precipitate out of solution and be unavailable for plant uptake.) Second, the binding and chelating of metals by HS helps counteract metal toxicity in fish and plants (see page 14). Both of these effects would occur both in the substrate and in the water.

2. Nitrification

Nitrification is the two-step process whereby ammonia, which is toxic (see page 20), is converted to nitrate, which is not toxic.[4] Nitrification is the critical component of 'biological filtration' in aquariums. The bacteria responsible for nitrification would be expected to colonize every surface in the established aquarium. However, they accumulate in the aquarium filter where they are provided with lots of attachment sites and plentiful oxygen from the moving water. (In 'wet-dry' or 'trickle' filters where the filter media is continuously exposed to air oxygen, nitrification is even more enhanced.)

The nitrifying bacteria of freshwater aquariums, once believed to be the same *Nitrosomonas* and *Nitrobacter* species found in nature, are as yet unidentified.[5] Although nitrifying bacteria are found in almost all soils and natural waters, they play a secondary, non-critical role in many natural ecosystems [19].[6]

Nitrifying bacteria are chemoautotrophic and differ from heterotrophic bacteria in that they oxidize inorganic chemicals (ammonium and nitrite) to obtain their energy. (Other chemoautotrophic bacteria are H_2S-oxidizing bacteria.) Chemoautotrophic bacteria differ from the vast majority of bacteria, which are heterotrophic in that they obtain their energy from the decomposition of organic compounds, such as proteins and sugars.

Because the requirements of nitrifying bacteria are so different than ordinary (i.e., heterotrophic) bacteria, early scientists had trouble cultivating them in the laboratory. Nitrifying bacteria simply would not grow on the organic nutrient media that had worked so well for other bacteria;

---

[4]For example, Spotte [17] reports that 400 mg/l of NO_3-N did not affect the growth or mortality of two freshwater fish, largemouth bass and channel catfish. Few aquariums would have nitrate concentrations even approaching these levels.

[5]Investigators [18] analyzed the nitrifying bacteria of 6 freshwater and 3 seawater aquaria using ribosomal RNA hybridization techniques. *Nitrosomonas europaea* was detected in all 13 samples from the seawater aquaria. However, in the freshwater aquariums, the common ammonia-oxidizing bacteria from the β subdivision of the *Proteobacteria* typified by the genera *Nitrosomonas, Nitrosococcus, Nitrosospira,* and *Nitrosolobus* were conspicuously absent. None of the usual *Nitrobacter* were found in any aquaria. (Previous studies, which often depended on isolating and culturing the organisms, may have been influenced by bacterial growth rates and culture conditions.)

[6]Plants in established forests and grasslands sometimes secrete allelochemicals that specifically inhibit nitrification. Rice [20] suggests that the plants do this, because they are better off without nitrification, which removes ammonium from ecosystems.

in fact, organic compounds inhibited the bacteria. It was not until 1890 that the Russian scientist Winogradsky discovered that if he used a simple inorganic media containing mainly ammonium and calcium carbonate, the bacteria would grow. Winogradsky had hypothesized correctly that the bacteria required an inorganic carbon source such as bicarbonate [21].

Actually, nitrifying bacteria are similar to plants in that they synthesize the large organic compounds they are made of (proteins, sugars, etc.) from small inorganic compounds like CO_2, iron, phosphates, etc. Plants use light energy to fuel the process (photosynthesis); nitrifying bacteria use chemical energy to fuel the process (chemosynthesis).

In the first step of nitrification one bacterial group converts ammonium to nitrite:

$$NH_4^+ + 1\frac{1}{2} O_2 \Rightarrow 2 H^+ + NO_2^- + H_2O$$

In the second step another bacterial group converts nitrite to nitrate:

$$NO_2^- + \frac{1}{2} O_2 \Rightarrow NO_3^-$$

The overall nitrification reaction $(NH_4^+ + 2 O_2 = NO_3^- + H_2O + 2 H^+)$ generates acid and consumes oxygen. Indeed, nitrifying bacteria require more oxygen than ordinary bacteria, up to 100 oxygen atoms per carbon atom fixed [21]. Thus, nitrifying bacteria may capriciously interfere with municipal water purification; during sewage treatment, if ammonium levels reach 2 mg/l, nitrification may consume all oxygen [22].

Nitrifying bacteria are helpful, if not essential, in tanks without plants. However, in planted tanks they compete with plants for ammonia. The energy nitrifying bacteria gain from oxidizing ammonium to nitrates is an equivalent energy loss to plants (see page 111).

3. Denitrification

Denitrification is a common process in soils and sediments that converts nitrate to N_2 gas:

Nitrate	$\Rightarrow$	Nitrite	$\Rightarrow$	Nitric oxide	$\Rightarrow$	Nitrous oxide	$\Rightarrow$	Nitrogen gas
NO_3^-		NO_2^-		NO		N_2O		N_2

Many ordinary bacteria (*Pseudomonas, Achromobacter, Escherichia, Bacillus, Micrococcus*, etc.) can denitrify [25,26]. The most common organisms are various strains of *Pseudomonas, Flavobacterium, and Alcaligenes* [27].

Although denitrification occurs anywhere there are nitrates, organic matter, and anaerobic conditions, it is often linked to nitrification [23,28]. Nitrification provides the nitrates, and by consuming oxygen, provides the anaerobic environment.

Nitrification-denitrification can result in substantial losses of N to aquatic ecosystems. In aquaculture ponds, one investigator found that only 43% of the added fishfood nitrogen could be recovered in water, soil, and fish; the remaining 57% of added N was believed to be lost through denitrification [29]. Lake Tanganyika is believed to be N-limited due to linked nitrification-denitrification [30]. Other investigators [31] studying nitrogen cycling in a Rhode Island bay concluded that denitrification reduced about 50% of the N loading from rivers, land, and sewage.

One investigator [32] closely followed N losses in nutrient-rich wastewater. Nitrate and ammonium were added to 100 gal treatment tanks containing sediment, wastewater, and various aquatic plants. Nitrogen distribution between water, substrate, and plants was measured at the end of 27 days (**Table IV-3**).

Table IV-3. Recovery of N Fertilizers in Tank Systems after 27 Days [32]. (or "Where did the N that was added to the tanks go?") Both nitrates and ammonium (0.010 ppm N of each) were added to all the tanks. In the first set of 4 tanks, only ammonium was labeled with ^{15}N (radioactive nitrogen), while in the second set of 4 tanks, only the nitrates were labeled with ^{15}N. By measuring the radioactivity in the water, soil, and plants, the investigator was able to monitor the fate of the additions. Each treatment was done in duplicate. I reported values for different tanks that were not significantly different as ranges of reported values.

N Source Monitored	Tank System	N in Water	N in Sediment	N in Plants (or algae)	Lost N
NH_4^+	Pennywort	0-3 %	8-9 %	67 %	24%
	Water hyacinth	0-3	8-9	41-44	47-54
	Cattail-Elodea	0-3	8-9	41-44	47-54
	Control (algae)	21	21	5	47-54
NO_3^-	Pennywort	0-0.1	6	13	81
	Water hyacinth	12	6	39	43-48
	Cattail-Elodea	0-0.1	29-31	24	43-48
	Control (algae)	36	29-31	4	29

Even though plants took up some of the added N, much of it could not be accounted for. For example, 24-54% of added ammonium (NH_4^+) was lost in the first set of 4 tanks (where ammonium-N was monitored). Some of the N loss was attributed to the escape of ammonia gas ('ammonia volatilization'). (During heavy photosynthesis when the pH climbed above 8.0 in these tanks, considerable NH_4^+ would convert to NH_3 gas.) In the second set of tanks where nitrate (NO_3^-) was monitored, N losses were even greater– 29 to 81%. The investigators attributed most nitrate losses to denitrification.

Denitrification can also reduce nitrogen levels in aquariums. Thus, one hobbyist [33] reduced water nitrate levels in his marine reef tanks by simply adding sand to the bare bottom. (The sand would provide numerous attachment sites and an anaerobic area for denitrifying bacteria.)

"In my own 15 gallon reef aquarium, when I maintained it without sand, using small live rocks, anemones, and soft corals on the bottom, the nitrate level averaged between 5 and 20 ppm as nitrate ion... pretty high. Even after water changes the nitrate rapidly climbed to this, the aquarium's "natural" level. Within a few weeks after I installed a thin (1/4") layer of sand, the nitrate level fell to about 1 ppm as nitrate ion. When I added a little more sand, bringing the thickness to about 1/2", the nitrate "disappeared" (now it is less than 0.01 ppm as nitrate-nitrogen). This is the aquarium's new natural level, since denitrification in the sand prevents nitrate from accumulating."

Thus, for aquarium hobbyists, denitrification is a harmless bacterial process that helps prevent nitrate accumulation.

4. Nitrite Accumulation

Nitrites, which are quite toxic to fish (see page 22), may accumulate from several different bacterial processes, not just one. The most probable candidates for causing nitrite accumulation are nitrate respiration and incomplete nitrification. However, two other bacterial processes (DAP and denitrification) might also release nitrites. All of these separate bacterial processes could contribute to nitrite accumulation in aquariums.

a) Nitrate Respiration

Nitrate respiration is a common bacterial process carried out by a variety of ordinary bacteria under anaerobic conditions. The reaction whereby bacteria use nitrate (NO_3^-) for respiration is:

$$NO_3^- + 2\,H^+ + 2\,e- \Rightarrow NO_2^- + H_2O$$

Unlike denitrification where nitrite is further converted to the gases (N_2O and N_2), nitrites are the endproduct of this reaction. Nitrate respiration is a major anaerobic process carried out by a wide variety of ordinary bacteria. Thus, in an extensive survey [27] of sediment and soil bacteria, about 80% of the bacteria capable of growing under anaerobic conditions were nitrate-respiring bacteria (produced nitrites when isolated and cultured). The remaining 20% of the anaerobic bacteria were denitrifying bacteria (i.e., produced N_2 but no nitrites when isolated and cultured with nitrate).

Q. Can you suggest some rapid growing, nitrate-consuming aquatic plants. My tanks need nitrate reduction, which I cannot seem to accomplish by changing 25 % of the water weekly.

A. I wouldn't count on plants to solve your nitrate accumulation problem. Even hobbyists with phenomenal plant growth can't control nitrate accumulation without the help of denitrification.

Assuming your tank is not overcrowded with fish, I would try to encourage denitrification in your tanks. Ordinary denitrification takes place in any aquarium filter where some debris has accumulated.

However, the substrate may be even more important than the filter in encouraging denitrification. I've had problems with nitrate accumulation in tanks with a bare glass bottom, even though the filter was okay and I had plenty of plants growing on rocks and in pots. Substrates with soil particles and mulm (lots of surface area) encourage denitrification.

In my tanks with soil substrates, there is no substantial nitrate accumulation, even after months of heavy fish feeding and virtually no water changes.

b) Incomplete Nitrification

When aquariums are first set up, there may be several weeks during which nitrites accumulate in the water. This is because bacteria that convert ammonium to nitrite establish themselves first in the aquarium. An additional 4 weeks may be required for the bacteria that convert nitrites to nitrates to establish themselves. (Nitrification is not fully functional until after about 8 weeks [23,24].)

Nitrification does not always go to completion. This often happens when environmental stresses (acidity, low temperature, etc) inhibit the bacteria responsible for nitrite oxidation more than the bacteria responsible for ammonia oxidation. Nitrite accumulation occurs when the second step of nitrification ($NO_2^- \Rightarrow NO_3^-$) no longer processes the nitrites produced by the first step ($NH_4^+ \Rightarrow NO_2^-$).

c) Incomplete DAP and Incomplete Denitrification

Bacteria use nitrates in yet another pathway besides denitrification and nitrate respiration. Apparently, numerous bacteria convert nitrates to ammonium by a pathway called 'dissimilatory ammonium production' or DAP. This pathway is linked to fermentation and energy production; therefore, it occurs even when there is adequate ammonium.[7] The reaction for DAP is:

Nitrates	$\Rightarrow$	Nitrite	$\Rightarrow$	Nitrous oxide	$\Rightarrow$	Ammonium
NO_3^-		NO_2^-		N_2O		NH_4^+

DAP produces substantial ammonium in some sediments, both freshwater and marine. Investigators tracing the fate of added nitrates have found that DAP often rivals denitrification in nitrate processing [34,35,36]. Although much of the ammonium produced by DAP is recycled back to nitrates (via nitrification), DAP appears to be a major bacterial process in the nitrogen cycle.

Sometimes DAP does not go to completion; when this happens nitrites may accumulate. Thus, one soil bacterium (*Citrobacter* sp) converted 97% of added nitrates to nitrite under certain conditions [37]. (Under other conditions, it produced N_2O and NH_4^+.)

Similarly, denitrification (see page 63) does not always go to completion either. Incomplete denitrification may result in transient nitrite accumulation [25]. Conceivably and under the right conditions, both DAP and denitrification, could contribute to nitrite accumulation in aquariums.

5. Reduction of Iron and Manganese

When oxygen and nitrates are gone, many substrate bacteria can use iron (Fe) or manganese (Mn) to accept the electrons generated by their metabolism. This 'chemical reduction' of Fe and Mn solubilizes the two metals allowing them to be taken up by plant roots. Thus, anaerobic bacteria are critical in providing plants with Fe and Mn.

Although there is less Mn than Fe in soils, oxidized Mn is a better electron acceptor than oxidized Fe (see page 128). Therefore, if Mn is available, it will be used before Fe. The following reaction describes Mn reduction by the electrons generated by bacterial metabolism:

$$MnO_2 + 4\,H^+ + 2\,e- \Rightarrow Mn^{2+} + 2\,H_2O$$

---

[7] DAP differs from 'assimilatory nitrate reduction' whereby bacteria convert nitrates to ammonium, which can then be assimilated (incorporated) into amino acids and proteins [34]. Bacteria use this pathway when ammonium isn't available.

In the above reaction, Mn goes from an oxide precipitate (MnO_2) to a soluble cation (Mn^{2+}) that can now enter plant roots. Apparently, a wide range of bacteria and microfungi can use MnO_2 as an electron acceptor [4].

When MnO_2 is exhausted, bacteria use ferric iron to accept electrons:

$$Fe(OH)_3 + 3 H^+ + e- \Rightarrow Fe^{2+} + 3 H_2O$$

As with Mn, an insoluble oxide precipitates, in this case $Fe(OH)_3$, is converted to a soluble ion (Fe^{2+}). Plant roots readily take up the Fe^{2+} form of iron.

6. Hydrogen Sulfide Production

Hydrogen sulfide (H_2S), which is readily formed in aquarium substrates, is a foul-smelling gas that is extremely toxic (see page 133). Indeed, it was found to be more toxic to small mammals than ammonia [38].

There are two sources of H_2S. One is from the ordinary decomposition of proteins by heterotrophic bacteria during which the protein's SH group is released as H_2S:

$$Protein-SH + H^+ + e^- \Rightarrow H_2S$$

The second source of H_2S is the specialized reduction of sulfates by *Desulfovibrio* and *Desulfotomaculm* bacteria. Sulfate is used as an electron acceptor by these bacteria during the anaerobic decomposition of organic matter:

$$SO_4{}^{2-} + 10 H^+ + 8 e^- \Rightarrow H_2S + 4 H_2O$$

The sulfate-reducing bacteria are strictly anaerobic [39].[8] Their activity is associated with severely anaerobic conditions (sediment redox of -120 mvolts to -300 mvolts) [40]. (See page 128 for an explanation of Redox.) The combination of plentiful sulfates and organic matter in the substrate encourages these bacteria and H_2S production.

7. Hydrogen Sulfide Destruction

In the presence of oxygen, various bacteria rapidly oxidize hydrogen sulfide (H_2S) to sulfates. (This reaction is analagous to the nitrification reaction where a very toxic molecule is converted to a harmless salt.) The overall reaction for H_2S oxidation is:

$$H_2S + 2 O_2 \Rightarrow HSO_4^- + H^+$$

H_2S oxidation is carried out aerobically by chemoautotrophic bacteria, such as *Thiobacillus*, *Thiothrix*, and *Beggiatoa*, or anaerobically in the presence of light by photosynthetic bacteria (*Chlorobacteriaceae* and *Thiorhodaceae*) [4,41].

---

[8]Oxygen is toxic to sulfate-reducing bacteria in that they do not have the cytochromes and catalases necessary to prevent the deadly build-up of hydrogen peroxide in the presence of oxygen.

The chemoautotrophic bacteria are the ones that are the most useful in aquariums. First, they protect plant roots by destroying toxic H_2S in the substrate (see page 152).

Second, they protect fish. The H_2S gas generated within the substrate or in any pockets of anaerobic debris is rapidly oxidized by H_2S-oxidizing bacteria. These bacteria inhabit the substrate's surface layer and probably oxidize any H_2S generated from below.

8. Fermentation and Methanogenisis

Under severely anaerobic conditions, organic matter is only partially metabolized by bacteria resulting in the accumulation of ethanol and various organic acids. (In contrast, when oxygen is present, bacteria metabolize organic matter to CO_2 and water.) In lake sediments large quantities of organic matter are degraded by the linked processes of fermentation and methanogenisis [4,42]. This happens when inorganic electron acceptors (NO_3^-, Fe^{3+}, Mn^{4+}, SO_4^{2-}) are no longer available. After oxygen and inorganic electron acceptors are depleted, the organic matter itself releases and receives electrons. (One portion of the organic molecule is oxidized, while another portion of the same molecule is reduced.)

Fermentation involves the breakdown of organic matter into various fatty acids, alcohols, acetic acid, hydrogen gas, and CO_2 by fermentative bacteria. Some of the organic acids and alcohols moderately inhibit plant roots (see page 134).

Methanogenisis is carried out by four major genera: *Methanobacterium*, *Methanobacillus*, *Methanococcus*, and *Methanosarcina*. These bacteria, which are strictly anaerobic, use the acetic acid, hydrogen gas, and CO_2 produced during fermentation to produce methane, CO_2, and water. The two reactions they use are:

$$CO_2 + 4\,H_2 \Rightarrow CH_4 \text{ (methane)} + 2\,H_2O$$

$$CH_3COOH \text{ (acetic acid)} \Rightarrow CH_4 \text{ (methane)} + CO_2$$

In the aquarium, methanogenisis and fermentation occur mainly in the substrate. While these two processes might have some negative impact on plant growth, overall they probably benefit aquarium ecosystems in that substrate organic matter is being processed into nutrients that plants can use.

Methane is released from the substrate by diffusion into the water as well as by gas bubbling [43].

9. Methane Oxidation

Methane-oxidizing bacteria, such as *Methanomonas methanica, Pseudomonas methanica, and Thioploca* species, are common and widely distributed [44,45]. They are located in the surface layer of sediments and quickly convert methane released from anaerobic sediments into CO_2. For example, approximately 91% of the methane produced in a peat sediment of the Florida Everglades was oxidized to CO_2 and water [4]. The overall reaction for methane oxidation is:

$$5\,CH_4 + 8\,O_2 \Rightarrow 2\,(CH_2O) + 3\,CO_2 + 8\,H_2O$$

Aquatic plants undoubtedly enhance methane oxidation by providing a home for these bacteria. Thus, one investigator [46] showed that in the emergent plant *Pontederia cordata*, methane-oxidizing bacteria were not only attached to the root surface but also lived **within** the roots themselves.

In aquariums, methane oxidation insures that methane generated in the substrate is made available to plants. Methane, which plants cannot use, is converted to CO_2, which plants can use. Since carbon is often the limiting plant nutrient in aquariums, methane-oxidizing bacteria are helpful.

Q. I added potting soil to my tank as an underlayer and I noticed that a lot of gas bubbled from the substrate. Are these gases similar to 'marsh gas'? I am concerned that these gases may be harmful to the fish?

A. I wouldn't worry about substrate gases, which could contain CO_2, H_2, N_2, N_2O, CH_4, and H_2S. Only if plant roots are stunted, mushy, and black, and/or the fish have lost their appetites would I be concerned. The substrate bubbling is helpful, because it allows oxygenated water to enter the substrate and keep it from becoming too anaerobic. The bubbling indicates that the substrate is 'alive'.

B. Biofilms

Many ideas about bacteria are based on laboratory studies where bacteria exist as individuals suspended in nutrient-rich media. However, the same bacteria in the natural world behave much differently than those in the laboratory. This is because nature, where predation is common and nutrients are not so plentiful, is a much harsher environment than the laboratory. To survive, bacteria have learned to attach themselves to surfaces, to associate cooperatively with other species, and to protect themselves from their enemies. This microcosm, which is held together by polysaccharide 'gums' produced by the bacteria, is called a biofilm.

Biofilms are the norm in the natural world. Aquarium hobbyists are familiar with filter debris or 'scum' on the water surface; these are examples of biofilms. The most well-studied ones are, of course, those that create problems: (1) dental plaque; (2) chronic lung infections of cystic fibrosis patients; (3) the corrosion of water pipes and ship hulls, and (4) the contamination of contact lenses, artificial hearts and other medical implant devices [47,51].

The reason bacteria attach and form biofilms on surfaces is that surfaces are where nutrients congregate. This is because all surfaces have a negative charge that attracts cations and dissolved organic carbon (DOC). The congregation of positively charged compounds, in turn, attracts negatively charged compounds. Thus, even in nutrient-depleted water, often enough organic compounds will adhere to surfaces to support some bacterial growth [48]. When organic compounds collect at the water surface, they attract various feeding bacteria, algae and protozoa, which may over time develop into a biofilm, sometimes called 'neuston' [49].

Bacteria stick to surfaces by various strategies. Some bacteria are sticky to begin with; they are essentially 'glueballs' covered with sticky lipopolysaccharide capsules or proteinaceous appendages. Other bacteria only synthesize the attachment components when a surface is present. For example, within 15 min of *Pseudomonas aeruginosa*'s encountering a glass surface, a gene (*AlgC*) critical for polysaccharide synthesis was stimulated [50].

Once the bacteria are attached to a surface, they divide and continuously produce large quantities of polysaccharides to form a 'mature' biofilm. A mature biofilm may be 600 to 900 μm thick [23], which is several hundred times thicker than an individual bacterium. (A bacterium is about 1 μm long [51].) The biofilm is not an amorphous, gelatinous mass of polysaccharides and bacteria as was once supposed; it has organization and structure. Even the densest area of a biofilm is permeated by water channels. Water flows through mushroom-like structures of clumped bacteria thereby bringing the inhabitants food and carrying away their wastes [47].

Apparently, the internal structure of biofilms does not happen by chance. Investigators [53] showed that active communication between bacteria insures that the biofilm develops properly. (Mutant bacteria that weren't able to communicate formed abnormal biofilms.)

Nor do biofilms consist of uniform layers of aerobic bacteria on top of uniform layers of anaerobic bacteria. Because of the water channels, anaerobic and aerobic bacteria coexist in microniches throughout biofilms. Thus, investigators [23] were surprised to find dentrification occuring in a supposedly aerobic filter used for wastewater treatment. (This filter would be similar to a 'trickle filter'.) They found similar proportions of aerobic heterotrophs, nitrifying bacteria, denitrifiers, and anaerobic heterotrophs at both the bottom and the top (**Fig. IV-2**). And in additional experiments, they found the metabolic activities of nitrifying (aerobic) and denitrifying bacteria (anaerobic) were the same in the bottom layer as in the top layer.

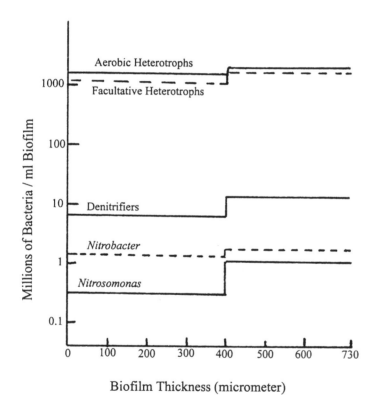

Fig. IV-2. Bacterial Populations in a Wastewater Biofilm. Investigators sliced a mature biofilm of about 730 μm thickness into three horizontal layers. (Thicknesses of the 3 layers was: top layer = 400 μm, middle layer = 200 μm; and bottom layer = 130 μm.). The layers were homogenized and the numbers of aerobic hetertrophs, facultative heterotrophs, nitrifying bacteria (*Nitrosomonas* sp., *Nitrobacter* sp.), and denitrifying bacteria were counted. (Facultative heterotrophs are bacteria that can metabolize under both aerobic and anaerobic conditions.) Figure from Masuda [23] redrawn and used with permission from Elsevier Science.

Probably nitrifying bacteria and other bacteria have worked out tight and mutually beneficial relationships in the biofilms of biological filters. As ordinary heterotrophs release ammonia during the decomposition of organic compounds, nitrifying bacteria can use the ammonia as its energy source. In turn, denitrifying bacteria, which consume acid, probably protect nitrifying bacteria, which are particularly sensitive to acidity.

Bacteria in biofilms have many advantages over those suspended freely in water. First, they share genetic information and metabolites. For example, in dental plaque biofilms, *Veillonella* bacteria use the lactate generated by *Streptococcus* bacteria [52]. Second, biofilm bacteria are protected from predators and destructive chemicals. In aquatic systems, biofilms protect bacteria from protozoa, various predatory algae (dinoflagellates) and predatory bacteria (Myxobacteria).

In human disease, biofilms protect bacteria from antibiotics, chemicals, antibodies, immune cells, etc. Thus, suspended cells of *Pseudomonas aeruginosa* were killed by 0.050 mg/ml of the antibiotic tobramycin, whereas 20 times more (1.0 mg/ml) could not kill this same bacterium when it was part of a biofilm [51]. And when the nitrifier *Nitrosomonas europaea* was exposed to 5 µg/ml of the inhibitory chemical nitrapyrin, bacterial growth in biofilm cultures was unaffected, whereas bacteria growth in suspended cultures was reduced 82% [54]. The investigators used their results to explain why nitrapyrin has not been as effective in blocking nitrification for farmers as predicted by laboratory studies. Thus, while nitrapyrin might be a potent inhibitor of *N. europaea* growing as suspended cells in nutrient media in the laboratory, it would not work as well under field conditions where the bacteria would attach to soil particles and reside within a protective biofilm.

Q. New problem: Surface scum. The tank is now completely covered by a scummy film thick enough that oxygen bubbles from the plants are getting trapped under it. Water current is evident just below the surface, but the surface itself is held motionless by this film. What is this film? What can I do about it?

A. This scum, which is an ecosystem of bacteria, algae and protozoa, is basically harmless. If you really want to get rid of it, you can just increase the surface agitation. I do this by temporarily putting the filter's spray bar above the water surface.

Q. Why did you write about biofilms? It doesn't seem very relevant to aquarium hobbyists.

A. The subject of biofilms gives us a glimpse into the natural and real world of bacteria. However, biofilms are relevant to hobbyists for two reasons.

First, biofilms explains why denitrification readily takes place alongside nitrification in ordinary aquarium filters. There is no need for hobbyists to buy 'denitrators' for denitrification.

The second reason is that biofilms prevent turbidity when soil is used in the aquarium. As bacteria within the soil spin their polysaccharide webs, they bind soil particles together. This binding of soil particles keeps even the tiniest clay from entering and clouding the water (see pages 134-135).

C. Bacteria Processes in the Aquarium

Bacteria affect nutrient cycling and the production (and destruction) of inhibitory compounds, such as ammonia, nitrites, acetic acid, and hydrogen sulfide. The fact that we cannot easily see bacteria should not discount their importance in aquariums.

Probably the most important bacterial process in the planted aquarium is simply the decomposition of organic matter. The gradual decomposition of organic matter by heterotrophic bacteria into plant nutrients is a natural and continuous process. It seems to work well in my aquariums. While CO_2 and other nutrients may be added artificially to obtain good plant growth, controlled decomposition by heterotrophic bacteria converts excess fishfood and debris into nutrients that plants can use. Without recycling by heterotrophic bacteria, organic matter would simply accumulate and be unavailable for plants.

In aquariums containing soil, the decomposition of the soil's organic matter by bacteria can provide plants with a generous initial supply of CO_2. Indeed, I calculated that an 'average' soil substrate would provide the plants with enough CO_2 for about 11 months (see page 83).

Table IV-4 lists some the main effects that the bacterial processes described in this chapter have in the planted aquarium.

Table IV-4. Effects of Bacterial Processes on Aquarium Ecosystems.

Bacterial Process	Where Found	Asset(s)	Drawback(s)
Nitrification	surface of filter, substrate, plants, etc.	detoxifies ammonia	competes with plants for ammonium, may cause pH declines, nitrate or nitrite accumulation
H_2S oxidation	surface of substrate	detoxifies H_2S	
Methane oxidation	surface of substrate	converts methane to CO_2 that plants can use	
Aerobic decomposition	surface of filter, substrate, plants, etc.	converts organic matter to plant nutrients	
Anaerobic decomposition	substrate and filter	converts organic matter to plant nutrients and humus	
*Nitrate respiration	substrate and filter		generates nitrites
*Denitrification	substrate and filter	removes nitrates from the tank	
*Manganese reduction	anaerobic soil substrate	provides manganese for plants	
*Iron reduction	anaerobic soil substrate	provides iron for plants	
*Sulfate Reduction	severely anaerobic substrate		produces toxic H_2S
*Fermentation	severely anaerobic substrate	provides CO_2 for plants	produces acetic acid and other inhibitory organic compounds
*Methanogenisis	severely anaerobic substrate	removes inhibitory acetic acid	

*Processes that occur along with anaerobic decomposition by heterotrophic bacteria.

Bacteria and fish both use oxygen. During the aerobic decomposition of organic matter, bacteria consume one oxygen molecule (O_2) for every CO_2 molecule they release. Thus, oxygen consumption can cause problems in deep tanks or ponds without water circulation and which contain large quantities of organic matter (fallen leaves, mulm, etc). Most serious are the acute problems brought on by large influxes of highly labile (readily digestible) organic matter. In aquariums, the sudden death and decomposition of large quantities of bacteria due to a malfunctioning filter may kill the fish.

I use signs of labored breathing by the fish in the early morning, when oxygen levels are lowest, to gauge whether oxygen is sufficient for my tanks. Although the easiest way to increase oxygenation is to add an air-stone, I would use only the amount of aeration that is necessary. For excessive aeration can remove all CO_2 from the water and deprive the plants of a much needed nutrient. In the beginning, I had to reduce the number of fish in each aquarium so that oxygen would be adequate for the way I feed and maintain my tanks.[9] Adjustment is rarely necessary now. There appears to be an innate stability to the aquariums whereby the oxygen needs of fish and heterotrophic bacteria are matched by oxygen inputs from plant photosynthesis and air/water mixing.

Q. How clean do you keep your planted tanks?

A. Tanks with good plant growth don't need much cleaning. Typically, I change 25 to 50% of the water about once every 6 months. I don't vacuum the gravel. I clean the filters only when they stop flowing. Usually that's once a year for the canister filters or every two months for the spillway type filters.

I do remove excess plant growth about once a month snipping off leaves of Amazon Swords and *Cryptocoryne* and removing excess floating plants from the tank. I consider pruning to be vital in that it insures that plants are continually growing. Plant growth that has stagnated from overcrowding will not purify the water for fish. Indeed, decaying plants may pollute the water rather than purify it.

Q. I try to control nutrient levels in the tank by feeding my fish sparingly. I would like to feed them more, but I don't want to pollute the water.

A. In tanks with good plant growth, you don't have to choose between feeding your fish well and keeping the water pure for them.

All of my fish get fed well twice a day. I consider excess fishfood and meat juices not taken up by the fish to be a rich source of nutrients for plants, thanks to decomposition by heterotrophic bacteria. Thus, when I feed my fish, I generally toss in a little extra for the plants. Invariably, these extra scraps of food are gone the next day. (While I cannot see the bacteria, I know that they are there.)

[9]I generally keep my aquariums lightly or moderately stocked with fish. For example, for several years, I kept six *Tropheus duboisi* (about 4" in length) in my 45 gal tank.

REFERENCES

1. Mills AL and Powelson DK. 1996. Bacterial interactions with surfaces in soils. In: Fletcher M (ed), Bacterial Adhesion, John Wiley (NY), pp 25-57.
2. Wetzel RG. 1983. Limnology (Second Ed.). Saunders College Publishing (Philadelphia, PA), p. 591.
3. Mann KH. 1972. Macrophyte production and detritus food chains in coastal waters. Mem. Ist. Ital. Idrobiol., 29 (Sup.): 353-383.
4. Westermann P. 1993. Wetland and swamp microbiology. In: Ford TE (ed.). Aquatic Microbiology. An Ecological Approach, pp 205-238.
5. Wetzel 1983, p. 667-668.
6. Wetzel 1983, p. 743.
7. Watson EV. 1981. British Mosses and Liverworts (3rd Ed). Cambridge University Press (Cambridge, England), p. 132.
8. Rheinheimer G. 1985. Aquatic Microbiology (3rd ed.). John Wiley (NY), p. 147.
9. Wetzel 1983, p. 610.
10. Cole JJ, Caraco NF, Kling GW, and Kratz TK. 1994. Carbon dioxide supersaturation in the surface waters of lakes. Science 265: 1568-1570.
11. Barko JW and Smart RM. 1983. Effects of organic matter additions to sediment on the growth of aquatic plants. J. Ecol. 71: 161-175.
12. Thurman EM. 1985. Organic Geochemistry of Natural Waters. Martinus Nijhoff/Dr W. Junk (Boston).
13. Haslam E. 1989. Plant Polyphenols. Vegetable Tannins Revisited. Cambridge Univ. Press (NY), p. 191.
14. Graneli W, Lindell M, and Tranvik L. 1996. Photo-oxidative production of dissolved inorganic carbon in lakes of different humic content. Limnol. Oceanogr. 41: 698-706.
15. Gundersen DT, Bustaman S, Seim WK, and Curtis LR. 1994. pH, hardness, and humic acid influence aluminum toxicity to rainbow trout (*Oncorhynchus mykiss*) in weakly alkaline waters. Can. J. Fish. Aquat. Sci. 51: 1345-1355.
16. Graneli W, Lindell M, and Tranvik L. 1996. Photo-oxidative production of dissolved inorganic carbon in lakes of different humic content. Limnol. Oceanogr. 41: 698-706.
17. Spotte S. 1979. Fish and Invertebrate Culture. Second Ed. Wiley-Interscience Publications (NY), p. 117.
18. Hovanec TA and DeLong EF. 1996. Comparative analysis of nitrifying bacteria associated with freshwater and marine aquaria. Appl. Environ. Microbiol. 62: 2888-2896.
19. Rheinheimer 1985, p. 146.
20. Rice EL. 1992. Allelopathic effects on nitrogen cycling. In: Rizvi SJH and Rizvi V, Allelopathy, Basic and Applied Aspects, Chapman and Hall (NY), pp 31-58.
21. Thimann KV. 1963. The Life of Bacteria (2nd ed.). The MacMillan Co. (NY), p. 399-411.
22. O'Connor JT. 1971. Iron and manganese. In: The American Water Works Assoc., Inc (ed), Water Quality and Treatment (3rd ed). McGraw-Hill Book Co (NY), pp 378-396.
23. Masuda S, Watanabe Y, and Ishiguro M. 1991. Biofilm properties and simultaneous nitrification and denitrification in aerobic rotating biological contactors. Water Sci. Technol. 23: 1355-1363.
24. Spotte 1979, p. 10.
25. Payne WJ. 1973. Reduction of nitrogenous oxides by microorganisms. Bacteriol. Rev. 37: 409-452.
26. Wetzel 1983, p. 237.
27. Gamble TN, Betlach MR, and Tiedje JM. 1977. Numerically dominant denitrifying bacteria from world soils. Appl. Environ. Microbiol. 33: 929-939.

28. Kemp WM, Sampou P, Caffrey J, and Mayer M. 1990. Ammonium recycling versus denitrification in Chesapeake Bay sediments. Limnol. Oceanogr. 35: 1545-1563.

29. Boyd, CE. 1995. Bottom Soils, Sediment, and Pond Aquaculture. Chapman & Hall (NY), p. 141.

30. Edmond JM, Stallard RF, Craig H, Craig V, Weiss RF, and Coulter GW. 1993. Nutrient chemistry of the water column of Lake Tanganyika. Limnol. Oceanogr. 38: 725-738.

31. Seitzinger SP, Nixon SW, and Pilson MEQ. 1984. Denitrification and nitrous oxide production in a coastal marine ecosystem. Limnol. Oceanogr. 29: 73-83.

32. Reddy KR. 1983. Fate of nitrogen and phosphorus in a waste-water retention reservoir containing aquatic macrophytes. J. Environ. Qual. 12: 137-141.

33. Sprung J. 1994. Reef Notes. Freshwater and Marine Aquarium, Jan 1994, p. 104.

34. Sorensen J. 1978. Capacity for denitrification and reduction of nitrate to ammonia in a coastal marine sediment. Appl. Environ. Microbiol. 35: 301-305.

35. Gilbert F, Souchu P, Bianchi M, and Bonin P. 1997. Influence of shellfish farming activities on nitrification, nitrate reduction to ammonium and denitrification at the water-sediment interface of the Thau lagoon, France. Mar. Ecol. Prog. Ser. 151: 143-153.

36. Jones JG and Simon BM. 1981. Differences in microbial decomposition processes in profundal and littoral lake sediments, with particular reference to the nitrogen cycle. J. Gen. Microbiol. 123: 297-312.

37. Smith MS. 1982. Dissimilatory reduction of NO_2^- to NH_4^+ and N_2O by a soil *Citrobacter* sp. Appl. Environ. Microbiol. 43: 854-860.

38. Bowen HJM. 1979. Environmental Chemistry of the Elements. Academic Press (NY), p. 149.

39. Rheinheimer 1985, p. 116.

40. Connell WE and Patrick WH. 1968. Sulfate reduction in soil: Effects of redox potential and pH. Science 159: 86-87.

41. Wetzel 1983, p. 324-325.

42. Wetzel 1983, p. 599-600.

43. Thurman 1985, p. 223.

44. Wetzel 1983, p. 602

45. Rheinheimer 1985, p. 117.

46. Calhoun A and King GM. 1997. Regulation of root-associated methanotrophy by oxygen availability in the rhizosphere of two aquatic macrophytes. Appl. Environ. Microbiol. 63: 3051-3058.

47. Potera C. 1996. Biofilms invade microbiology. Science 273: 1795-1797.

48. Marshall KC. 1996. Adhesion as a strategy for access to nutrients. In: Fletcher M (ed), Bacterial Adhesion, John Wiley (NY), pp 59-87.

49. Wetzel 1983, p. 139.

50. Fletcher M. 1996. Bacterial attachment in aquatic environments: a diversity of surfaces and adhesion strategies. In: Fletcher M (ed), Bacterial Adhesion, John Wiley (NY), pp 1-24.

51. Costerton JW, Cheng KJ, Geesey GG, Ladd TI, Nickel JC, Dasgupta M, and Marrie TJ. 1987. Bacterial biofilms in nature and disease. Annu. Rev. Microbiol. 41:435-464.

52. London J and Kolenbrander PE. 1996. Coaggregation: Enhancing colonization in a fluctuating environment. In: Fletcher M (ed), Bacterial Adhesion, John Wiley (NY), pp 249-279.

53. Davies DG, Parsek MR, Pearson JP, Iglewski BH, Costerton JW and Greenberg EP. 1998. The involvement of cell-to-cell signals in the development of a bacterial biofilm Science 280: 295-298.

54. Powell SJ and Prosser JI. 1992. Inhibition of biofilm populations of *Nitrosomonas europaea*. Microb. Ecol. 24: 43-50.

Chapter V.

SOURCES OF PLANT NUTRIENTS

In my aquariums, the three main sources of required nutrients are fishfood, water, and soil. I will compare these nutrient sources using one of my own aquariums as a study model.

I began the following study attempting to pinpoint potential nutrient deficiencies in my aquarium plants. At the time, I was concerned that my plants might need micronutrient fertilizers, which seemed to be expensive and hard to obtain.

A. Representative Aquarium and Methodology

As the model for my calculations, I used my 50 gal tank containing Rainbow fish (see book cover). Because the aquarium contains adult fish and is well-established, I didn't have to be concerned with nutrient accumulation by growing fish, plants and bacteria just getting started in a new aquarium.

Major nutrient removal from this tank was from periodic (every 2-3 weeks) plant pruning. I do not believe that other means of nutrient removal were significant, because I keep cleaning and water changes to a minimum.

For uniformity and simplicity, all data in this chapter is expressed and calculated on the basis of dry weight and expressed in terms of elements.

Fishfood Additions: For a week of ordinary twice-a-day feeding, I kept track of the fishfood I added to the tank. The weight of fishfood I added was 9.3 g, representing about 40 g per month.

Water and Water Changes: The 50 gal tank contains about 175 l (liters) of hardwater. (My tapwater shows 137 ppm of $CaCO_3$ hardness and a GH = 17.) Every 3 months, I change about 40% of the water, which is about 75 l for an average of 25 l per month. Water additions to the tank, to replace losses due to evaporation, are a separate 15 l per month. Thus, we could say that the tank gets an average monthly water input of 40 liters (25 l plus 15 l).

Soil Substrate: I layered the bottom of the tank with approximately 10 kg (1 inch layer) of garden soil covered with 20 to 30 kg of gravel (1½ to 2 inch layer).

Plant Pruning– For this study, I dried and weighed all plant prunings collected over a 13 week period. The collected prunings weighed 61 g, representing about 20 g per month.

Thus, there had to be enough nutrients in the tank (or going into the tank) to support 20 g of plant growth each month. To calculate how much of each element was in the 20 g, I used the minimum concentration of each element that would be expected to be found in the dried plant matter, that is, the element's *critical concentration* (see pages 104-105). Because plants store excess nutrients, my plants invariably contain more than the critical concentration of each element. However, I wanted to base my later calculations of nutrient supply only on what the plants need, not the excess they happen to accumulate in their tissues. **Table V-1** shows the amount of each element my plants require to support 20 g of plant growth.

B.   Fishfood

All fishfood, whether live, frozen, or dried, is composed of organisms or the remnants of organisms (wheat germ, shrimp meal, etc), not plastics or bottled inorganic chemicals. Because all organisms share an underlying chemical uniformity and a similar need for certain elements, fishfood contains all the nutrients that plants need.

1. Chemical Uniformity of Living Things

While there are enormous differences in appearance and behavior between organisms, there is a chemical uniformity that is truly remarkable. Because many of the underlying chemical mechanisms are the same, organisms contain similar concentrations of the elements [2]. For example, while fish, plants, fungi, and worms may not look the same, they all contain about 40-50 % carbon. And of the 17 elements required by plants, only boron is not required by animals, bacteria, algae, invertebrates, and fungi [3,4].

The reason for this chemical uniformity is simply that some elements are more useful to organisms than others. The element carbon (C) is wonderful for creating structures. Like a tinker toy, C atoms can be bound together to form an infinite variety of sizes and shapes. Because none of the other 100 plus elements on the planet can do this, carbon is a popular element. The average C concentration in organisms is about 430,000 mg/kg or 43% [1,5].

While C is ideal for making structures, other elements, such as iron and zinc, are better for function. The cells of all living things, whether a bacterium or the cells that make up plants and fish, need to move electrons quickly and efficiently. Indeed, the cellular metabolism of all organisms is based on energy extraction from electron movement and transport (see page 81). Iron and zinc just happen to have the atomic properties necessary to 'capture and release' electrons effi-

Table V-1. My Plant's Element Requirements.[1]	
ELEMENT	**What My Plants Need** (mg/mo.)
B (boron)	0.026
C (carbon)	8,000
Ca (calcium)	56
Cu (copper)	0.03
Fe (iron)	1.2
K (potassium)	160
Mg (magnesium)	20
Mn (manganese)	0.08
Mo (molybdenum)	0.003
N (nitrogen)	320
P (phosphorus)	28
S (sulfur)	16
Zn (zinc)	0.16

---

[1] Quantities for 'What My Plants Need' shown in Table V-1 were calculated by dividing critical concentration values for *Elodea occidentalis* by 50 (20 g is 1/50 of a kg). C value of 8,000 is based on the fact that aquatic plants are about 40% carbon [1], that is, contain 400,000 mg C/kg plant dry wt.

ciently. In contrast, similar metals such as nickel and aluminum are too slow to be useful [6]. Thus, iron and zinc are used and required by all organisms, while the others are either used rarely (nickel) or not at all (aluminum).

Table V-2 shows element concentrations in various fishfoods and live foods. All 6 represent either living organisms or preparations from living organisms. Here, one sees great fluctuations in element concentration, the norm throughout the scientific literature. Fluctuations reflect nutrient levels in each organism's environment, not the organism's requirements. (Organisms often accumulate more nutrients than they need.) The important thing is that the values **must** be above the organism's requirements; otherwise, the organism would not have lived long enough to become food for fish.

Table V-2. Elements in Prepared Fishfoods and Live Foods.[2]

ELEMENT (mg/kg dry wt.)	Trout Grower	Salmon Pellets	'Brand X' Fishfood	Crustacea	Live Brine Shrimp	Live Daphnia
B	-	15	48	15	-	-
Ca	22,000	25,000	32,000	20,000	300	-
Cu	14	19	15	65	16	30
Fe	200	363	220	85	270	400
K	10,000	13,000	12,000	13,000	13,000	-
Mg	2,300	4,600	1,700	2,000	1,500	-
Mn	56	13	23	850	14	8
Mo	-	-	1.3	0.6	-	0.2
N	-	-	82,000	84,000	-	-
P	15,000	15,000	23,000	9,000	1,100	-
S	-	-	5,100	6,000	-	-
Zn	95	120	110	140	120	120

---

[2]'Trout Grower' numbers were taken from a mineral analysis of 38 European feeds [7]. 'Salmon Pellets' are the mean of 12 different formulas for rearing salmon in Oregon [8].

'Brand X' is a hypothetical fishfood. Like most real fishfoods, I planned that it would be composed of 50% fish matter and 50% high protein plant matter. For the element contribution of fish matter, I averaged the element composition of 6-9 different fish meals reported by the NAS [9]. For elements (B, K, Mo, N, S) not included in the fish meal analysees, I used values reported for marine fish [10]. To represent the element contribution of the plant matter, I averaged NAS values for the element composition of soybean seeds and yeast. Again, for elements not reported by the NAS (B, K, Mo, N, S), I used those for woody angiosperms [11]. Finally, I averaged fish and plant matter values to provide my numbers for a typical aquarium food (e.g. 'Brand X').

Values for 'Crustacea' are the averages from broad ranges [10]. Those for 'Brine Shrimp' are from an analysis of *nauplii* [12]. 'Daphnia' values are from a specific analysis of *Daphnia pulex* [13].

'Salmon Pellets' and 'Brand X' were not supplemented with minerals; formulation of the 'Trout Grower' was not described.

The only real 'elemental' differences between various organisms are the smaller amounts of nitrogen (N) and sulfur (S) in plants as compared to animals. Producers (plants and algae) have 3% N and 0.5% S, while predators (animals, fish, invertebrates, etc.) have about three times more (10 % N and 1.3% S) [5]. Other than this exception, based on the higher protein content of predators, all organisms have similar element needs, and therefore, have the same potential (as a fishfood ingredient) to provide plant nutrients.

2. Fishfood as a Source of Nutrients

All fishfood contains the elements required by plants, but will it contain enough? **Table V-3** shows the supply of elements that the 40 g of fishfood provides for the 20 g plant growth in the model aquarium. Carbon is the nutrient least provided by fishfood. In the model aquarium, fishfood provides only a 2 month supply. (In contrast, fishfood provides an 80 month supply of the trace-element manganese.)

Hobbyists can use the ten-fold excess of N to gauge the relative supply of other fishfood-derived nutrients. For example, if the N in the aquarium is in excess, then boron must also be in excess. This is because the boron supply from fishfood (40 months) is four times greater than the nitrogen supply of 10 months.

3. Nutrients Go from Fishfood to Aquarium Plants

Elements reside in fish only temporarily. All healthy adult animals regulate the intake of nutrients into their bodies by homeostatic control mechanisms, so that required elements do not accumulate to toxic levels [14]. Thus, as the fish extracts energy from fishfood's large organic compounds, it excretes the breakdown products, small inorganic compounds, which are the nutrients plants can use. For example, the N, S, and C that are in fishfood proteins will be converted to ammonia, sulfates and carbon dioxide, which can be taken up immediately by plant leaves. And whatever fish don't eat and excrete, will be digested in essentially the same way by bacteria.

Table V-3. Fishfood Supply of Elements for Plant Growth.[3]

ELEMENT	Average Fishfood (mg/kg)	Nutrient Supply (# mo.)
B	26	40
C	430,000	2
Ca	20,000	14
Cu	27	36
Fe	260	9
K	12,000	3
Mg	2,400	5
Mn	160	80
Mo	0.7	9
N	83,000	10
P	13,000	19
S	5,600	14
Zn	120	30

---

[3] For the 'Average Fishfood', I averaged the element concentration of each of the 6 foods in Table V-2. I will use boron (B) as an example of how I calculated 'Nutrient Supply'. Since a kg of the average fishfood contains about 26 mg of B, the 0.040 kg (40 g) of fishfood I add each month would contain 1.04 mg of B (0.04 kg X 26 mg/kg). The 20 g of plant growth during the same month required a minimum of 0.026 mg of B (see Table V-1, p. 78). The 1.04 mg input of B divided by the 0.026 mg requirements is 40. This means that the 40 g of fishfood is, theoretically, providing the plants with a 40 month supply of boron.

This is because organisms, whether bacteria, plants, fish or humans, share the same metabolic mechanisms for extracting energy from food.[4] (Basically, metabolism is simply the reverse of photosynthesis.) As organic compounds (such as glucose) and oxygen are consumed, carbon dioxide, water, and energy are released.

$$C_6H_{12}O_6 \ + \ 6\,O_2 \ \Rightarrow \ 6\,CO_2 \ + \ 6\,H_2O \ + \ \text{energy}$$

Intertwined with biological cycling in aquariums is a great deal of purely chemical cycling– solubilization, precipitation, binding, and unbinding of elements. However, the elements themselves remain unchanged. Thus, the iron contained in the living shrimp that is dried into shrimp meal and then processed mechanically into shrimp pellets is just as good as if it were added to the tank as a component of living shrimp. Elements are 'rock stable'.

Some elements are excreted from fish directly into the water, so plants can easily take them up. (Fish excrete most digested B, K, Mg, Mo, N, S, and C as water-soluble compounds from their urine or gills.)

In contrast, other elements tend to be excreted by fish as solids. Thus, much of the Ca and P in fishfood would pass through the fish as solids in the feces. Metals Cu, Fe, Mn, and Zn, would be even less available to plants than Ca and P, because very little of these elements are excreted in the urine or gills.[5]

> **Q.** I'd like to just let the fish fertilize the plants, but I don't have many fish in the tank. Should I add more fish?
>
> **A.** No, you can just add more fishfood to the tank. You see, fish by themselves don't add nutrients to the tank. They only process (metabolize) what you add in the fishfood. Aerobic bacteria do the same thing— break down organic matter into the nutrients that plants can use.
>
> Thus, I add fishfood to each of my tanks based on the tank's size, not the number of fish in it. Generally, I add more food than the fish can eat but not so much that I ever see leftover food rotting on the bottom the next day. Snails are a big help, because they break the fishfood down into smaller particles that bacteria can digest more easily.

They would need to accumulate as fish mulm before plant roots could take them up. Thus, the route of Cu, Fe, Mn and Zn from fishfood to plants might be a lengthy and circuitous one, involving the processing of accumulated feces by numerous bacteria and fungi in the substrate. The lag time for the four metals may explain why plants often will not grow in a pure gravel substrate until sufficient mulm has accumulated.

------

[4]What may appear to be exceptions to the above are simply variations of this unifying theme. For example, while plants make their own food using light, and chemoautotrophic bacteria make their own food using chemical energy, both organisms metabolize food for energy exactly as animals do. And in the absence of oxygen, some bacteria may use other electron acceptors during metabolism. However, the mechanism of energy generation (ATP formation from electron transport) is the same.

[5]For example, 97% of N, 94% of S, 64% of P, and 17% of Ca is excreted by humans as soluble compounds in the urine [15]. In contrast, very little of the 4 metals are excreted as soluble compounds-- 1.4% for Cu; 1.6% for Fe; 0.81% for Mn; and 3.6% for Zn. (Fish would be expected to have an excretion pattern similar to humans.)

82

Q.   I think it's really funny how lately every article you read about plants says they just don't do really well without adding micronutrients to the water. And then you try to find them and they're totally unheard of, or they're too expensive and out of my price range. There must be another way to get iron and these trace elements into the tank without hurting the fish, so what is it?

A.   Soil and fishfood...
    Most 'ordinary' soils contain a huge reservoir of iron and other trace elements. Also, once a soil is submerged in the tank, the anaerobic conditions insure that trace elements are readily available to plants.
    Fishfood is the perfect fertilizer. Not only does it contain all the nutrients that plants require, including carbon and trace elements but it is relatively safe. Because nutrients are released slowly in small increments by the metabolism of fish and bacteria, it's probably better for the plants than adding big doses of inorganic fertilizers at weekly or monthly intervals. And it's cheap.
    In my opinion, if an aquarium contains at least 2 mg/l (ppm) of nitrate-N and a layer of soil, there should be enough nutrients for the plants. The hobbyist must use some judgement about how much tank cleaning is necessary. But certainly, there is little to be gained from restricting the nutrient levels in the aquarium by underfeeding fish, changing water frequently, and cleaning gravel, but then adding it all back as plant fertilizers. (Sounds like a lot of work to me.)

Q.   I have no idea where your idea of carbon in fishfood going to CO_2 comes from? It is unlikely that carbon is just floating around as a pure element. Carbon does not mean CO_2. From your assumption, we could just pour some charcoal into the tank and, boom, **lots of CO_2**, but this does not happen.

A.   The carbon that makes up charcoal, diamonds, and graphite is inert. Organisms are simply unable to break the strong carbon-carbon bonds of which these compounds are made. The carbon I'm talking about comes from the organic C in the biomolecules that make up organisms. Below are a few examples of biomolecules– a sugar, a nucleotide, and an amino acid. Organisms readily convert these compounds to CO_2.

Glucose 6-phosphate

Cytosine

$2\ HSCH_2CHCO^-$

cysteine

C.   Soil as a Source of Plant Nutrients

Ordinary soil is an extremely concentrated source of nutrients, especially trace elements. For example, 10 kg of a typical soil would provide plants in the 50 gal model aquarium with a 330,000 month supply of iron (**Table V-4**). Even if much of the iron is mostly insoluble iron oxides, soil should still provide plants with iron indefinitely.

In contrast, soil does not provide major nutrients like C, N, and P so generously. In addition, the nutrient supply from soil, unlike the one from fishfood or water, represents a fixed supply that at some point will be used up. Therefore, while the 25 month supply of carbon seems adequate, it will be gradually used up.

Much of the soil's carbon is in the organic form and is released as CO_2 during decomposition. As the CO_2 is slowly released into the water, plants take it up for their photosynthesis. To calculate about how fast a soil's carbon would be released, I used the CO_2 release rate of 0.23 g CO_2 per day per kg described for one natural lake sediment [17]. This sediment contained a moderate amount of organic matter (9.3%) and supported luxuriant aquatic plant growth. Using this rate of CO_2 release, I calculated that 10 kg of soil in a tank would give off 69 g of CO_2 per month:

0.230 g of CO_2/kg sediment/day X 10 kg sediment X 30 days/month = 69 g of CO_2 released/month

Table V-4. Supply of Elements from Soil in the Experimental Aquarium.[6]		
ELEMENT	Median Soil Concentration (mg/kg)	Nutrient Supply (# mo.)
B	20	7,700
C	20,000	25
Ca	15,000	2,700
Cu	30	10,000
Fe	40,000	330,000
K	14,000	875
Mg	5,000	2,500
Mn	1,000	125,000
Mo	1.2	4,000
N	2,000	63
P	800	290
S	700	440
Zn	90	5,600

Carbon makes up 27.3% of CO_2. Therefore, the 69 g of CO_2 represents 18.8 g of C released per month. If a kg of the average soil contains 20,000 mg of C (Table V-4), the total carbon reservoir in the 10 kg of soil in the experimental tank is 200,000 mg (200 g). If C is released from the soil at the rate of 18.8 g. per month, then the soil will provide carbon for the plants for about 11 months before it is used up (200 g ÷ 18.8 g = 10.6 mo.).

---

[6]'Median Soil Concentration' is from Bowen [16]. For the 'Nutrient Supply' calculations, I will use iron (Fe) as an example. If the average soil contains 40,000 mg of iron per kg dry soil, 10 kg of soil would contain 400,000 mg of iron (10 kg X 40,000 mg/kg). The 400,000 mg supply divided by the plant's 1.2 mg monthly requirement (see Table V-1) shows that the soil contains a 330,000 month supply of iron.

Iron concentrations (mg Fe per kg of soil) for various soils range from 2,000 to 550,000 [16]. Even if I had used 10 kg of the soil with the lowest concentration (2,000 mg/kg) of iron, it still would have provided my plants with a 17,000 month supply.

Q. I'm not having any luck growing plants in my 50 gal aquarium. The tank contains no algae and about half the recommended level of fish. It has about 4" of small gravel that I regularly vacuum to keep water ammonia levels down. The plants first lose their older leaves and then eventually just die away. I don't know what's wrong. Lighting is from two 30 watt fluorescent bulbs.

A. It sounds like your plants may be starving. Carbon makes up a large part (about 40%) of plant dry weight. The main source in tanks like yours and mine (without CO_2 injection) is the metabolism of organic matter (fishfood, debris, soil organic matter) by fish and/or bacteria. I suspect that your tank may be 'too clean' to support plant growth. (The absence of algae in your tank supports this hypothesis.)

For tanks without CO_2 injection, a soil underlayer helps greatly, because the decomposition of soil organic matter releases CO_2 into the water for several months after the tank is set up. Without soil in the tank, plants would depend almost solely on the fishfood carbon input. But it requires time to build up a substantial carbon reservoir from fishfood. (This would be in the form of dissolved organic carbon in the water and mulm in the substrate.) Moreover, the hobbyist too often prevents organic matter accumulation by tank cleaning measures (charcoal filtration, protein skimming, gravel vacuuming, etc.).

In your case, I would either be content with a fish-only tank or tear down the tank and set it up for plants as well as fish. This can be done with a soil underlayer, moderate filtration, and less tank cleaning.

Having a 'dirty' aquarium that will support good plant growth requires a leap of faith. The hobbyist must believe that plants can help purify the aquarium environment.

Q. I noticed a decline in plant growth in my 70 gal tank, which has a 5-year old peat/sand substrate. Green thread algae appeared as cottony clumps among the chain swordplants and long, stringy green threads draped on the stem plants.

I first tried adding calcium carbonate ($CaCO_3$) and baking soda ($NaHCO_3$). I got no response from the *Hygrophila*, but some *Vallisneria* came back from the dead and started to reproduce. Next, I added Epsom salts ($MgSO_4$) to boost the Mg and S concentration, but got no response.

Finally, I set up a yeast generator to add CO_2. CO_2 appears to be the missing ingredient. Within 1-2 weeks, the *Hygrophila* came back to life, all the bottom plants are putting out new growth, and the *Rotala macrandra* is doing well. All the plants are bubbling oxygen towards the end of the day. Also, the algae's growth rate seems to be decreasing.

The tank did great for years without CO_2 injection. Maybe the substrate's C supply is gone?

A. I think you're right– that plant growth in your tank declined due to a gradual depletion of substrate carbon. The first clue was that when you added $CaCO_3$ and $NaHCO_3$, the *Vallisneria* was stimulated. (*Vallisneria* can use bicarbonates as a carbon source.)

Your peat substrate probably did not degrade. The CO_2 it was providing via degradation of the peat organic matter gradually tapered off over the years. Apparently, the fishfood you add to your tank was not enough to replenish the substrate carbon reservoir indefinitely.

I calculated that substrate bacteria would release a 25 month supply of carbon within 11 months. However, this is a strictly theoretical calculation based on one particular lake sediment. CO_2 release would vary greatly depending on the amount and type of organic matter. Peat has a lot of organic matter but it also has a very acidic pH (~pH 4 - 5), which would inhibit decomposition, thereby slowing CO_2 release considerably. Thus, your experience– that carbon release from a peat/sand substrate may take several years– is not surprising.

D.   Water as a Source of Plant Nutrients

About half of the U.S. population, often those in rural areas, gets their drinking water from ground water (private and public wells); the other half, often from cities, gets their drinking water from surface water (rivers, reservoirs, etc) that has been treated. It is hard to make generalizations about the nutrient level of drinking water, because element concentrations vary greatly depending on the water source (well v. reservoir), how it is handled (water treatment, metal pipes, etc), and the regional geography. However, for a given region groundwater will probably contain more nutrients, especially Ca, Fe, K, Mg, Mn, S, and Zn than city water. Moreover, some water treatment procedures will remore heavy metals, including substantial Fe, Mn, Cu, and Zn, from the water. **Table V-5** provides some data on levels of plant nutrients that drinking water might contain.

Table V-5. Nutritive Elements in Drinking Water.[7]

ELEMENT (ppm)	Ground Water (ppm)		Muncipal Water (ppm)	
	Median	Range	Median	Range
B	-	-	0.03	0.003- 0.6
C (as HCO_3^-)	-	-	9.0	0- 75
Ca	36	0.5- 230	26	0- 145
Cu	0.004	0.1- 3	0.008	<0.001- 0.3
Fe	0.10	0.04- 6,000	0.02	0.005- 0.1
K	2.4	0.5- 4.0	1.6	0- 30
Mg	12	0.2- 70	6.3	0.0- 120
Mn	0.05	0.1- 110	0.003	0.001- 0.01
Mo	-	0.4- 40	0.001	0- 0.07
N	-	-	0.1	0.08- 1
P	-	0.1- 10	0.02	0.01-0.2
S	22	0.1- 10,000	8.7	0- 83
Zn	0.1	0.01- 240	0.003	0.001- 0.01

---

[7]For 'Ground Water', I combined data from a 1984 study of U.S. groundwater [18] with data from two local private wells plus the 1997 ground water analysis reports of two major cities. For 'Municipal Water' I combined data from a 1962 study of the 100 largest U.S. cities [18] and 1997 water analysis reports from several major U.S. cities.

1. Water Hardness and the 'Hardwater Nutrients'

Technically speaking, *water hardness* is a measure of water's Ca and Mg concentrations, with Ca generally dominating.[8] It says nothing about the bicarbonate, Cl, K or S concentrations. However, these nutrients are often linked with water hardness [19] such that hardwater often contains ample quantities of Ca, HCO_3^-, Cl, K, Mg, and S (i.e., the 'hardwater nutrients'). (This relationship is not true, however, for other nutrients N, P, Fe, and Mn.) Thus, municipal drinking water from Portland, which is quite soft, contains much lower levels of several major nutrients than Chicago's harder water (**Table V-6**).

Variable (all ppm)	Portland OR	Chicago (S. district)
Hardness (as $CaCO_3$)	6.3	137
HCO_3^-	4.8	58
Ca	1.6	36
Cl	1.0	13
K	0.2	1.5
Mg	0.6	11
S	<0.2	9.7

Table V-6. Water Hardness and the 'Hardwater Nutrients' in Two Cities. Data from 1997 water analysis reports published by the water departments of the two cities.

2. Water as a Source of Plant Nutrients

I add 40 liters of water to the model aquarium each month (see page 77). **Table V-7** shows the hypothetical nutrient supply that water additions would provide plants in the model aquarium. Whether the water is hard or soft would be critical in supplying plants with major nutrients Ca, Mg, K, and S. Since the calculations for 'Nutrient Supply' were based on median values, plants in softwater would get less, and in some instances, maybe not enough.

I would caution hobbyists to use water hardness whenever possible to classify their tapwater. It is the water hardness, not the pH or the alkalinity that counts. Although all three parameters are often correlated in nature, under artificial tapwater conditions they may not be. For example, some hobbyists report that their city tapwater has a very high pH and alkalinity, but has little hardness. This is because municipal treatment plants may add bicarbonates to acidic softwater to prevent corrosion of metal pipes. This water with its artificial alkalinity is still 'softwater' and, therefore, deficient in many hardwater plant nutrients (e.g., Ca, Mg, K, and S).

Q. The Amazon Sword plants in my 100 gal Rainbow fish tank get holes in the leaves and then just disintegrate. I think there is enough light. The water is soft and the plants are in pure gravel. What is happening?

A. The plants may be suffering from a deficiency in one of the hardwater nutrients. Soft water is almost always deficient in K, Ca, and Mg. Amazon Swordplants are greedy plants that

---

[8] *Water hardness* is the Ca and Mg concentration, often expressed as GH or ppm calcium carbonate ($CaCO_3$) (see page 185 for water hardness categories). In nature, water hardness usually correlates positively with pH, salinity, specific conductance, and alkalinity.

require lots of nutrients. Thus, they often don't do well in tanks with softwater, that is, water with a GH < 4 and/or a hardness of 60 ppm $CaCO_3$ or less (see page 185).

For calcium you can add $CaCO_3$. One hobbyist routinely adds a calcium supplement designed for human consumption to his 70 gal tank. For magnesium, you can add Epsom's salts, which is $MgSO_4 \cdot 7H_2O$. Even though Ca and Mg are relatively harmless, it is probably best to monitor water hardness as you make the additions. Hobbyist test kits for water hardness are inexpensive and readily available. You could also keep a mesh bag of dolomite gravel in the filter. (Mesh bags can be made by tying off sections of old panty hose.) To provide potassium, you can use 'potash' from farm supply stores or 'salt substitute' from grocery stores (both are KCl). If you add a 'pinch' (or about 1/8 tsp) to every 10 gal, you should end up with 10 ppm K, which is plenty. [In calculating the KCl dosage, take note that 1 level tsp. of KCl weighs about 5 g. (or 5,000 mg) and that about half of the weight is Cl.]

Reply.   I added oyster grit from a farm supply store to the filters and the substrate in my tanks. The Amazons are doing fine now.

ELEMENT	Concentration (mg/l)	Nutrient Supply (# mo.)
B	0.03	46
C	9	0.05
Ca	31	22
Cu	0.006	8
Fe	0.06	2
K	2	0.5
Mg	9	18
Mn	0.03	15
Mo	0.001	13
N	0.1	0.01
P	0.02	0.03
S	15	38
Zn	0.05	13

Table V-7. Nutrient Supply from Water Additions to the Model Aquarium. For 'Water Concentrations' of elements, I used median values from Table V-5. To show the calculations for 'Nutrient Supply', I will use K (potassium) as an example. Since drinking water contains about 2 mg/l of K (Table V-5), 40 liters of added water would contain 80 mg K. The plants in the model aquarium require 160 mg/month of K (see Table V-1, p. 78). Monthly water additions of 80 mg divided by the 160 mg required by plants provide a 0.5 month supply of K.

E.   Availability of Plant Nutrients in the Aquarium

Table V-8 summarizes all the data presented earlier by comparing the nutrient supply provided to plants in the 50 gal model aquarium by fishfood, soil and water. Apparently, my concerns about micronutrient deficiencies were unnecessary. The soil in the model aquarium was shown to provide many micronutrients, including a huge excess of iron. The occasional mild chlorosis I saw in my plants was probably not due to iron deficiency but to other factors, such as allelopathy and metal toxicity.

Carbon, which is not well-supplied by any source, is probably **the limiting nutrient for the submerged growth of aquatic plants in aquariums.**[10] Soil organic matter would be expected to provide adequate carbon for several months, but afterwards, fishfood would be the primary source. However, the fishfood carbon input is small (in comparison to other nutrients) and can easily be lost by CO_2 gas escaping into the air. The inevitable carbon shortage explains why procedures that provide plants with more carbon (e.g., CO_2 injection and allowing amphibious plants to grow emergent) so greatly stimulates plant growth.

In softwater tanks, potassium, magnesium, and calcium deficiencies might occur in some plant species. Iron and manganese would only be deficient in tanks without soil substrates or mulm accumulations. Mulm is probably a rich source of iron, manganese, copper, zinc, phosphorus, and calcium. Planted tanks without adequate fishfood additions would probably become rapidly depleted of major nutrients nitrogen, potassium, and phosphorus. I concluded that adding plant fertilizers to my aquariums was unnecessary.

Table V-8. Fishfood, Soil, and Water as Nutrient Sources in the Model Aquarium.[9]

ELEMENT	Nutrient Supply (# mo.) from:		
	Fishfood	Soil	Water
B	40	7,700	46
C	2	25	0.05
Ca	14	2,700	22
Cu	36	10,000	8
Fe	9	330,000	2
K	3	875	0.5
Mg	5	2,500	18
Mn	80	125,000	15
Mo	9	4,000	13
N	10	63	0.01
P	19	290	0.03
S	14	440	38
Zn	30	5,600	13

---

[9] 'Number of Month's Supply' for fishfood, soil, and water were taken from tables earlier in the chapter (i.e., Table V-3, p. 80, Table V-4, p. 1 and Table V-7, p. 87).

[10] Plants in ponds would be less likely to be carbon-limited, because they have carbon inputs in addition to fishfood, water, and soil. For example, bugs, tree leaves, etc falling into ponds bring in organic carbon. Furthermore, ponds usually contain water lilies and other emergent plants. These plants bring carbon from the air into the pond. They use air CO_2 for photosynthesis and when parts of these plants decompose, the carbon that originated from the air is released into the water as CO_2 that the submerged plants can use.

REFERENCES

1. Peverly JH. 1979. Elemental distribution and macrophyte growth downstream from an organic soil. Aquat. Bot. 7: 319-338.
2. Sposito G. 1986. Distribution of potentially hazardous trace metals. In: Sigel H (ed), Metal Ions in Biological Systems (Vol 20). Marcel Dekker (NY), pp 1-20.
3. Davies BE and Jones LHP. 1988. Micronutrients and toxic elements. In: Wild A (ed), Russell's Soil Conditions and Plant Growth (11th Edition). John Wiley (NY), pp. 780-814.
4. Bowen HJM. 1979. Environmental Chemistry of the Elements. Academic Press (NY), pp. 132-133.
5. Bowen 1979, p. 69.
6. Martin RB. 1986. Bioinorganic chemistry of metal ion toxicity. In: Sigel H (ed), Metal Ions in Biological Systems (Vol 20). Marcel Dekker (NY), pp. 21-45.
7. Tacon AGJ and DeSilva SS. 1983. Mineral composition of some commercial fish feeds available in Europe. Aquaculture 31: 11-20.
8. Crawford DL and Law DK. 1972. Mineral composition of Oregon pellet production formulations. Prog. Fish-Cult. 34: 126-130.
9. NAS. 1977. Nutrient Requirements of Warmwater Fishes. National Academy of Sciences (Washington, DC).
10. Bowen 1979, Table 6.3.
11. Bowen 1979, Table 6.2.
12. Bengston DA , Beck AD and Simpson KL. 1985. Standardization of the nutrition of fish in aquatic toxicological testing. In: Mackie AM and Bell JG (eds). Nutrition and Feeding in Fish. Academic Press (NY), pp 431-445.
13. Tarifeno-Silva E, Kawasaki LY, Yu DP, Gordon MS and Chapman DJ. 1982. Aquacultural approaches to recycling of dissolved nutrients in secondarily treated domestic wastewaters- III. Uptake of dissolved heavy metals by artificial food chains. Water Res. 16: 59-65.
14. Mertz W (ed.). 1987. Trace Elements in Human and Animal Nutrition— Fifth Ed. Vol. 1. Academic Press (NY).
15. Bowen 1979, Table 7.6.
16. Bowen 1979, Table 4.4.
17. Barko JW and Smart RM. 1983. Effects of organic matter additions to sediment on the growth of aquatic plants. J. Ecol. 71: 161-175.
18. van der Leeden F, Troise FL, and Todd DK. 1990. The Water Encyclopedia, Second Ed., Lewis Publishers (Boca Raton LA).
19. Wetzel RG. 1983. Limnology (Second Ed.). Saunders College Publishing (Philadelphia, PA), p. 179-201.

Chapter VI.

CARBON

Carbon dioxide (CO_2) is more than a plant nutrient. In its bicarbonate form (HCO_3^-), it is also the major pH buffer of natural freshwaters.

A. Water Alkalinity, pH, and CO_2

For most natural freshwaters, alkalinity is determined mainly by the water's bicarbonate concentration.[1] More bicarbonates mean more alkalinity, which means more pH buffering. **Fig VI-1** shows how alkalinity buffers large daytime pH changes in aquaculture ponds. Ponds with low alkalinity show a major pH rise during the late afternoon due to photosynthesis. Ponds with moderate or high alkalinity show much smaller pH changes.

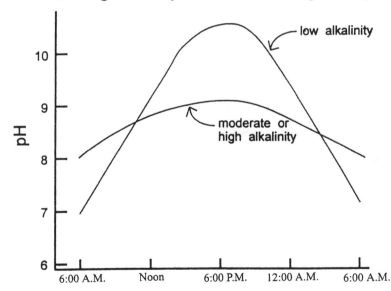

Figure VI-1. Effect of Alkalinity on Daily pH Changes in Aquaculture Ponds. 'Low alkalinity' was defined as less than 20 (as ppm $CaCO_3$). Moderate or high alkalinity was 50-300. Figure from Boyd [2] redrawn and used with kind permission from Kluwer Academic Publishers.

---

[1]*Alkalinity* is strictly defined as milliequivalents (meq) of acid required to shift a water's pH to the alkaline side of neutral. While alkalinity could be influenced by other ions (silicates, phosphates, borates, etc), the water's bicarbonate concentration usually determines most of the alkalinity [1]. Many water treatment plants express alkalinity as ppm $CaCO_3$, with 1 meq H_2CO_3 equivalent to 50 ppm $CaCO_3$ alkalinity. However, hobbyist test kits usually express it as KH (German degree of Carbonate Hardness). One KH is equal to 17.9 ppm of $CaCO_3$ alkalinity.

Alkalinity's pH buffering action is based on the following equilibrium reactions for dissolved inorganic carbon (DIC):

$$CO_2 + H_2O \Leftrightarrow H_2CO_3 \Leftrightarrow H^+ + HCO_3^- \Leftrightarrow CO_3^{2-} + 2 H^+$$

When the CO_2 or H^+ levels change, most of that change is absorbed by bicarbonate (HCO_3^-). For example, when acid (H^+) is generated in the water, say during nitrification, some of that H^+ combines with HCO_3^-. Thus, despite the addition of H^+ to the water, the pH may not go down immediately.

The reaction above also shows the relationship between pH and CO_2. Thus, when CO_2 is added to the water, such as during CO_2 injection, the above reaction moves to the right and H^+ (acid) is produced, and the pH tends to go down. (How fast the pH goes down is moderated by the water's alkalinity.) Conversely, when CO_2 is removed from the water, such as during photosynthesis or water-air mixing, the reaction moves to the left. As a result, H^+ is consumed, and the pH tends to go up. Again, how fast the pH goes up is moderated by the water's alkalinity.

Not only does CO_2 affect the pH, but pH affects the CO_2 concentration. For pH determines the relative proportions of CO_2, bicarbonates (HCO_3^-), and carbonates (CO_3^{2-}) (**Fig. VI-2**). At an acidic pH of 5 and below, most of the water's DIC is CO_2. At pH 6.5 the water contains about equal amounts of CO_2 and bicarbonate, while at pH 8.5, almost all of the CO_2 has converted to bicarbonates. When the water reaches pH 10, about 24% of the bicarbonates have, in turn, converted to carbonates.

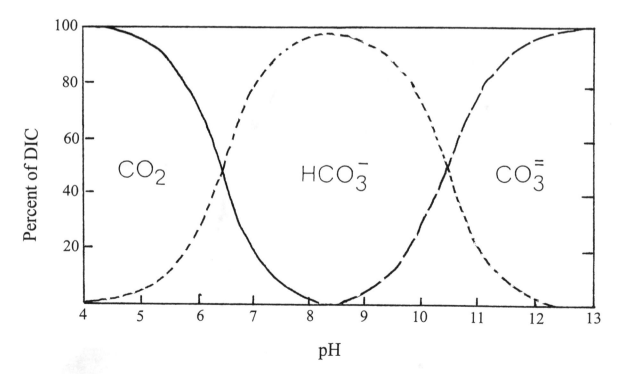

Figure VI-2. pH's Effect on the Relative Proportions of CO_2, Bicarbonates, and Carbonates. Figure from Wetzel [3] slightly modified.

Alkalinity also represents a carbon reservoir for plants. Alkalinity has been likened to a 'bicarbonate battery' that stores CO_2 [4]. During the day, plants draw on the battery and deplete the water of bicarbonates. Alkalinity goes down. At night, though, the 'battery' is recharged with fresh CO_2 from the respiration of plants, fish, and bacteria. Alkalinity goes back up.

B. Carbon Limits the Growth of Submerged Plants

Aquatic plants in nature (and aquariums) are often limited by CO_2. The difficulties submerged plants have in obtaining enough CO_2 are believed to be responsible for their inherently slow growth and low productivity. Air-grown plants (terrestrial annuals, emergents, and rain forest plants) are much more productive than freshwater submerged plants (**Table VI-1**). For example, freshwater emergent plants are shown to be over four times more productive than freshwater submerged plants– 7.5 versus 1.7 kg.

> **Q.** In the store we have a 40 gal plant tank. pH is about 7.2. Only R.O. (reverse osmosis) water is used. I have recently added CO_2 injection to this system, and it seems to have made a positive difference for the plants. However, the visual tester usually indicates there is too much CO_2 in the water. I have switched to mouth-breathing fish (gouramis and bettas), because the Kribensis and Congo tetras were gasping at the surface.
>
> My question– Under these circumstances is it bad to slightly overdose on CO_2?
>
> **A.** Your fish are in grave and imminent danger.[2] Adding CO_2 to R.O. water can easily kill them. (R.O. water contains almost no salts, including bicarbonates, so the water would not have enough alkalinity to buffer the added CO_2.)
>
> If you use CO_2 injection, you simply must maintain a certain alkalinity in the water. The addition of hard tapwater or baking soda ('Arm & Hammer'™) are ways to increase alkalinity. One of these additions, which must be done on a periodic basis, should bring the alkalinity up to normal test levels. Your tank should have a carbonate hardness (KH) above 3 or 4.

The low productivity of submerged plants is not because there is less CO_2 in water than in air. (On average, most natural waters have about three times more mg/l CO_2 than air [8,9]). It is because CO_2 diffuses so slowly in water (i.e., 10,000 times slower than in air). This simple physical phenomenon inevitably limits CO_2 uptake, because the CO_2 molecules just don't contact the plant's leaf fast enough to meet the plant's needs.

Plant Type (all tropical)	Productivity (kg dry wt/m^2/yr)
Freshwater submerged plants	1.7
Freshwater emergent plants	7.5
Marine submerged plants	3.5
Terrestrial annual plants	3.0
Rain forest plants	5.0

Table VI-1. Productivity of Various Plants. From Wetzel [7].

---

[2] It may not be helpful to plants either. Investigators [5] showed that CO_2 fertilization above 50 mg/l inhibited the photosynthesis of *Elodea densa*. Apparently, excessive CO_2 decreases the normally alkaline pH within the plant's cells, so that the plant's main photosynthetic enzyme (RUBISCO) stops working [6].

However, if CO_2's slow movement in water were the only problem for submerged plants, then marine plants should be just as unproductive as freshwater plants. However, **Table VI-1** shows that submerged plant productivity in the marine environment is much greater than in the freshwater environment (i.e., 3.5 versus 1.7 kg/m²/yr). Thus, two submerged marine plants, eelgrass and turtle grass, were found to be 50 to 200% more productive than *Hydrilla verticillata* and *Myriophyllum spicatum,* two 'fast-growing' freshwater species [10].

The difference is because marine plants are assured of an ample and constant carbon supply from the 115-143 mg/l of bicarbonates in seawater [11]. Investigators [12] hypothesize that marine plants have been able to match their photosynthetic systems very nicely to this stable carbon supply. Thus, their photosynthetic systems generally run at maximum capacity and efficiency.

In contrast, submerged plants in stagnant freshwater must contend with capricious variations in CO_2 levels ranging from 0 to over 14 mg/l [13]. In lake areas of dense vegetation, CO_2 may be depleted in the afternoon by heavy photosynthesis and then slowly return to normal levels at night. Extreme fluctuations in water CO_2 may explain why aquatic plants do not have the stable C_3 and C_4 photosynthetic systems of terrestrial plants; they exist in a continuum of photosynthetic states depending on growth conditions [13]. It appears that submerged freshwater plants are constantly scrambling to adapt their photosynthetic machinery to match the enormous and sometimes hourly fluctuations in CO_2.

In order to compete, submerged plants have had to invest in costly photosynthetic equipment (enzymes) to rapidly capture CO_2 when it is available. When water CO_2 is depleted, though, such as in the afternoon during intense photosynthesis, this equipment lies idle. Indeed, the typical photosynthetic rate for freshwater plants runs at only 38% of maximum capacity, much less than for marine seagrasses and macroalgae [12]. Plants must still maintain underused or idle equipment; this maintenance drains energy from the plant in the form of increased respiration. The result is a reduction in photosynthetic efficiency– and ultimately growth– of the freshwater plant.

C.   Carbon's Scarcity in Natural Freshwaters

Freshwater aquatic plants face major problems in getting the carbon (both CO_2 and bicarbonates) they need for their photosynthesis. Carbon is often scarce in freshwater and levels fluctuate rapidly. During rapid photosynthesis, aquatic plants and algae often deplete lake waters of carbon by midday. Photosynthesis will often be highest in midmorning and gradually decrease throughout the rest of the day, even when light and other nutrients are plentiful [14].

Plant photosynthesis removes CO_2 directly from the water and in turn drives the pH up so high that any remaining CO_2 is converted to bicarbonates. Bicarbonates are also drawn on, so that the alkalinity declines. **Fig. VI-3** depicts a stagnant pond with patchs of heavy plant growth. It shows that the pH is much higher and the alkalinity is much lower in the plant patchs.

pH changes due to photosynthesis are especially dramatic in non-alkaline water where there is less bicarbonate buffering. For example, in a softwater lake the pH climbed from an acidic 5.7 in the morning to 9.6 at noon (**Table VI-2**). By then, CO_2 had been reduced from 81% of DIC to a mere 0.01%. Photosynthesis was fastest at 10:00 A.M when light and CO_2 were plentiful. During the two hours between 10:00 A.M. and noon, photosynthesis decreased sharply from 16 µg C/l/hr to 2.5 µg C/l/h. At noon we can assume that photosynthesis was not limited by light; it probably was limited by DIC, not just CO_2. By late afternoon, DIC and CO_2 levels were recovering, but photosynthesis dropped off to a low of 0.4 μg C/l/h.[2]

Time	pH	DIC (mg/l)	CO_2 (% of DIC)	Photosynthesis (μg C/l/hr)
8:00 A.M.	5.7	6.5	81	5.2
10:00 A.M.	5.7	2.6	76	16.
Noon	9.6	0.6	0.01	2.5
2:00 P.M.	8.3	0.9	2.0	2.9
4:00 P.M.	6.4	2.0	54.	0.4

DIC = Dissolved Inorganic Carbon (CO_2 + HCO_3^- + CO_3^{2-})

Table VI-2. Daytime Fluctuations in a Softwater Lake [16]. Star Lake (VT) is a softwater lake of low alkalinity (<10-20 mg/l of $CaCO_3$). Photosynthesis rates of phytoplankton were measured on a summer day at a 0.5 meter depth using ^{14}C-labeled CO_2 and HCO_3^-.

Figure VI-3. Changes in pH and Alkalinity due to Heavy Plant Growth. Cross-hatched boxes represent areas of dense growth of Hornwort in the pond. Measurements were made along a 50 meter transect of Sangwin Pond on a summer afternoon (June). Figure from Wetzel [15] modified.

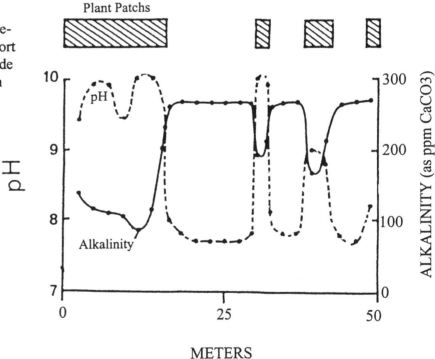

[2]Wetzel [14] attributes afternoon declines in photosynthesis, which are typical, to oxygen accumulation. Oxygen buildup within the plant and in the water surrounding the plant induces *photorespiration*, a wasteful process that decreases photosynthetic efficiency.

However, the drop-offs may also be due to the organism's internal circadian rhythm. For example, there was no afternoon drop-off in photosynthesis in *Euglena gracilis* when the alga's normal circadian rhythm was inactivated by manipulating extracellular Ca concentrations [17].

D.   Plant Strategies to Increase Carbon Uptake

The faster an aquatic plant species can take up carbon from the water, the faster it will grow. For example, investigators [18] sought to find a reason for the extreme variation in growth rates of 14 different aquatic plant species. (Growth doubling times ranged from 6 to 95 days.) So the investigators compared growth rates with photosynthesis rates, leaf chlorophyll concentration, leaf biomass, leaf surface area, and carbon affinity. The only factor that correlated significantly with growth was carbon affinity. Thus, the fastest growing plant (*Sparganium erectum*) had the greatest carbon affinity and the slowest growing plant *Lobelia dortmanna* had the lowest carbon affinity (**Table VI-3**).

Plant Species	Plant Growth (units bio-mass/day)	Carbon Affinity ('End pH')
Sparganium erectum	0.109	9.6
Batrachium aquatile	0.097	9.5
Potamogeton pectinatus	0.094	9.1
Potamogeton densus	0.094	9.0
Callitriche cophocarpa	0.088	8.8
Elodea canadensis	0.086	9.4
Potamogeton panormitanus	0.067	9.3
Potamogeton crispus	0.052	9.3
Myriophyllum spicatum	0.046	8.8
Sparganium emersum	0.042	8.8
Myosotis palustris	0.030	8.9
Berula erecta	0.020	9.0
Littorella uniflora	0.009	8.4
Lobelia dortmanna	0.007	8.2

Table VI-3. Plant Growth and Carbon Uptake [18]. To determine carbon affinity, individual plants were placed in sealed bottles filled with growth media of pH 8.0 and high alkalinity (3.8 mM bicarbonates). After 24 hours of continuous light and water mixing, the pH was measured. A greater pH increase would inevitably correlate with greater carbon affinity (CO_2 and bicarbonate removal from the water.) 'Plant Growth' was measured in a separate 4-6 week experiment.

Because obtaining carbon is often a problem for aquatic plants, many aquatic plants have devised ingenious strategies to increase its uptake. There are five known strategies [13,20]: (1) storage of CO_2 as malate; (2) refixation of respired CO_2; (3) bicarbonate uptake; (4) sediment CO_2 uptake by roots; and (5) aerial growth.

1.   Storage of CO_2 as Malate

Instead of taking up CO_2 only during the day during photosynthesis, some aquatic plants will take up CO_2 whenever it is available, especially at night. Plants convert night-time CO_2 to the carbohydrate malate, and then during the day, use the malate to generate CO_2 for their photosynthesis. This allows plants to photosynthesize in environments where CO_2 may be scarce during the day.

This strategy is not as common in aquatic plants as it is in terrestrial plants.[4] It is used by the prolific *Hydrilla verticillata* under summer growth conditions and by Isoetid-type plants (see page 98).

2.   Fixation of Respired CO_2

When water levels of CO_2 are consistently low, some plant species, mostly Isoetid-type plants, can recycle the CO_2 generated by their own respiration. The plant collects respiratory CO_2 in its large internal gas chambers (lacunae). In the few species studied, 30 to 40% of this internal CO_2 is recycled in photosynthesis [20].

3.   Bicarbonate Use

CO_2 is scarce and bicarbonates are plentiful in alkaline water. Thus, plants that can use bicarbonates (in addition to CO_2) have an enormous advantage in alkaline water. About half of the aquatic plants that have been tested can use bicarbonates [12]. **Table VI-4** lists a few examples of plant species that can and cannot use bicarbonates.

Table VI-4. Bicarbonate Use in Aquatic Plant Species.

Bicarbonate Users	Non-users of Bicarbonates
Ceratophyllum demersum [23]	*Callitriche cophocarpa* [24]
Chara [12]	*Ceratopteris* sp. [23]
Egeria densa [23]	*Echinodorus paniculatus* [23]
Elodea canadensis [23]	*Echinodorus tenellus* [23]
Hydrilla verticillata [23]	*Isoetes* sp. [10]
Myriophyllum spicatum [23]	*Ludwigia natans* [23]
Potamogeton crispus [24]	*Myriophyllum brasiliensis* [23]
Potamogeton lucens [23]	*Myriophyllum hippuroides* [23]
Potamogeton pectinatus [24]	*Myriophyllum verticillatum* [23]
Potamogeton perfoliatus [23]	*Nuphar lutea* [23]
Stratiotes aloides [23]	*Riccia fluitans* [23]
Vallisneria spiralis [23]	*Sparganium simplex* [24]
	Sphagnum cuspidatum [22]

In general, plants like *Myriophyllum spicatum* that can use bicarbonates come from alkaline waters in nature (see pages 112-113). However, some stream plants (*Callitriche stagnalis* and *Sparganium simplex*), despite being unable to use bicarbonates, apparently extract enough CO_2 from flowing alkaline hardwater streams to compete effectively with bicarbonate users [24].

---

[4]Crassulacean Acid Metabolism (CAM) is used by many desert plants to collect CO_2 at night. Thus, they can keep their stomatas closed during the day to minimize water loss.

Aquatic plants show some flexibility in whether or not they can use bicarbonates. Thus, *Callitriche cophocarpa* can use bicarbonates, but only if the concentration is high enough [21]. Plants that apparently cannot use bicarbonates at all are the bryophytes (e.g., aquatic mosses and liverworts) [10]. Usually, these plants come from soft acidic waters, where CO_2 prevails.

Because many amphibious plants cannot use bicarbonates well, it has been suggested that they may have 'chosen' over the course of evolution an aerial strategy (rather than bicarbonate uptake) to enhance carbon gain [13,25]. (However, there is at least one exception as the amphibious pondweed *Potagmogeton gramineus* can use bicarbonates quite effectively [26].

Plants prefer CO_2 to bicarbonates 10 to 1 [27], probably because bicarbonate uptake requires work. Even the ultimate hardwater plant *Potamogeton pectinatus* was shown to use bicarbonates with a much lower efficiency than it used CO_2 [24]. And *Elodea canadensis* in a rich bicarbonate media grew twice as fast when the media was injected with CO_2 [28]. Overall, freshwater aquatic plants use bicarbonates much less effectively than many algae (see page i).

Some bicarbonate users polarize their leaves during bicarbonate uptake. Polarized bicarbonate uptake has been described for *Potamogeton lucens* [26]: The plant excretes H^+ (acid) on the leaf's underside to generate a pH of about 6. This acidity converts bicarbonate to CO_2, which diffuses into the leaf to be used for photosynthesis. In order for the plant to maintain its internal charge balance, H^+ is taken up by the plant on the leaf surface resulting in a high, localized pH (about 10) and a high hydroxide (OH^-) concentration.

The OH^- combines with calcium bicarbonate [$Ca(HCO_3)_2$] in the water causing the precipitation of calcium carbonate ($CaCO_3$) on the top of the leaf. In hard, alkaline water, this reaction, which is called 'biogenic decalcification', may be so great that crusts of precipitated $CaCO_3$ may weigh more than the underlying plant [29]. I have seen $CaCO_3$ deposited as small white 'pimples' on the leaves of *Egeria densa* and *Ludwigia repens* when they were grown in hardwater under intense light.

Some aquatic plants (e.g., *Myriophyllum spicatum* and *Vallisneria spiralis*) that use bicarbonates do not polarize their leaves during bicarbonate uptake [23].

4.   Sediment CO_2 Uptake

The sediment water generally contains much higher concentrations of CO_2 than the overlying water– often 50-100 times more. Logically, one would expect that many plants would extract CO_2 from the sediment and use it for their photosynthesis.

However, that does not appear to be the case. For slow CO_2 diffusion rates both within the sediment water and within the plant make using sediment CO_2 much more difficult for plants than leaf uptake [12]. Thus, sediment CO_2 use is generally restricted to Isoetid-type plants— *Isoetes, Eriocaulon, Littorella uniflora, Lobelia dortmanna,* and to a lesser extent, *Juncus bulbosus* [30]. These slow-growing, evergreen species are common in softwater lakes that are severely depleted of CO_2 and other nutrients. Usually, the plants grow as rosettes with short thick leaves that contain extensive longitudinal lacunal channels. (These channels enhance CO_2 movement from roots to leaves.)

Sediment CO_2 uptake may be so instrinsic to adapted plant species that they may actually prefer this strategy over ordinary leaf CO_2 uptake. Thus, when *Juncus bulbosus* was grown in split chambers (see page 106), if roots were fertilized with CO_2, leaf uptake of CO_2 was immediately and substantially reduced [31].

5. Aerial Leaf

Amphibious aquatic plants will send up aerial leaves in order to gain direct access to air CO_2. In general, aerial leaves are produced in response to summer growth conditions and light spectral changes [13]. The aerial leaf strategy conveys major advantages to aquatic plants (see Chapter IX).

6. Miscellaneous Strategies

Hydrilla verticillata often dominates other aquatic plants in nature. This species can photosynthesize at low light levels, which gives it a strong competitive advantage in obtaining CO_2 over species that require more light.[5] Thus, in the early morning when the light is low but CO_2 is generally high, *Hydrilla* can begin photosynthesizing. By mid-morning when the light intensity is high enough for other plants, *Hydrilla* may have removed much of the CO_2. Competing species have light but not CO_2.

Hydrilla verticilla, a strong competitor. Drawing from IFAS [19].

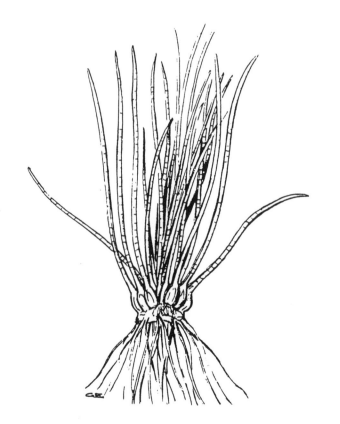

Isoetes lacustris. *I. lacustris*, which comes from acidic softwater habitats severely depleted of CO_2, has developed at least three ingenious strategies (malate storage, refixation of respiratory CO_2, and sediment CO_2 uptake) to obtain precious inorganic carbon. This species represents the 'Isoetid lifestyle', which is shared by several other genera [32]. These unrelated species, which are often found growing together, have a similar plant morphology, habitat type, and physiology. Drawing from Preston [32].

---

[5]Light compensation points for *Hydrilla verticillata*, *Ceratophyllum demersum*, *Myriophyllum spicatum*, and *Cabomba caroliniana* are 15, 35, 35, and 55 μmol/m^2/sec, respectively [33].

E.   Carbon Sources for Plants

Lakes and rivers almost always have more CO_2 than one would expect from just equilibration with air [9]. The extra CO_2 is generated by decomposition (see pages 58-60). This CO_2 can be considerable, especially since natural waters contain lots of dissolved organic carbon (DOC). Much of this DOC is in the process of decay, and therefore, is a potential CO_2 source.

Many aquatic plants could not survive in nature without the CO_2 provided by decomposition. Water in equilibrium with air contains 0.5 mg/l CO_2. Yet, many aquatic plants require much higher CO_2 concentrations. For example, when CO_2 levels were less than 36 mg/l, the moss *Sphagnum cuspidatum* was found either dead or dying [22]. And *Callitriche cophocarpa* and *Ranunculus peltatus* were found to be limited by CO_2 in their stream environment containing 5 mg/l CO_2 [21]. Because these species cannot use bicarbonates, they depend on the CO_2 released from decomposition.

F. CO_2 in the Aquarium

CO_2 for plants in aquariums is ultimately derived from fishfood and soil organic matter (see Table V-8 on page 88). Both of these sources require either fish metabolism and/or decomposition to turn organic matter into CO_2.

If the hobbyist uses natural means (e.g. decomposition) to provide CO_2, it is especially important to limit CO_2 loss from the aquarium. CO_2, because it is a gas, will be lost by all measures that increase air-water

Q. What are your feelings on CO_2 injection systems. Do you feel they are worth the hefty price tag?

A. Whether a CO_2 injection system is worth the money is a personal choice. I don't use it, because I'm satisfied with my plants and aquariums.

Generally, aquarium plants will grow much better with added CO_2. This is because CO_2 is often the limiting nutrient in most aquariums including my own, if only because so many other nutrients, such as nitrogen and phosphorus, are so plentiful.

However, the down side is that with CO_2 fertilization, your tank will require much more work. Not all aquarium hobbyists like the frequent pruning and weeding that is associated with CO_2 fertilization. And because the nutrient carbon no longer limits plant growth, artificial fertilizers are often required. You will need to continuously monitor pH and KH to make sure that the alkalinity buffer is holding. If you have softwater, you will need to add sodium bicarbonate or calcium carbonate on a regular basis to maintain a KH that is safe for the fish. Even then, hobbyists occasionally report massive overnight fish kills from CO_2 overdoses.

Also, there may be long-term effects on the substrate by CO_2 fertilization.[6] Thus, some hobbyists describe miraculous plant growth with their new CO_2 injection systems, only to report an inexplicable collapse of their tanks a year or two later (see pages 48 and 140).

mixing, such as vigorous agitation of the water by spray bars, airstones, and 'wet-dry' filters. The

---

[6] CO_2 fertilization of experimental terrestrial ecosystems not only enhanced photosynthesis but also increased root release of DOC. More specifically, investigators measured a two-fold increase in DOC in the top 15 cm of soil plus significant changes in the soil's fungal community after increasing air CO_2 levels by 50% for three plant generations [34].

hobbyist must balance water movement that enhances nutrient uptake by plants, distributes heat, and brings oxygen to fish without driving off all the CO_2. Thus, I try to keep water agitation just sufficient for providing the fish with oxygen.

All organic matter in the tank is essentially a reservoir of potential CO_2. Examples of organic matter are substrate mulm and dissolved organic carbon (DOC) in the water. Cleaning measures (water changes, charcoal filtration, gravel vacuuming, filter cleaning) remove organic matter and its potential to provide plants with CO_2. Therefore, I don't clean the tanks or filters unless it is necessary.

Aquatic plants in their natural habitats have had to adapt to low and constantly changing levels of CO_2. Many plants have developed ingenious strategies to increase carbon uptake or to conserve what they have. The fact that there are so many strategies suggests that submerged freshwater plants often have trouble getting enough carbon.

The difficulties submerged aquatic plants have in obtaining CO_2 in their native environment carry over into the aquarium. Although hobbyists can dramaticaly improve plant growth by artificial means (CO_2 injection), I would suggest that hobbyists try more natural means (allow decomposition to provide CO_2 and encourage emergent growth).

REFERENCES

1. Wetzel RG. 1983. Limnology (Second Ed.). Saunders College Publishing (Philadelphia, PA), p. 207.

2. Boyd, CE. 1995. Bottom Soils, Sediment, and Pond Aquaculture. Chapman & Hall (NY), p. 262.

3. Wetzel 1983, p. 204.

4. King DL. 1972. Carbon limitation in sewage lagoons. In: Liken GE (ed.), Nutrients and Eutrophication: The Limiting Nutrient Controversy. Special Symposium, Am. Soc. Limnol. Oceanogr. 1: 98-110.

5. Weber JA, Tenhunen JD, Yocum CS, and Gates DM. 1979. Variation of photosynthesis in *Elodea densa* with pH and/or high CO_2 concentrations. Photosynthetica 13: 454-458.

6. Pokorny J, Ondok JP and Koncalova H. 1985. Photosynthetic response to inorganic carbon in *Elodea densa* (Planchon) Caspary. Photosynthetica 19: 366-372.

7. Wetzel 1983, p. 547.

8. Cole JJ, Caraco NF, Kling GW, and Kratz TK. 1994. Carbon dioxide supersaturation in the surface waters of lakes. Science 265: 1568-1570.

9. Titus JE, Feldman RS, and Grise D. 1990. Submersed macrophyte growth at low pH. 1. CO_2 enrichment effects with fertile sediment. Oecologia 84: 307-313.

10. Boston HL, Adams MS, and Madsen JD. 1989. Photosynthetic strategies and productivity in aquatic systems. Aquat. Bot. 34: 27-57.

11. Reiskind JB, Seamon PT, and Bowes G. 1989. Photosynthetic responses and anatomical features of two marine macroalgae with different CO_2 compensation points. Aquat. Bot. 33: 71-86.

12. Madsen TV and Sand-Jensen K. 1991. Photosynthetic carbon assimilation in aquatic macrophytes. Aquat. Bot. 41: 5-40.

13. Bowes G. 1987. Aquatic plant photosynthesis: Strategies that enhance carbon gain. In: Crawford RMM (ed), Plant Life in Aquatic and Amphibious Habitats. Blackwell Scientific Publications (Boston, MA), pp. 79-98.

14. Wetzel 1983, p. 533.

15. Wetzel 1983, p. 555.

16. Allen HL. 1972. Phytoplankton photosynthesis, micronutrient interactions, and inorganic carbon availability in a soft-water Vermont lake. In: Likens GE (Ed.), Nutrients and Eutrophication: The Limiting Nutrient Controversy. Special Symposium, Amer. Soc. Limnol. Oceanogr. 1:63-83.

17. Lonergan TA 1990. Steps linking the photosynthetic light reactions to the biological clock require calcium. Plant Physiol. 93: 110-115.

18. Nielsen SL and Sand-Jensen K. 1991. Variation in growth rates of submerged rooted macrophytes. Aquat. Bot. 39: 109-120.

19. Aquatic plant line drawings are the copyright property of the University of Florida Center for Aquatic Plants (Gainesville). Used with permission.

20. Wetzel RG. 1990. Land-water interfaces: Metabolic and limnological regulators. Verh. Int. Ver. Limnol. 24: 6-24.

21. Madsen TV and Maberly SC. 1991. Diurnal variation in light and carbon limitation of photosynthesis by two speecies of submerged freshwater macrophyte with a differential ability to use bicarbonate. Freshwater Biol. 26: 175-187.

22. Paffen BGP and Roelofs JGM. 1991. Impact of CO_2 and ammonium on the growth of submerged *Sphagnum cuspidatum*. Aquat. Bot. 40: 61-71.

23. Prins HBA, O'Brien J and Zanstra PE. 1982. Bicarbonate utilization in aquatic angiosperms. pH and CO_2 concentrations at the leaf surface. In: Symoens JJ, Hooper SS, and Compere P. Studies on Aquatic Vascular Plants. Royal Botanical Society of Belgium (Brussels Belgium), pp. 112-119.

24. Sand-Jensen K. 1983. Photosynthetic carbon sources of stream macrophytes. J. Exp. Bot. 34: 198-210.

25. Bristow JM. 1969. The effects of carbon dioxide on the growth and development of amphibious plants. Can. J. Bot. 47: 1803-1807.

26. Frost-Christensen H and Sand-Jensen K. 1995. Comparative kinetics of photosynthesis in floating and submerged *Potamogeton* leaves. Aquat. Bot. 51: 121-134.

27. Wetzel 1983, p. 219.

28. Smith CS. 1993. A bicarbonate-containing medium for the solution culture of submersed plants. Can. J. Bot. 71: 1584-1588.

29. Wetzel 1983, p. 206.

30. Raven JA, Handley LL, MacFarlane JJ, McInroy S, McKenzie L, Richard JH, and Samuelsson G. 1988. The role of CO_2 uptake by roots and CAM in acquisition of inorganic C by plants of the isoetid life-form: A review, with new data on *Eriocaulon decangulare* L. New Phytol. 108: 125-148.

31. Wetzel RG, Brammer ES, Lindstrom K, and Forsberg C. 1985. Photosynthesis of submersed macrophytes in acidified lakes. II. Carbon limitation and utilization of benthic CO_2 sources. Aquat. Bot. 22: 107-120.

32. Preston CD and Croft JM. 1997. Aquatic Plants in Britain and Ireland. B.H. & A. Harley Ltd (Essex, England).

33. Van TK, Haller WT, and Bowes G. 1976. Comparison of the photosynthetic characteristics of three submersed aquatic plants. Plant Physiol. 58: 761-768.

34. Jones TH, Thompson LJ, Lawton JH, Bezemer TM, Bardgett RD, Blackburn TM, Bruce KD, Cannon PF, Hall GS, Hartley SE, Howson G, Jones CG, Kampichler C, Kandeler E and Ritchie DA. 1998. Impacts of rising atmospheric carbon dioxide on model terrestrial ecosystems. Science 280: 441-443.

Chapter VII.

PLANT NUTRITION AND ECOLOGY

A. Required Nutrients

Because plants make their own food, their nutrient requirements are simple; they require but 17 chemical elements (**Table VII-1**).

Table VII-1. Elements Required by Plants and their Function [1,2].

Element:	Nutrient Form	Major Function in Plants
B (boron)	BO_3^{3-}	Cellular membrane function, normal root growth, and flowering
C (carbon)	CO_2, HCO_3^-	Structural component of all organic compounds
Ca (calcium)	Ca^{2+}	Enzyme activator, intracellular 'secondary messenger'; essential for cell membrane permeability and cell wall structure
Cl (chlorine)	Cl^-	Osmosis, charge balance, photolysis of water
Cu (copper)	Cu^{2+}	Component of enzymes for electron transport and other oxidation-reduction reactions
Fe (iron)	Fe^{2+}, Fe^{3+}	Component of enzymes for electron transport and other oxidation-reduction reactions
H (hydrogen)	H_2O	Structural component of all organic compounds
K (potassium)	K^+	Enzyme activator, charge balance
Mg (magnesium)	Mg^{2+}	Enzyme activator and a key component of chlorophyll
Mn (manganese)	Mn^{2+}	Enzyme activator, essential for photolysis of H_2O
Mo (molybdenum)	MoO_4^{2-}	Component of nitrate reductase, the enzyme essential for the chemical reduction of nitrates
N (nitrogen)	NH_3, NH_4^+, NO_2^-, NO_3^-	Component of proteins, nucleic acids, etc.
Ni (nickel)	Ni^{2+}	Essential component of the enzyme urease
O (oxygen)	CO_2, H_2O	Structural component of all organic compounds
P (phosphorus)	PO_4^-	Component of ATP, NADP, nucleic acids, membrane phospholipids
S (sulfur)	SO_4^{2-}	Component of proteins
Zn (zinc)	Zn^{2+}	Component of 60 enzymes

B.   Competitive Uptake of Nutrients

Nutrients compete for plant uptake so that a large excess of one may dimminish the uptake of another. Thus, excessive Mn, Zn, or Cu may induce iron deficiency in plants [3]. Conversely, excessive iron has been shown to reduce tissue manganeses levels in *Hydrilla* [4]. Under certain circumstances, if ammonium (NH_4^+) is added to duckweed cultures, the duckweed will release potassium (K^+) into the media [5]. Calcium and heavy metals compete for cellular uptake, such that water hardness can affect both metal toxicity and micronutrient availability.

C.   Nutrient Accumulation and the Critical Concentration

Plants require a minimum level of each nutrient in their tissues to grow normally. The *critical concentration* is the minimum concentration of a nutritive element in a plant's tissue that correlates with unrestricted growth. If a plant contains more than the critical concentration, it means the plant is getting enough of that particular nutrient and is storing the excess; if the plant contains less than the critical concentration, then the plant is not getting enough of that nutrient.

Although there is some variation in critical concentration values between plant species, the values that Gerloff [6] reported for *Elodea occidentalis* are often used by aquatic botanists to gauge nutrient deficiencies. Using *Elodea*'s critical concentration values, one can make tentative statements about nutrient availability in a plant's environment.

If a particular nutrient is abundant in the environment, plants will take up more than the critical concentration. Indeed, plants will even take up toxic elements like lead and cadmium that they don't need (see page 18). A chemical analysis of my aquarium plants (**Table VII-2**) shows that they are clearly getting plenty of all nutrients listed. For example, my plants are accumulating 104 times the 8 mg/kg critical concentration for zinc. Because all nutrients listed were found in excess in my plants, plant growth is probably limited by carbon, a hypothesis supported by my earlier analysis of fishfood, water and soil (see Ch V).

D.   Moderate Water Movement is Best.

Water movement is often helpful, because it brings CO_2 and other nutrients quicker and closer to the leaves. However, photosynthesis and growth may be reduced by excessively high flow rates, which induce mechanical stress for the plant and remove CO_2 from the water. For example, water movement of about 1 cm/sec stimulated photosynthesis in *Callitriche stagnalis*, but faster water movement (4 cm/sec) decreased photosynthesis by 13-29% [7]. And in a separate study, *Ramunculus aquatilis* showed maximal growth at moderate flow rates of 11 cm/sec; growth was reduced at lower velocity (< 2 cm/sec) and at higher velocity (23 cm/sec) [8].

E.   Sediment versus Water Uptake of Nutrients

In nature, most aquatic plants are found in relatively unpolluted waters. Here the sediment is often a more concentrated source of nutrients than the overlying water, and thus, becomes the primary nutrient source for rooted plants. This is particularly true for phosphorus, iron, and other trace elements [9]. In contrast, nutrients that are often associated with water hardness– potassium, calcium, magnesium, chloride, and sulfates (the 'hardwater nutrients')– are generally taken up from the water.

However, 'aged' aquarium water contains much higher concentrations of nutrients than most natural waters.[1] In aquariums then, one would expect the water to become a major nutrient source for plants.

ELEMENT	Critical Concentration (mg/kg)	Elements Found in My Plants (mg/kg)
B	1.3	27
Ca	2,800	9,100
Cu	0.8	21
Fe	60	200
K	8,000	45,000
Mg	1,000	6,600
Mn	4	350
Mo	0.15	0.6
N	16,000	39,000
P	1,400	5,600
S	800	4,900
Zn	8	834

Table VII-2. Nutrient Accumulation by My Aquarium Plants. The 'Critical Concentration' of each element are published values for *Elodea occidentalis* [6]. 'Elements Found in My Plants' is from a chemical analysis by the North Carolina State Agronomy laboratories. Numbers represent the average of 3 separate analyses of healthy miscellaneous stems/leaves from 3 of my aquariums.

1. Nutrient Translocation

Nutrient translocation allows aquatic plants to scour the water or the substrate for nutrients. Using radioisotope tracers, scientists can actually track a nutrient's movement within the plant.

For example, *Myriophyllum exalbescens* distributed the P absorbed by its roots throughout its stems and leaves within 8 hours. Similarly, P absorbed by the plant's shoots moved partially into the roots. There appears to be a pressure flow-through system within the plant, because part of the P taken up by *M. exalbescens* roots was released by the shoots into the water [11].

In submerged plants, nutrient translocation may be due to osmotic pressure generated in the roots.[2] (Sediment water has a higher osmostic pressure than the overlying water.) Indeed, one investigator using radiolabeled water, showed that a water transport system operated within

---

[1]Lakes with more than 1.5 ppm of N and 0.1 ppm of P are polluted and classified as 'hypereutrophic' [10]. My aquariums contain the same or higher concentrations of N and P.

[2] However, some of the transport apparently requires energy, because when the roots of *Sparganium emersum* were treated with metabolic inhibitors, transport slowed considerably. For example, lowering the root temperature from 15 to 10° C reduced the transport (temporarily) about 5 fold [12]. Similarly in *Myriophyllum exalbescens*, calcium translocation occurred only in the light; Ca was not transported in the dark [11], suggesting that Ca translocation requires energy, in this case photosynthetic energy.

two submerged plants (*Lobelia dortmanna* and *Sparganium emersum*) [12]. Water from the roots traveled through the xylem and was exuded out of the leaf tips into the overlying water. The flow rate, while not as fast as the transpiration-generated transport in terrestrial plants, is apparently fast enough to provide aquatic plants with enough sediment nutrients for growth [13].

2. Plants Prefer Root Uptake of Phosphorus

Many aquatic plants prefer root uptake of phosphorus (P). For example, investigators [13] showed that 3 aquatic plant species, given a choice, took up more P from the substrate than from the water. To test this, the investigators used radiolabeled P (^{32}P-phosphate) and grew plants in 'split-chambers' where the plant's leaves/stems were suspended in an upper chamber sealed off from a lower chamber containing the plant's roots. (The two chambers contained complete nutrient media with or without ^{32}P-phosphate.) The investigators found that most of the P in the new shoots was not absorbed from the upper leaf/stem chamber but was derived from the roots in the lower compartment. This was especially true for *Myriophyllum brasiliense*. This species took up over 90% of its P from the roots, while *M. spicatum*, and *Elodea densa* took up 59% and 74% of their P from the roots, respectively. In separate experiments the investigators also showed that P uptake by roots was faster than shoot uptake.

Other plants (*Myriophyllum alterniflorum*, *Potamogeton zosteriformis*, *Potamogeton foliosus*, *Callitriche hermaphroditica*, *Elodea canadensis*, and *Najas flexilis*) have been shown to prefer root uptake of P [15]; they took up all of their P from the sediments when water P levels were less than 0.03 ppm. In a later study, *Najas flexilis* was found to take up over 99% of its P from the sediment [16].

3. Plants Prefer Shoot Uptake of Potassium

Aquatic plants seem to greatly prefer water uptake of potassium (K). Thus, the shoots of *Elodea occidentalis* absorbed K over 5 times faster than its roots [6]. And *Potamogeton pectinatus* showed reduced growth and flowering when K was absent from the water, even though the sediment contained ample K (see page 114).

Indeed, leaf uptake of K predominates so much over root uptake, that some aquatic plants actually add potassium to sediments rather than remove it [18]. For example, while *Hydrilla* depleted N and P from one fertile substrate, it actually increased the already high K levels in the sediment by 61% following 12 weeks of growth [19]. This same K enrichment of the sediment was shown for *Myriophyllum spicatum* [20].

Investigators [18] have hypothesized that aquatic plants under N limiting-conditions may pump K from the water into the sediment to extract ammonium. The two nutrients K^+ and ammonium (NH_4^+) compete for binding sites on soil particles. Thus, if the plant's roots increase the soil's K^+ concentration, NH_4^+ will be released from soil binding sites and enter the soil solution where roots can take it up.

4. Aquatic Plants Prefer Leaf Uptake of Ammonium

Although the nitrogen requirements of aquatic plants can be provided by ammonium from the sediment alone, the water appears to be the preferred source [21,22]. For example, in a split-chamber experiment with *Zostera marina* [23], when ammonium was added to the leaf/stem compartment, root uptake was reduced by 77%. However, when ammonium was added to the root compartment, leaf uptake was not reduced.

Work with other plant species support the above findings. Apparently, the seagrass *Amphibolis antarctica* can take up ammonium 5 to 38 faster by the leaves than the roots [24]. And *Myriophyllum spicatum* planted in fertile sediment grew fine without any ammonium in the water. However, if ammonium was added to the water (0.1 mg/l N), plants took up more N from the water than the sediment [25].

F.   Nitrogen Nutrition in Aquatic Plants

1. Aquatic Plants Prefer Ammonium over Nitrates

Aquatic plants can use ammonium (NH_4^+), nitrite (NO_2^-) or nitrate (NO_3^-) as their nitrogen source. Many aquatic plants have been found to prefer ammonium over nitrates, and the extent of this preference is substantial. For example, *Elodea nuttallii* growing in a mixture of ammonium and nitrates, removed 50% of the initial ammonium after 8 hr but few nitrates (**Fig. VII-1**). Only when much of the ammonium was gone (i.e., at about 16 hr), did it begin to take up nitrates.

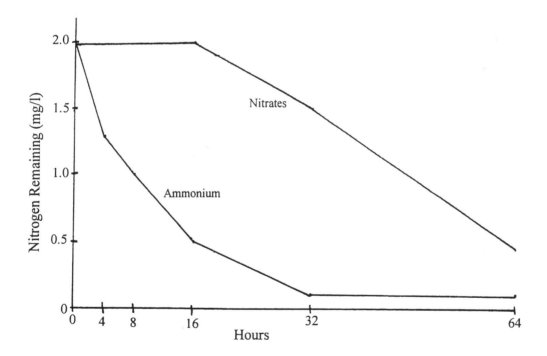

Figure VII-1. Uptake of Ammonium and Nitrates by *Elodea nuttallii*. Plants (0.5 g dry wt.) were placed in 1 liter of filtered lake water containing 2 mg/l each of NO_3-N and NH_4-N. Concentrations of ammonium and nitrates were measured at 4, 8, 16, 32 and 64 h. For each exposure period, 3 tanks with plants and 3 control tanks without plants were used. Control tanks (without plants) showed that there was little loss of either NH_4-N or NO_3-N due to bacterial processes. Figure from Ozimek [30] redrawn and used with kind permission from Kluwer Academic Publishers.

Aquatic plants take up ammonium more quickly than nitrates. For example, the 'turnover time' for ammonium (at 0.4 ppm N) in *Pistia stratiotes* was found to be just 4 hours, while nitrate turnover required a full 20 hours [39].

Ammonium often inhibits nitrate uptake and assimilation in a variety of organisms [44]. For example, algae doesn't take up nitrates if the ammonium concentration is more than 1 μM (0.018 mg/l) [46]. The prompt cessation of nitrate uptake when ammonium is added to nutrient solutions has been investigated extensively in duckweed [5,35,36]. The inhibition is typically reversible in that plants will take up nitrates a day or two after all ammonium is removed from the water.[3]

Of 33 aquatic plant species investigated, most were found to prefer ammonium over nitrates (**Table VII-3**). Because many terrestrial plants grow better with nitrates and some botanists successfully grow plants with nitrates should not weaken the fact that aquatic plants– given a choice– greatly prefer ammonium. Whether they grow better with ammonium is a separate issue– one that is not as critical to fish health or aquarium functioning. However, I would hypothesize that most aquatic plants probably grow better with ammonium.

2. Nitrogen Source for Best Growth

There are fewer studies comparing the effect of nitrates and ammonium on the **growth** of aquatic plants than their 'uptake preferences' discussed in the section above. The fact that plants take up ammonium preferentially from a mixture of ammonium and nitrates does not guarantee that they will grow better with ammonium.

Also, studies that show poor plant growth with ammonium may be confounded by ammonia toxicity (see page 20) and media acidification. (Plants release acid when they use ammonium.) Aquatic plants are sometimes grown in nutrient media that contains 30 to 60 ppm of nitrate nitrogen [6,47].

Table VII-3. Nitrogen Preference of Various Species.

Ammonium Preference:
  Agrostis canina [22]
  Callitriche hamulata [26]
  Ceratophyllum demersum [27][4]
  Drepanocladus fluitans [22]
  Eichhornia crassipes [28]
  Elodea densa [29]
  Elodea nuttallii [30]
  Fontinalis antipyretica [31]
  Hydrocotyle umbellata [32]
  Juncus bulbosus [22,33]
  Jungermannia vulcanicola [34]
  Lemna gibba [35,36,37]
  Lemna minor [5]
  Marchantia polymorpha [38]
  Myriophyllum spicatum [25]
  Pistia stratiotes [39]
  Ranunculus fluitans [26]
  Salvinia molesta [40]
  Scapania undulata [34]
  Sphagnum cuspidatum [41]
  Sphagnum fallax [41]
  Sphagnum flexuosum [22]
  Sphagnum fuscum [41]
  Sphagnum magellanicum [41]
  Sphagnum papillosum [41]
  Sphagnum pulchrum [41]
  Sphagnum rubellum [41]
  Spirodela oligorrhiza [42]
  Zostera marina [21,43]
Nitrate preference:
  Echinodorus ranunculoides [22]
  Littorella uniflora [22]
  Lobelia dortmanna [22]
  Luronium natans [22]

---

[3]The immediate (within 1 min) inhibition observed may be due to membrane depolarization and inhibition of the membrane H^+ extrusion pump by NH_4^+. (NO_3^- entry into the cell requires a simultaneous extrusion of H^+ from the cell.) The later inhibition observed, requiring at least one hour, may be due to the repression of nitrate reductase.

[4] *C. demersum* took up more nitrates during the day, but at night it took up ammonium exclusively. (Nitrate uptake requires light.)

When ammonium is substituted for nitrates at such high N concentrations, growth inhibition or plant death often occurs [48,49].

Elodea nuttallii has been shown to grow much better with ammonium than nitrates as its nitrogen source (**Fig. VII-2**). Plants in unfertilized lake water had the smallest increase in growth (~40%). (Initial dry wt was 410 mg, but after 2 weeks it increased to a final dry wt of about 560 mg.) Growth in the lake water may have been limited by N, because when nitrate (NO_3^-) was added to the lake water, plants grew better than unfertilized plants. However, plants grew much better when ammonium (NH_4^+) was added. While E. nuttallii clearly responded to nitrate fertilization, it did even better with ammonium fertilization.

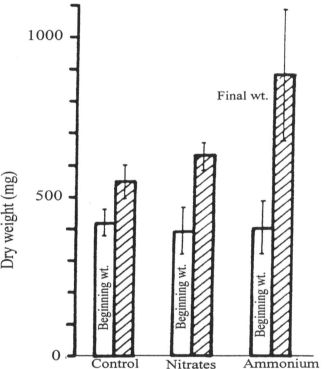

Figure VII-2. Effect of Nitrogen Source on the Growth of *Elodea nuttallii*. Five shoots of *Elodea nuttallii* were added to tanks containing 1 liter of filtered lake water. Columns in the figure show beginning dry wt. and final dry wt. for the 3 conditions. 'Control' tanks contained lake water without added nitrogen. 'Nitrates' are tanks that contained lake water plus 2 mg/l of NO_3-N. 'Ammonium' tanks contained lake water plus 2 mg/l of NH_4-N. 'Final Wts' were determined at the end of the 2 week growth period. Figure from Ozimek [30] redrawn and used with kind permission from Kluwer Academic Publishers.

Elodea nuttallii. *E. nuttalli* is a native of North America that like *E. canadensis* has since spread to the rest of the world. Although *E. nuttallii* seems to compete somewhat better than *E. canadensis* in polluted waters, the two species resemble each other and are occasionally found growing together in Britain [53]. Like many other aquatic plants, *E. nuttallii* prefers ammonium over nitrates as its N source.

110

Table VII-4 summarizes experimental studies comparing growth as a function of nitrogen source. When ammonium was tested at concentrations <40 mg/l, all plants grew better with ammonium or a mixture of ammonium and nitrate. Most likely, these results can be generalized to the majority of aquatic plants. For, if one assumes that a plant species has adapted to the N source in its particular native habitat, then aquatic plants should not only prefer ammonium but also grow better with it. (This assumption is explained in the following section.)

Table VII-4. Nitrogen Source for Best Growth.

Ammonium:
Ceratophyllum demersum [48]
Elodea nuttallii [30]
Marsilea drummondii [48]
Salvinia molesta [40]
Ammonium/Nitrate Mixture:
Eichhornia crassipes [28]
Marchantia polymorpha [38]

---

3. Ecology and Nitrogen Source Preferences

Both nitrates and ammonium have their own attributes as an N source for plants [50]. Whether a plant species grows better using one or the other depends on where the species evolved. Species from habitats where nitrate predominates do better with nitrates; species from habitats where ammonium predominates do better with ammonium.

Nitrates predominate in many drier terrestrial soils. This is because there is plentiful oxygen, which nitrifying bacteria use to rapidly convert ammonium to nitrates. Nitrates accumulate, because the oxygen discourages nitrate removal by denitrification (see page 63). Thus, many terrestrial plants, especially crop plants, have adapted well to their nitrate-rich environments, and in general, prefer nitrates or an ammonium/nitrate mixture over pure ammonium [50,51].

In the aquatic environment, however, ammonium predominates. This is because almost all sediments supporting aquatic plant growth are anaerobic. Ammonium, not nitrates, tends to accumulate, because anaerobic conditions discourage nitrification and encourage denitrification. Because ammonium predominates in the aquatic environment, most aquatic plant species have developed an ammonium-based nutrition.

Q. Are you suggesting that I add ammonium to my aquariums so that the plants can grow better?

A. No. I would never add ammonium to an aquarium; it is far too toxic to plants as well as fish. The typical aquarium ecosystem continuously generates low levels of ammonium. There is no need to add more.

My point is that plants readily take up ammonium from aquarium water and probably grow better using ammonium. This means that biological filtration (nitrification) can be de-emphasized in aquariums that contain healthy aquatic plants.

The exceptions, such as *Littorella uniflora*, *Lobelia dortmanna*, *Luronium natans*, and *Echinodorus ranunculoides*, come from environments that are severely nutrient-depleted ('ultraoligotrophic') [52]. These environments favor nitrification and nitrate accumulation. Moreover, the plants themselves encourage nitrification by releasing particularly large amounts of oxygen into the root area [33]. These four species apparently prefer root uptake of nitrates over the more common leaf uptake of ammonium [22].

4. Plants and Nitrifying Bacteria Compete

Plants, algae, and all photosynthesizing organisms use the N of ammonium (not nitrate) to produce their proteins.[5]

Nitrate conversion to ammonium by plants (e.g. 'nitrate reduction') requires energy and appears to be the mirror image of nitrification (page 62). Nitrifying bacteria gain the energy they need for their life processes solely from ammonium oxidation to nitrate; the total energy gain from the two-steps of nitrification is 84 Kcal/mol [55], and the overall reaction is:

$$NH_4^+ + 2\,O_2 \Rightarrow NO_3^- + H_2O + 2\,H^+$$

Plants must expend essentially the same amount of energy (83 Kcal/mol) to convert nitrates **back** to ammonium in the two-step process of nitrate reduction [50]. The overall reaction for nitrate reduction is:

$$NO_3^- + H_2O + 2\,H^+ \Rightarrow NH_4^+ + 2\,O_2$$

Plants use ammonium to synthesize their proteins. Thus, when nitrifying bacteria convert ammonium to nitrates, plants are forced– at great energy– to convert nitrates back to ammonium.

Q. Our three 300 liter High-tech tanks are heavily loaded with fish. Since we also feed heavily to keep the fish in prime condition, we believe that our systems require external biological filtration. Clearly, the lush plant growth is not consuming all the ammonium, since nitrates accumulate at the rate of 7-10 mg/l per week, requiring the use of denitrators and regular partial water changes to keep the average nitrate concentration less than 10 mg/l.

Two of the tanks have trickle filters for extra biological filtration, and one has an undergravel filter. As for your conjecture that "biological filtration may have a negative impact on plants", I can only say "I doubt it". If the filtration stunts our plants, presumably through a lack of ammonium due to rapid nitrification, I would truly hate to see how they would grow otherwise; we currently have to trim the faster growing plants every two weeks.

A. Your observation that your plants thrive despite the trickle filters does not prove that they couldn't do better without them. I suspect that whatever possible effect the trickle filters might have on the plants is dwarfed by the otherwise ideal growing conditions in your 'High-tech' tanks.

And the fact that nitrates accumulate in your tanks does not mean that your plants are not taking up ammonium. The plants are predictably ignoring the less desirable nitrates as they compete with the filter bacteria for the ammonium. Only by measuring ammonia levels (not nitrates)

---

[5]The first step in the important GS-GOGAT metabolic pathway is the binding of NH_3 to a carbohydrate. (GS and GOGAT are acronyms for the enzymes glutamine synthetase and glutamine-oxoglutarate aminotransferase.) GOGAT works with the enzyme glutamine synthetase to bind ammonia to glutamic acid to form glutamine. From this glutamine all other amino acids will be synthesized and then eventually combined to form the plant's proteins [54].

as you gradually reduced biological filtration could you determine how much nitrification is really necessary for the fish load in your tanks.

The relatively rapid nitrate accumulation in your tanks may be more a function of the heavy biological filtration than the heavy fish load. Your plants would probably remove more total N and prevent nitrate accumulation if you didn't have the trickle filters. This is because plants may accumulate more N in their tissue when it is given to them as ammonium than when it is given to them as nitrate [39].

In my planted tanks I have been surprised at how little biological filtration is actually required. When I decreased biological filtration (by removing the filter media in the canister filters), I had fewer problems with nitrate accumulation and water acidification.

Although nitrification is essential in tanks without plants, it is much less important in planted tanks. My point is not to advocate dispensing with filters altogether, but I would urge readers to believe in their plants more than trickle filters.

G.   Water Hardness and Plant Ecology

As one travels down the river systems of the Carolinas to the coast, the water changes from softwater bogs, Cypress swamps, and blackwater streams with almost no water hardness to hard, saline waters due to the tidal influx of seawater.[6] The vegetation changes as well. Common aquarium plants like *Echinodorus tenellus*, *Ludwigia repens*, *Bacopa caroliniana*, and *Sagittaria graminea* in the softwaters give way to *Bacopa monnieri*, *Sagittaria subulata*, and *Riccia fluitans* in hard and/or brackish waters [56].

Aquatic plant species have 'learned' to survive in their particular environment by developing adaptive physiological mechanisms.[7] After a time, these mechanisms become, to a lesser or greater degree, genetically 'fixed'. Thus, aquatic plant species are not alike in their requirements. Many softwater species and amphibious species can only use CO_2; they are unable to use bicarbonates. Hardwater species often can use bicarbonates, but seem to need more calcium in the water than softwater species.

Water hardness is a major unifying theme. Although, strictly speaking, Ca and Mg concentrations determine water hardness, other macronutrients (K, Na, S, Cl, bicarbonates), and other factors (alkalinity, pH, specific conductance[8]) are usually associated with water hardness in natural freshwaters.

One investigator [59] surveyed the water chemistry and aquatic plant species in 700 diverse habitats in Japan where the water ranged from soft to extremely hard, brackish water. Whether the pH, alkalinity, Ca, and specific conductance were higher (or lower) where the plants were present or where they were absent was recorded. Of the 20 species studied, most plants showed a significant association with all four parameters. For example, *Myriophyllum spicatum*

---

[6] Seawater contains 412 ppm Ca and 1,300 ppm Mg, making it hard as well as 'salty'.

[7] For example, *Bacopa monnieri*, an aquarium plant that originates from brackish waters, is known to tolerate high levels of salts. Thus, investigators successfuly acclimated plants (over a 12 week period of exposure to increasing salt concentrations) to 15,000 mg/l NaCl [57].

[8] Specific conductance is an exact measure of electrical conductance in water by ions, but it also reflects levels of the 'hardwater nutrients'[58]. This is because the hardwater nutrients exist in water as ions (e.g. Ca^{2+}, Mg^{2+}, K^+, Na^+, Cl^-, HCO_3^-, HSO_4^-), all of which would conduct electricity in water.

was found in hardwater habitats with a high specific conductance and *Brasenia schreberi* was found in softwater habitats with a low specific conductance (**Table VII-5**).

Although there is some overlap between the two species in all 4 parameters, what differentiates the two are the extremes. *Myriophyllum spicatum* is found in water with a conductivity of 15,100 μmhos, whereas *Brasenia schreberi* wasn't found in any waters with conductivity above 238 μmhos. And the hardwater *M. spicatum* was not found in water with less than 2.7 mg/l calcium, whereas the softwater *B. schreberi* was found growing in water with only 0.4 mg/l Ca. (Not surprisingly, several hardwater plants have an absolute requirement for 1-2 ppm water Ca (see next section).

Water Chemistry	*Myriophyllum spicatum* (range)	*Brasenia schreberi* (range)
Alkalinity (as ppm CaCO$_3$)	13 - 145	2.5 - 47
Calcium (mg/l)	2.7 - 61	0.4 - 22
pH	6.5 - 9.6	5.6 - 8.7
Conductivity (μmhos, 25° C)	55 - 15,100	15 - 238

Table VII-5. Natural Habitats of *Myriophyllum spicatum* and *Brasenia schreberi* [59].

The water shield *Brasenia schreberi*. *B. schreberi* is a water lily type of plant whose underwater petioles are covered with a gelatinous slime. This species has been found all over the world in very softwater – water in which hardwater plants could probably not survive. Thus, softwater plants, many of which are slow-growers, may have found an ecological niche in nutrient-depleted environments. Drawing from IFAS [62].

1. Requirements of Hardwater Plants

Aquatic plants from hardwater are rarely found in soft, acidic water, because they require a certain level of Ca, bicarbonates, K, and Mg in the water (e.g. the 'hardwater nutrients').

For example, water Ca, Mg, and K were shown by Huebert [68] to greatly affect the growth, survival, and flowering of the hardwater plant *Potamogeton pectinatus* (**Table VII-6**). Plants grown in nutrient media where N was omitted from the water grew and flowered just as well as plants in the control tank. This was also true of plants grown in tanks without S or tanks without micronutrients in the water. (They could get all of these nutrients from the rich sediment in which they were planted.) However, plants grown in media without K grew and flowered about half as well as controls. Mg omission from the water had a similar effect. The most dramatic effect, though, was on plants grown in Ca-deficient media. Plants without Ca (~2 ppm) died within one week.

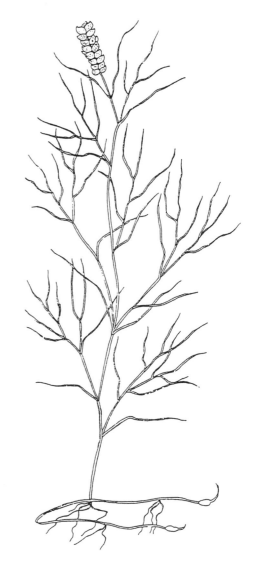

Table VII-6. Effect of Omitting Nutrients from the Water on *Potamogeton pectinatus* [68]. Plants were grown in cups containing the same rich lake sediment but put into tanks with different nutrient media. The sediment was covered with 1" of sand. (Investigators detected no leaching of sediment nutrients into the water.)

Nutrients Omitted from the Water	Growth (% of Control)	Flowering (flower clusters/g of plant dry wt)
None (control tank with all nutrients)	100 %	1.6 - 3
Nitrogen	100	1.6 - 3
Sulfur	100	1.6 - 3
Micronutrients (Fe, Cu, Zn, Mn, etc)	100	1.6 - 3
Potassium	45	0.7
Magnesium	53	0.7
Calcium	Death	Death

The Sago pondweed *Potamogeton pectinatus*. *P. pectinatus* requires Mg, K, and Ca in the water, not just the substrate. In fact, without some calcium in the water it will die. This may explain why *P. pectinatus*, which has a world-wide distribution, is never found in softwater habitats. Other hardwater species have been shown to have a similarly compelling requirement for water Ca.

Indeed, calcium's absence in the water often results in death for hardwater plants. Water-hyacinth plants without water Ca died within 2 weeks [69]. (The absence of other nutrients N, K, P, Mg, S, and Fe merely resulted in deficiency symptoms and slower growth.) *Lemna trisulca* reportedly died or became deformed when put into nutrient media without 1 ppm Ca [70].

The water lily *Nymphoides peltata* is never found in softwater habitats. Investigators [71] showed that this plant must have some Ca in the water for normal petiole extension. Without about 1 ppm Ca, young plants were unable to get their leaves above the water surface and they died, probably from suffocation.[9]

Generally, most plants that come from hardwater can use bicarbonates as an alternate carbon source (see page 97). However, some hardwater plants seem to need bicarbonates in the water for more than just photosynthetic carbon. Thus, even when fertilized heavily with CO_2, *Vallisneria americana* grew 40% better when the nutrient media contained bicarbonates than when it did not. And *Myriophyllum spicatum* was much less susceptible to fungal attack when bicarbonates were added to the nutrient media [72].

Heavy metals, which include micronutrients like iron and copper, are often scarce in alkaline hardwater, because they form (or co-precipitate with) metal oxides [73]. For example, in one study, Fe^{2+} remained in solution for 13 h at pH 6.3, but only 3.4 min at pH 8 [74]. Once the metals precipitate, they then become less available to plants. Most likely, the inhabiting plants have, over time, adapted to these conditions by developing powerful physiological mechanisms for scavenging scarce micronutrients from their environment. Thus, hardwater plants probably require fewer water micronutrients than softwater plants.

At the same time, however, hardwater plants would not have 'learned' how to protect themselves from an excess of heavy metals and may be particularly susceptible to metal toxicity (see page 17).

2. Requirements of Softwater Plants

Unfortunately, there is much less experimental data on softwater plants, many of which are the tropical plants used in aquariums. But I would still like to hypothesize about their ecology and requirements. First, softwater plants come from habitats severely depleted of hardwater nutrients like Ca, Mg, K, and S. As a consequence, they have been forced to develop highly efficient mechanisms for scavenging these nutrients from their environment.

Thus, I compared the growth of a softwater plant (*Bacopa carolinana*) and a hardwater plant (*Bacopa monnieri*) in nutrient media with and without added Ca. (In this experiment plants were grown in separate bottles containing potting soil covered with gravel and were allowed to grow emergent.) Without Ca, *B. monnieri* disintegrated. (With Ca it grew quite well.) In contrast, the softwater plant (*B. caroliniana*) grew well and appeared normal under both experimental conditions.

Acidity is often associated with calcium-depleted habitats, and acidic water contains few bicarbonates. *Eriocaulon decangulare* and other Isoetid-type plants (see page 98), which come from extremely softwaters, cannot use bicarbonates as a carbon source [75].

---

[9]Water lilies depend on aerating their substrate efficiently in order to survive in the severely anaerobic substrates where they are often found. They must have at least two leaves above the water to ventilate the root area (see page 151).

116

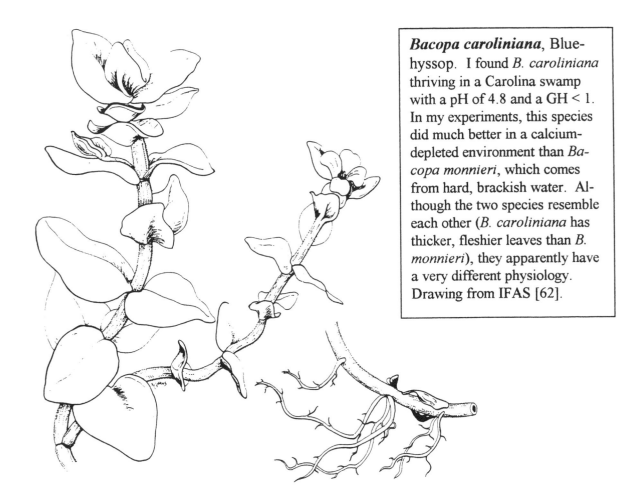

Bacopa caroliniana, Blue-hyssop. I found *B. caroliniana* thriving in a Carolina swamp with a pH of 4.8 and a GH < 1. In my experiments, this species did much better in a calcium-depleted environment than *Bacopa monnieri*, which comes from hard, brackish water. Although the two species resemble each other (*B. caroliniana* has thicker, fleshier leaves than *B. monnieri*), they apparently have a very different physiology. Drawing from IFAS [62].

In understanding what softwater plants require, one question arises. Do softwater plants actually prefer the water and soil conditions of their native habitat, despite the fact that it is often nutrient-depleted and prone to excessive heavy metals?

I decided to test this hypothesis by comparing the growth of various hardwater and soft-water species in two quite different soil/water conditions. (Each plant species got its own experimental bottle, so it didn't have to compete with other plant species.) The 'acidic condition' consisted of a softwater nutrient media and an acidic substrate (1:2 mixture of *Sphagnum* peat moss and sand with a final pH of 4). The 'alkaline condition' consisted of a hardwater nutrient media and an alkaline soil (desert soil from Arizona with a final pH of 8.0). Plant growth during the 6-week experiment is shown in **Table VII-7**.

Two species from softwater habitats, *B. caroliniana* amd *S. graminea*, grew moderately well under acidic conditions but grew even better under the alkaline conditions of my experiment. For example, the average growth increase of *B. caroliniana* under alkaline conditions was 84%, whereas under acidic conditions it was 43%. The other softwater plant *Ludwigia repens* did not grow at all under acidic conditions, but grew well under alkaline conditions.

The results for the hardwater plants were mixed. *Vallisneria spiralis*, as expected due to its hardwater origins, grew splendidly under alkaline conditions with the 3 original, medium-sized plants increasing their biomass 520% and reproducing vigorously. Under acidic conditions, however, 'Val' was clearly struggling, if not dying, by the end of the experiment (**Fig. VII-3**). *Bacopa monnieri*, another hardwater plant, grew slowly and stayed submerged under both acidic and alkaline conditions, probably from CO_2 deficiencies.

Figure VII-3. Growth of *Vallisneria spiralis* under Acidic v. Alkaline Conditions. Most *Vallisneria* come from hardwater habitats. In an experiment where I grew *V. spiralis* in hardwater and an alkaline desert soil, a single small plant increased its biomass over 500% and produced an average of 8 babies after 6 weeks (righthand bottle). In contrast, *V. spiralis* in softwater and an acidic peat substrate (lefthand bottle) disintegrated.

Plant Species	Growth (% Increase)	
	Acidic Conditon	Alkaline Condition
Bacopa caroliniana	43	84
Bacopa monnieri	22	49
Sagittaria graminea	68	145
Ludwigia repens	-4	78
Vallisneria spiralis	0	520

Table VII-7. Growth of Various Species under Acidic v. Alkaline Conditions. Each experimental unit (bottle containing plants) was replicated three times. At the end of 6 weeks, whole plants were cleaned, dried, and weighed. Final weight was compared with a beginning dry weight determined earlier. For *B. caroliniana*, *L. repens*, and *V. spiralis*, the differences in average growth between the two conditions were statistically significant ($P < 0.05$).

When I began this experiment, I had assumed that softwater plants would prefer the conditions of their natural habitat. After all, that is what they are used to. However, the softwater plants behaved counter to my assumption. They did best under alkaline conditions that must have been quite unfamiliar to them.

The explanation for this anomaly may be that softwater plants are found in softwater habitats in nature, because that is the only habitat where they can compete effectively against hardwater plants, many of which use bicarbonates and can grow much faster.

H.   Nutrition in the Aquarium

My experiment (**Table VII-7**) and the fact many nursery growers of aquatic plants successfully grow softwater *Cryptocoryne*, *Aponogeton*, etc in hard, alkaline water contradict the well-meaning attempts of aquatic gardeners to cater to softwater plants by using softwater. The idea that softwater is optimal for many aquarium plants is pervasive. I have heard many hobbyists denounce their hard tapwater as the reason for the poor plant growth in their aquariums.

In my opinion, the only thing that would hold softwater plants back in hard water is the limited CO_2. (The typically high pH would convert most CO_2 to bicarbonates, and softwater plants generally can't use bicarbonates.) Thus, if softwater plants are forced to compete with hardwater plants for carbon in the same tank, softwater plants may do poorly.

However, exceptions abound. For example, if softwater amphibious plants, such as *Ludwigia repens*, are allowed to grow partially emergent and to tap into air CO_2, they should do fine.

Comment.   Well, what you have written in this chapter is interesting, but not very useful. It doesn't tell me what fertilizers to use or how to get my plants to grow better.

Reply.   If your water is not too soft and you use soil in your tank, feed your fish well, and keep tank cleaning/water changes to a minimum, your plants will get all the nutrients they need. Fertilizers are really only needed in certain situations, such as growing plants in tanks with CO_2 injection and/or softwater.

I see three 'take-home messages' in this chapter. First, biological filtration (nitrification) can be de-emphasized in a planted aquarium, because plants readily take up ammonium.

Second, softwater is nutrient-depleted water and is not ideal for plants, even plants that come from softwater. Indeed, hardwater plants may not be able to survive in it.

Third, I would urge beginning hobbyists, especially those with hardwater, not to discriminate against fast-growing, hardwater plants. Hobbyists with hardwater could do worse than take advantage of prolific growers like Hornwort, *Elodea* and *Vallisneria*.

REFERENCES

1. Hopkins WG. 1995. Introduction to Plant Physiology. John Wiley (NY), Ch. 4.

2. Glass ADM. 1989. Plant Nutrition: An Introduction to Current Concepts. Jones & Bartlett Publishers (Boston), Ch. 8.

3. Wild A and Jones LHP. 1988. Mineral nutrition of crop plants. In: Wild A (ed), Russell's Soil Conditions and Plant Growth (11th Edition). John Wiley (NY), pp 69-112.

4. Basiouny FM, Garrard LA and Haller WT. 1977. Absorption of iron and growth of *Hydrilla verticillata* (L.F.) Royle. Aquat. Bot. 3: 349-356.

5. Beck T and Feller U. 1991. Ammonium-stimulated K release from *Lemna minor* L. grown on a medium containing nitrate as N-source. Aquat. Bot. 255-266.

6. Gerloff GC. 1975. Nutritional Ecology of Nuisance Aquatic Plants. National Environmental Research Center (Corvallis OR), 78 pp.

7. Madsen TV and Sondergaard M. 1983. The effects of current velocity on the photosynthesis of *Callitriche stagnalis* Scop. Aquat. Bot. 15: 187-193.

8. Boeger RT. 1992. The influence of substratum and water velocity on growth of *Ranunculus aquatilis* L. (Ranunculaceae). Aquat. Bot. 42: 351-359.

9. Barko JW, Gunnison D, and Carpenter SR. 1991a. Sediment interactions with submersed macrophyte growth and community dynamics. Aquat. Bot. 41: 41-65.

10. Wetzel RG. 1983. Limnology (Second Ed.). Saunders College Publishing (Philadelphia, PA), pp. 232, 256.

11. DeMarte JA and Hartman RT. 1974. Studies on absorption of ^{32}P, ^{59}Fe, and ^{45}Ca by Water-Milfoil (*Myriophyllum exalbescens* fernald). Ecology 55: 188-194.

12. Pedersen O. 1993. Long-distance water transport in aquatic plants. Plant Physiol. 103: 1396-1375.

13. Pedersen O and Sand-Jensen K. 1997. Transpiration does not control growth and nutrient supply in the amphibious plant *Mentha aquatica*. Plant Cell Environ. 20: 117-123.

14. Bristow JM and Whitcombe M. 1971. The role of roots in the nutrition of aquatic vascular plants. Am. J. Bot. 58: 8-13.

15. Carignan R and Kalff J. 1980. Phosphorus sources for aquatic weeds: Water or sediments? Science 207: 987-988.

16. Moeller RE, Burkholder JM, And Wetzel RG. 1988. Significance of sedimentary phosphorus to a rooted submersed macrophyte (*Naja flexilis* (Willd.) Rostk. and Schmidt) and its algal epiphytes. Aquat. Bot. 32: 261-281.

17. Fassett NC. 1957. A Manual of Aquatic Plants. The University of Wisconsin Press (Madison WI).

18. Barko JW, Smart RM, McFarland DG, and Chen RL. 1988. Interrelationships between the growth of *Hydrilla verticllata* (L.F.) Royle and sediment nutrient availability. Aquat. Bot. 32: 205-216.

19. Sutton DL and Latham WGH. 1996. Analysis of interstitial water during culture of *Hydrilla verticillata* with controlled release fertilizers. Aquat. Bot. 54: 1-9.

20. Carignan R. 1985. Nutrient dynamics in a littoral sediment colonized by the submersed macrophyte *Myriophyllum spicatum*. Can. J. Fish. Aquat. Sci. 42: 1303-1311.

21. Iizumi H and Hattori A. 1982. Growth and organic production of eelgrass (*Zostera marina* L.) in temperate waters of the pacific Coast of Japan. III. The kinetics of nitrogen uptake. Aquat. Bot. 12: 245-256.

22. Schuurkes JAAR, Kok CJ, and Hartog CD. 1986. Ammonium and nitrate uptake by aquatic plants from poorly buffered and acidified waters. Aquat. Bot. 24: 131-146.

23. Thursby GB and Harlin MM. 1982. Leaf-root interaction in the uptake of ammonia by *Zostera marina*. Mar. Biol. 72: 109-112.

24. Pedersen MF, Paling EI, and Walker DL. 1997. Nitrogen uptake and allocation in the seagrass *Amphibolis antarctica*. Aquat. Bot. 56: 105-117.

25. Nichols DS and Keeney DR. 1976. Nitrogen nutrition of *Myriophyllum spicatum*: Uptake and translocation of ^{15}N by shoots and roots. Freshwater Biol. 6: 145-154.

26. Schwoerbel VJ and Tillmanns GC. 1972. Adaptation to ammonia *in situ* by submerged macrophytes. Arch. Hydrobiol. 42: 139-141. (German)

27. Toetz DW. 1971. Diurnal uptake of NO_3 and NH_4 by a *Ceratophylllum*-periphyton community. Limnol. Oceanogr. 16: 819-822.

28. Reddy KR and Tucker JC. 1983. Productivity and nutrient uptake of water hyacinth, *Eichhornia crassipes*. I. Effect of nitrogen source. Econ. Bot. 37: 237-247.

29. Reddy KR, Tucker JC, and DeBusk WF. 1987. The role of *Egeria* in removing nitrogen and phosphorus from nutrient enriched waters. J. Aquat. Plant Manage. 25: 14-19.

30. Ozimek T, Gulati RD, and van Donk E. 1990. Can macrophytes be useful in biomanipulation of lakes: The Lake Zwemlust example. Hydrobiologia 200: 399-407.

31. Schwoerbel VJ and Tillmanns GC. 1974. Assimilation of nitrogen from the medium and nitrate reductase activity in submerged macrophytes: *Fontinalis antipyretica* L. Arch. Hydrobiol. Sup. 47: 289-294.

32. Reddy KR. 1983. Fate of nitrogen and phosphorus in a waste-water retention reservoir containing aquatic macrophytes. J. Environ. Qual. 12: 137-141.

33. Roelofs JGM, Schuurkes JAAR, and Smits AJM. 1984. Impact of acidification and eutrophication on macrophyte communities in soft waters II. Experimental studies. Aquat. Bot. 18: 398-411.

34. Miyazaki T and Satake K. 1985. *In situ* measurement of uptake of inorganic carbon and nitrogen by the aquatic liverworts *Jungermannia vulcanicola* Steph. and *Scapania undulata* (L.) Dum. in an acid stream, Kashiranashigawa, Japan. Hydrobiologia 124: 29-34.

35. Ingemarsson B, Johansson L, and Larsson C-M. 1984. Photosynthesis and nitrogen utilization in exponentially growing nitrogen-limited cultures of *Lemna gibba*. Physiol. Plant. 62: 363-369.

36. Ullrich WR, Larsson M, Larsson CM, Lesch S, and Novacky A. 1984. Ammonium uptake in *Lemna gibba* G 1, related membrane potential changes, and inhibition of anion uptake. Physiol. Plant. 61: 369-376.

37. Porath D and Pollock J. 1982. Ammonia stripping by duckweed and its feasibility in circulating aquaculture. Aquat. Bot. 13: 125-131.

38. Katoh K, Ishikawa M, Miyake K, Ohta Y, Hirose Y, and Iwamura T. 1980. Nutrient utilization and requirement under photoheterotrophic growth of *Marchantia polymorpha*: improvement of the culture media. Physiol. Plant. 49: 241-247.

39. Nelson SG, Smith BD, and Best BR. 1980. Nitrogen uptake by tropical freshwater macrophytes. Technical Report by Water Resources Research Center of Guam Univ. Agana. (Available from National Technical Information Service (NTIS), Springfield VA 22161 as PB80-194228.)

40. Cary PR and Weerts PGJ. 1983. Growth of *Salvinia molesta* as affected by water temperature and nutrition. 1. Effects of nitrogen level and nitrogen compounds. Aquat. Bot. 16: 163-172.

41. Jauhiainen J, Wallen B, and Malmer N. 1998. Potential NH_4^+ and NO_3^- uptake in seven *Sphagnum* species. New Phytol. 138: 287-293.

42. Ferguson AR and Bollard EG. 1969. Nitrogen metabolism of *Spirodela oligorrhiza* 1. Utilization of ammonium, nitrate and nitrite. Planta 88: 344-352.

43. Short FT and McRoy CP. 1984. Nitrogen uptake by leaves and roots of the seagrass *Zostera marina* L. Bot. Mar. 27: 547-555.

44. Kansas State Teachers College. 1967. Common Aquatic weeds of Kansas Ponds and Lakes. The Emporia State Research Studies.

45. Guerrero MG, Vega MJ, and Losada M. 1981. The assimilatory nitrate-reducing system and its regulation. Annu. Rev. Plant Physiol. 32: 169-204.

46. Dortch Q. 1990. The interaction between ammonium and nitrate uptake in phytoplankton. Mar. Ecol. Prog. Ser. 61:183-201.

47. Kane ME, Gilman EG, Jenks MA, and Sheehan TJ. 1990. Micropropagation of the aquatic plant *Cryptocoryne lucens*. HortScience 25: 687-689.

48. Edwards PSJ and Allsopp A. 1956. The effects of changes in the inorganic nitrogen supply on the growth and development of *Marsilea* in aseptic culture. J. Exp. Bot 7: 194-202.

49. Best EPH. 1980. Effects of nitrogen on the growth and nitrogenous compounds of *Ceratophyllum demersum*. Aquat. Bot. 8: 197-206.

50. Lewis OAM. 1986. Plants and Nitrogen. Edward Arnold Publishers, LTD. Baltimore, MD, pp. 27-29.

51. Hageman RH. 1980. Effect of form of nitrogen on plant growth. In: Meisinger JJ, Randall GW, and Vitosh ML (eds). Nitrification Inhibitors— Potentials and Limitations. Am.Soc. of Agronomy (Madison WI), pp. 47-62.

52. Arts GHP, Roelofs JGM, and De Lyon MJH. 1990. Differential tolerances among soft-water macrophyte species to acidification. Can. J. Bot. 68: 2127-2134.

53. Preston CD and Croft JM. 1997. Aquatic Plants in Britain and Ireland. B.H. & A. Harley Ltd (Essex, England).

54. Lewis 1986, pp. 34-41.

55. Wetzel 1983, pp. 235.

56. Botanist Patrick McMillan (personal communication 1997).

57. Ali G, Purohit M, Saba, Iqbal M, and Srivastava PS. 1997. Morphogenic response and isozymes of *Bacopa monniera* (L.) Wettst cultures grown under salt stress. Phytomorphology 47: 97-106.

58. Wetzel 1983, p. 182.

59. Kadono Y. 1982. Occurrence of aquatic macrophytes in relation to pH, alkalinity, Ca^{++}, Cl^- and conductivity. Jpn. J. Ecol. 32: 39-44.

60. Catling PM, Freedman B, Stewart C, Kerekes JJ, and Lefkovitch LP. 1986. Aquatic plants of acid lakes in Kejimkujik National Park, Nova Scotia; floristic composition and relation to water chemistry. Can. J. Bot. 64: 724- 729.

61. Seddon B. 1972. Aquatic macrophytes as limnological indicators. Freshwater Biol. 2: 107-130.

62. IFAS Aquatic plant line drawings are the copyright property of the University of Florida Center for Aquatic Plants (Gainesville). Used with permission.

63. Coulter GW. 1991. Lake Tanganyika and its Life. Oxford University Press (NY), pp 215- 218.

64. Ferguson RL, Rivera JA, and Wood LL. 1989. Submerged aquatic vegetation in the Albemarle-Pamlico Estuarine System. Project No. 88-10 of the National Marine Fisheries Service, NOAA, (Beaufort NC).

65. Fraser D, Morton JK, and Jui PY. 1986. Aquatic vascular plants in Sibley Provincial Park in relation to water chemistry and other factors. Can. Field-Naturalist 100: 15-21.

66. Pip E. 1984. Ecogeographical tolerance range variation in aquatic macrophytes. Hydrobiologia 108: 37-48.

67. Moyle JB. 1945. Some chemical factors influencing the distribution of aquatic plants in Minnesota. Am. Mid. Nat. 34: 402-420.

68. Huebert DB and Gorham PR. 1983. Biphasic mineral nutrition of the submersed aquatic macrophyte *Potamogeton pectinatus* L. Aquat. Bot. 16: 269- 284.

69. Newman S and Haller WT. 1988. Mineral deficiency symptoms of waterhyacinth. J. Aquat. Plant Manage. 26: 55-58.

70. Huebert DB and Shay JM. 1991. The effect of external phosphorus, nitrogen and calcium on growth of *Lemna trisulca*. Aquat. Bot. 40: 175-183.

122

71. Smits AJM, Schmitz GHW, and van der Velde G. 1992. Calcium-dependent lamina production of *Nymphoides peltata* (Gmel.) O. Kuntze (Menyanthaceae): Implications for distribution. J. Exp. Bot. 43: 1273-1281.

72. Smith CS. 1993. A bicarbonate-containing medium for the solution culture of submersed plants. Can. J. Bot. 71: 1584-1588.

73. Wetzel 1983, p. 309.

74. Anderson MA and Morel FMM. 1982. The influence of aqueous iron chemistry on the uptake of iron by the coastal diatom *Thalassiosira weissflogii*. Limnol. Oceanogr. 27: 789-813.

75. Raven JA, Handley LL, MacFarlane JJ, McInroy S, McKenzie L, Richard JH, and Samuelsson G. 1988. The role of CO_2 uptake by roots and CAM in acquisition of inorganic C by plants of the isoetid life-form: A review, with new data on *Eriocaulon decangulare* L. New Phytol. 108: 125-148.

Chapter VIII.

SUBSTRATE

Using soil in aquariums is a strong ideological barrier for many aquarium hobbyists. Here, I am specifying soils that ordinary gardeners grow plants in— gardens soil or potting soil. (I'm not talking about subsoils, vermicullite, pottery clay, kitty litter or gravel additives.)

I think that the risks of using soils in aquariums have been greatly exaggerated. If a soil can support the growth of terrestrial plants, whether they are weeds or flowers, then it can grow aquatic plants. And problems that soils sometimes cause are generally temporary and can be gotten around.

Certainly, using an unknown soil in the aquarium entails risk. Even if the soil is okay, it still may not work. (Soil coupled with inappropriate lighting and/or unsuitable plants can be a disaster.) However, the standard method– using plain, washed gravel– almost guarantees failure with growing plants in the aquarium.

Q. My plants never seem to thrive. Amazon Sword plants produce successively smaller shoots until they wither away. *Anubias* grow slowly and the leaves rot soon after emerging. *Cryptocoryne* spread from the roots but remain small and squatty.

The 45 gal tank is 1 ½ year old with 17 Angel fish and 13 various bottom feeders. Set-up includes 4" of gravel, an undergravel filter, and a double bulb reflector with two 40 watt fluorescent bulbs. I give 12+ hours of light/day and do a 30% water change weekly. What should I do?

A. Your plants are probably starving. But if you add fertilizers to the water, you will probably just get rampant algal growth.

Chances are good that you won't ever get good plant growth in this tank. The substrate is not fertile enough or it may be too aerobic with the undergravel filter. Your situation is typical. I would either set up the tank with a soil under-layer or forget about growing plants.

A.   Components of Soils and Sediments

Soils (terrestrial) and sediments (aquatic) consist of: (1) mineral particles; (2) organic matter; (3) precipitated inorganic matter; and (4) microorganisms.

1. Mineral Particles [1,2]

The four most common elements of the earth's crust– oxygen, silicon, aluminum, and iron– form the mineral 'backbone' (sand, silt, and clay) of all soils. Sand, silt and clay are not only different in size, but also in composition. In general, sand is broken pieces of quartz (silicon dioxide). Silt may be either broken-down rock or aggregates of clay. Clay, on the other hand, consists of tiny sheets of aluminum silicate.

Other minerals like iron, aluminum, and manganese oxides may bind to the clay particles or form separate precipitates. Soil scientists consider these oxide precipitates to be part of the clay fraction. In tropical and other old, highly weathered soils, iron and aluminum oxides often make up a large part of the soil's clay fraction.

2. Organic Matter

Organic matter is biological in origin. The remains of algae, bacteria, plants, dead leaves, and fish following decomposition constitute typical sediment organic matter. Although organic matter may represent only a small fraction of a soil's weight, perhaps only 2%, it may cover 90% of the surface area of soil particles [3].

Organic matter eventually decomposes into humic substances (i.e., 'humus'), which have multiple negative charges that attract and bind nutrient cations like Fe^{3+} and Cu^{2+} (see Fig. II-2 on page 15). The origin of humus' negative charge (and nutrient binding ability) is its various hydroxy, carboxylic, and phenolic groups (**Fig. VIII-1**).

Humus makes up 60-80% of the organic matter of terrestrial soils [5] and about 25% of the total organic matter in lake sediments [6]. It benefits plants by making nutrients in the soil solution more available and by protecting plant roots from metal toxicity.

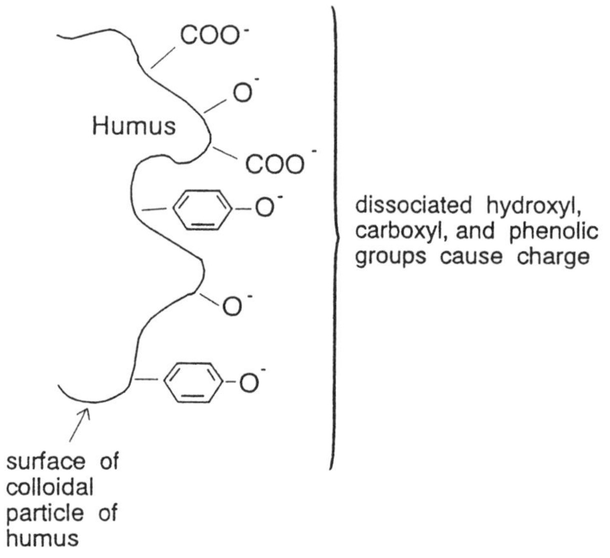

3. Precipitated Inorganic Matter

Precipitated inorganic matter originates from organisms, such as the calcium silicate shells of diatoms. In aquariums, where there is a continual input of fishfood, there might be large deposits of insoluble iron phosphates, calcium phosphates, and calcium carbonates. For example, most fishfood contains ground-up fish ('fish meal'), which contains the calcium phosphate of fish bones and teeth. This calcium

Figure VIII-1 Negative Charged Groups on the Humus Surface. Figure from Boyd [4] and used with kind permission from Kluwer Academic Publishers.

phosphate passes intact through the fish gut and accumulates in the aquarium substrate as part of fish mulm.

4. Microorganisms

The substrate surface, in comparison to the overlying water, is home to many microorganisms. For example, lake sediments have been shown to contain about a billion bacteria per gram of sediment [7]. And bacteria in sand filters of established aquariums, both marine and freshwater, number about 10 million per gram of sand [8].

Aquatic substrates contain not just bacteria but protozoa, fungi, algae, and yeast [9]. Microorganisms live in tightly packed colonies attached to substrate particles. **Fig. VIII-2** shows a typical colonization of a sand grain whereby small colonies of 10 to 100 individuals often appear in patches between large barren areas. The colonies are often found near hollows and cracks in patches of attached organic matter.

Microbial colonization of sand particles is actually rather sparse in comparison to that of finer sediment particles (clay and humus). For example, one study showed most bacteria colonize organic particles rather than sand, even though the organic particles represented only a fraction of the available surface area [11]. Thus, clay and organic matter (not silt or sand) are where the vast majority of bacteria are found.

B.   Characteristics of Soils and Sediments

1.   Nutrient Binding

Soil particles, especially clay, are invariably negatively charged.[1] Because the interior is negatively charged, the outside 'shell' of soil particles attract and bind cations

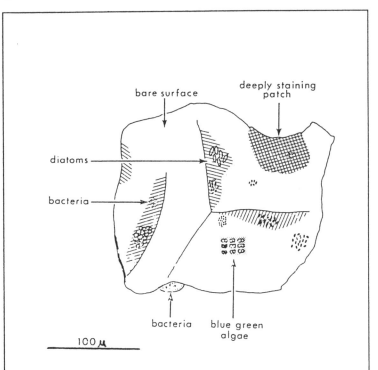

Fig. VIII-2. Diagram of Aquatic Microorganisms on a Sand Grain. Hatching indicates areas that stained when the sand was treated with various histological stains; stained areas most likely represent attached organic matter. Bar represents 100 μ (i.e., μm), which would be equivalent to 0.1 mm. [Reprinted with permission from *Nature* [10] Copyright (1966) Macmillan Magazines Limited.]

---

[1] This is because the silicone ion (Si^{4+}) within the original soil structure is gradually replaced by other cations (e.g., Na^+ and K^+) with fewer positive charges.

including important plant nutrients like Ca^{2+}, NH_4^+, Mg^{2+}, and K^+ (**Fig. VIII-3**) (Cations are atoms or small molecules with a positive charge.)

Clay has 10,000 times more surface area than sand [12], which gives clay a much greater capacity to bind plant nutrients than sand. Thus, only clay and humus, not sand or silt, contribute significantly to a soil's cation-binding capacity.

Soil binding of cations keeps substrate nutrients from entering the water. Indeed, soil particles can even pull nutrients like copper out of the overlying water [13].

Soils particles also bind negatively charged nutrients, 'anions' such as phosphates (HPO_4^{2-} and $H_2PO_4^-$). (This is because anions are attracted to the cations associated with soil particles.)

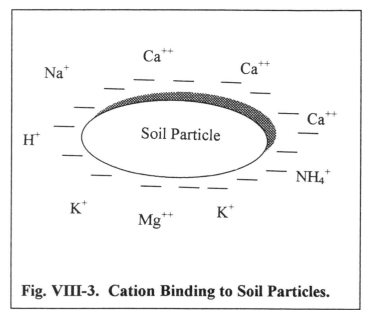

Fig. VIII-3. Cation Binding to Soil Particles.

Thus, phosphate is readily adsorbed onto iron oxides, or it may react directly with iron [14]. Indeed, if a soil sample is shaken with a concentrated phosphate solution, it will remove the phosphate [15].

Thus, sediments typically contain much higher concentrations of phosphates than the overlying water [14]. For example, in aquaculture ponds used for the commercial farming of fish and shrimp there is often a large disparity between the phosphorus concentration in the water and in the sediment. In one pond the overlying water contained very little P, only 0.04 ppm (**Fig VIII-4**). In contrast, there was 1,000 mg of soil-bound P for every kg of sediment (1,000 ppm). One could say that the soil had a P concentration 25,000 times higher than the water.[2]

Some plant nutrients, especially micronutrients like Fe^{2+}, Zn^{2+}, and Cu^{2+}, bind to DOC in the soil solution. This binding encourages nutrient uptake by plant roots. (Nutrients that are bound to humic substances and organic acids are much more available to plants than if they were locked away in metal oxide precipitates.)

Nutrients like phosphate, copper, molybdate, and zinc are often buried in metal oxide precipitates. Plants can open up these precipitates by ordinary root respiration. That is, the respiratory CO_2 released at the root tip acidifies the soil solution, which slowly dissolves the precipitates. Plant roots also actively release organic acids, such as citric, oxalic, and caffeic acids [16,17], which help solubilize nutrients like iron and phosphate. When metal oxide precipitates are broken up, the associated micronutrients and phosphates enter the soil water [18]. Then plant roots can readily take up these nutrients.

---

[2] And this difference is not just because the soil had a higher starting concentration of P. It is the result of active P absorption by soil particles. Thus, when phosphorus was added as fertilizer to an aquaculture pond (to stimulate algal growth to feed the fish and/or shrimp), the added P was removed from the water within a few weeks, such that water P levels returned to earlier levels. Although algae took up some of the water P, most P removal was due to soil absorption [20].

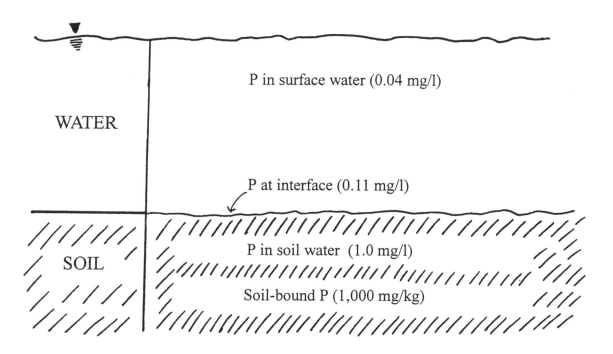

P in surface water (0.04 mg/l)

WATER

P at interface (0.11 mg/l)

SOIL

P in soil water (1.0 mg/l)

Soil-bound P (1,000 mg/kg)

Figure VIII-4. Phosphorus (P) Distribution in a Pond. Redrawn from Boyd [19] and used with kind permission from Kluwer Academic Publishers.

2. Anaerobic Nature of Substrates

A common theme running through discussions about the fertility or toxicity of substrates is how 'aerobic' or 'anaerobic' they are. Invariably, natural sediments (and aquarium substrates) are devoid of oxygen, so the term 'anaerobic', meaning without oxygen, is essentially meaningless. What anaerobic sediments do differ in, though, is their capacity to accept electrons.

For example, a substrate with lots of fresh organic matter and a neutral pH encourages bacterial activity and electron release (see page 58). Such a substrate accumulates electrons,

Q. Why won't plants grow in my tank with an undergravel filter (UGF)?

A. The substrate may be too 'aerobic', because the undergravel filter circulates oxygen-containing water constantly through the gravel. Micronutrients like iron stay 'locked up' in their oxide precipitates, which plants cannot use.

While some hobbyists report that their plants grow in older tanks with a UGF, this is usually because some mulm has accumulated underneathe. Water is no longer flowing evenly across the filter plate but 'channeling' inbetween pockets of mulm. Plant roots find the nutrients and anaerobic conditions they require in these mulm pockets.

Without a UGF, pure gravel substrates inevitably collect organic matter, become anaerobic, and release numerous toxins. A UGF keeps the gravel aerobic, so that it actually becomes a biological filter (nitrifying bacteria colonize the gravel). This is why undergravel filters work so well in 'fish-only' tanks.

Unfortunately, some hobbyists desiring to grow plants (but with an aversion to soil) set up their tanks with pure gravel substrates but without undergravel filters. This is a bad compromise. In this situation hobbyists should be prepared for poor plant growth and lots of gravel vacuuming.

and therefore, has a dimminished capacity to accept new electrons. In contrast, a sandy substrate with less organic matter would accumulate less electrons, and therefore, have a greater capacity to accept new electrons. While both substrates might be similarly devoid of oxygen, the organic substrate would probably have a much lower 'Redox' than the sandy substrate.

Redox or 'Oxidation-Reduction Potential' is a precise and numerical description of a solution's capacity to accept electrons. It is simply the voltage difference (expressed as millivolts or mV) between a platinum electrode and a reference hydrogen electrode placed in a solution.

The relationship between Redox and electron acceptors in a hypothetical planted aquarium can be described as follows: Because aquarium water must have oxygen for fish, the water has lots of the optimal electron acceptor (i.e., oxygen), and thus, a high Redox (+800 mV). This changes abruptly as we move into the substrate. Within the gravel layer, aerobic bacteria have used up most of the oxygen, so the Redox has declined from + 800 to +200 mV. Even though this layer is depleted of oxygen, it is still rich in efficient electron acceptors like nitrates, which many bacteria readily use. As we proceed down under the gravel surface, though, efficient electron acceptors have become increasingly depleted. At the bottom of the soil layer, the Redox may have declined to almost -200 mV. Here specialized bacteria use sulfates or the organic matter itself to accept electrons in various fermentation processes.

The oxidation-reduction potentials of typical water and soil reactions are listed in **Table VIII-1** in order of decreasing efficiency. Thus, bacteria gain more energy when they use nitrate (the second reaction listed) than iron (the fourth reaction listed) to accept their electrons.

Table VIII-1. Redox of Typical Chemical Reactions in Water and Sediment [21].

Redox (mV)	Reaction	Characteristic
+816	$O_2 + 4 H^+ + 4 e- = 2 H_2O$	Oxygen-saturated water
+421	$NO_3^- + 2 H^+ + 2 e- = NO_2^- + H_2O$	Denitrification (first step)
+396	$MnO_2 + 4 H^+ + 2 e- = Mn^{2+} + 2 H_2O$	Manganese solubilization
-182	$Fe(OH)_3 + 3 H^+ + e- = Fe^{2+} + 3 H_2O$	Iron solubilization
-215	$SO_4^{2-} + 10 H^+ + 8 e- = H_2S + 4 H_2O$	Hydrogen sulfide production
-244	$CO_2 + 8 H^+ + 8 e- = CH_4 + 2 H_2O$	Methane gas production
-413	$2 H^+ + 2 e- = H_2$	Hydrogen gas production

Sediments with a high Redox are not ideal. For example, when investigators [22] lowered the sediment Redox in several Norweigan lakes from +250 to +50 mV, nutrients were released into the sediment water and aquatic plant growth was 13 times greater. (Vegetation dominated by small Isoetids was replaced by massive stands of *Juncus bulbosus*.)

Conversely, a substrate Redox that is too low (below -100 mv) is difficult for plants. Roots may be forced to use fermentation, a very inefficient process, to obtain their energy. Hydrogen sulfide and heavy metals may also become problems. One investigator concluded that a sediment Redox ranging between +70 and +120 mV range is optimal for plants [18].

3. Oxidized Microzone Keeps Nutrients and Toxins in Sediments

The oxidized microzone is the top layer of sediment. It separates the sediment environment from the aerobic overlying water. Even though it may be only a few mm thick, it is critically important. First, it prevents nutrients from diffusing into the overlying water [23]. For example, soluble iron (Fe^{2+}) diffusing upwards from sediment depths forms insoluble iron oxides (FeOOH) in the oxidized microzone. Because phosphate readily binds to iron oxides, phosphate is trapped by iron in the oxidized microzone. Thus, seasonal increases in FeOOH (oxidized iron) were found to control water P levels in one coastal marine environment [24].

Second, the oxidized microzone is the site of rampant bacterial activity, some of which benefits aquatic ecosystems (including aquariums). Here various bacteria neutralize ammonium and hydrogen sulfide generated in the lower sediments and keep these toxins from entering the overlying water. Methane oxidizers convert methane to CO_2 that plants can use. Heterotrophic bacteria convert organic matter to nutrients that plants can use.

If this surface layer is anaerobic rather than oxidized, it can cause problems in aquatic ecosystems (see page 136).

4. Stability of Sediments and Submerged Soils

Sediments and long-time submerged soils are very stable in terms of Redox and pH [18]. For example, one study investigating the effects of acid rain showed that even when the water's pH was lowered to pH 5.0 for 60 days, the sediments maintained their ambient alkaline pH [25].

Neutral pH in the substrate is desirable. If the pH is too high, metal oxides form and nutrients like iron become less available to plants. If the pH is too low, there is too much solubilization of metal oxides, releasing aluminum, iron, etc into the sediment water resulting in metal toxicity to plants. A sediment pH of 6.6 is considered [18] to be ideal for plants; it represents a balance between nutrient availability and metal toxicity.

Much of the scientific literature on the toxicity of flooded soils is based on short-term studies of waterlogged or flooded terrestrial soils [26]. Indeed, the initial submergence of a terrestrial soil sets off a large number of chemical and biological reactions that can be detrimental to plants and fish. However, if the soil stays submerged, these reactions slow, and the soil begins to stabilize within a few months. Eventually, the pH gravitates to neutral and the Redox stops plunging. This stability is due to both biological and chemical forces.[3]

---

[3]Bacterial activity slows as fresh organic matter and efficient electron acceptors become depleted in the submerged terrestrial soil. Moreover, the reversible reaction between $Fe(OH)_3$ and ferroso-ferric hydroxide $Fe_3(OH)_8$ is believed to stabilize the redox and pH of acidic soils, while the calcium carbonate buffering system tends to stabilize alkaline soils [21].

Figure VIII-5 shows that the pH of various terrestrial soils gravitated towards a relatively neutral pH within 2 to 4 weeks following submergence. Thus, alkaline soils became less alkaline, and acid soils became less acidic.

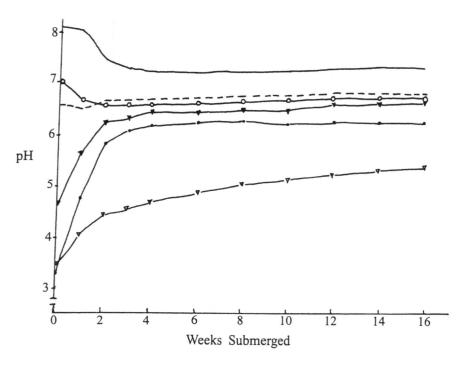

Figure VIII-5. pH Stabilization in Six Different Terrestrial Soils following Submergence. Fig. 4 from Ponnamperuma [18] redrawn and used with permission from Springer-Verlag.

C.   Chaos in Freshly Submerged Terrestrial Soils

The chemical and biological instability of terrestrial soils during the first couple months following submergence has been well documented [18,21]. Although this temporary instability will be influenced by the pH, the organic matter content, etc of the soil, the following events consistently occur when a terrestrial soil is flooded.

First, the oxygen supply to the submerged soil is cut off almost immediately; within days the remaining oxygen is rapidly consumed by bacteria and soil chemicals. Thereupon, soluble iron (Fe^{2+}) and manganese (Mn^{2+}) flood the soil water displacing cations (Na^+, K^+, Ca^{2+}, Mg^{2+}, etc) from the soil particles. These cations accumulate in the soil water as measured by large increases in specific conductance. Finally, bacterial decomposition of sediment

> **Q.**   I put soil into my new pond and all the fish died. Is there any way to prevent this?
>
> **A.**   I would be careful the first few days and weeks after submerging an 'unknown' terrestrial soil. There may be an initial release of ammonia, metals, etc that could kill your fish. I would change the water completely at least once before I added any fish. I would also add a water conditioner that contains EDTA. If you suspect that the soil might contain pesticides, you might want to keep charcoal in the filter the first few weeks. Gradually, and within about two months, the terrestrial soil in your pond should achieve the inherent stability characteristic of all natural sediments.

organic matter under anaerobic conditions releases ammonia, hydrogen sulfide, and organic acids (acetic, formic, butyric, and propionic acids) into the soil water.

Figure VIII-6 shows the actual time course of some of the above events in one submerged soil. Various chemicals flood the soil solution during the first few weeks, but at about 8 weeks these chemicals start to disappear from the soil solution as the soil 'settles down'.

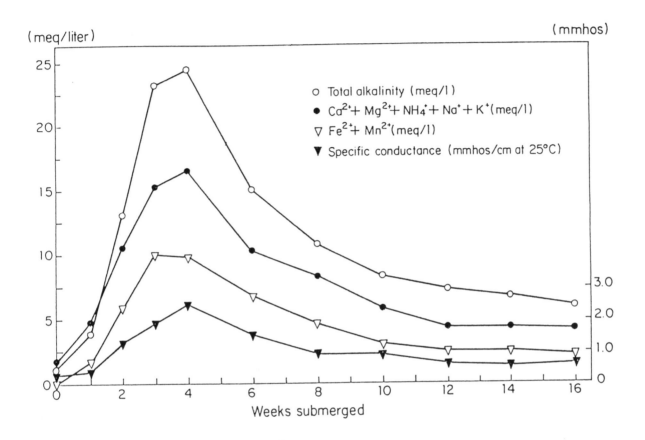

Figure VIII-6. Changes in the Soil Water of a Freshly Submerged Soil. Fig. 6 from Ponnamperuma [18] used with permission from Springer-Verlag.

Does this chemical chaos have any effect on plant growth? To test this, I did a small experiment to see whether the length of soil submergence time would affect the growth of *Vallisneria spiralis* (**Table VIII-2**). *Valisneria spiralis* grew well in freshly submerged soil, but it grew even faster (about 40%) in soil that had been submerged an entire 6 weeks before planting. No advantage was gained by soaking the soil less than 6 weeks.

Soil Submergence Time (weeks)	Ave. Growth Increase (%)
0	160
2	170
4	160
6	230

Table VIII-2. Effect of Soil Submergence Time on *Vallisneria spiralis* Growth. I added 1 cup garden soil, 1 cup sand, and 1.5 quarts tapwater to three 2 liter bottles every 2 weeks. (Bottles were stored in the dark at about 80 °F.) At 6 weeks, I changed the water and planted all 12 bottles with one small *V. spiralis*. Plants were grown for 4 weeks before harvesting plants and getting their dry weights.

D.   Terrestrial Soils and Sediments for Growing Aquatic Plants

Investigators have repeatedly shown that aquatic plants grow much better in sediment or soil than in sand [31,32]. Aquatic botanists may use fine-textured inorganic sediments containing mostly silt [27] or terrestrial soils rich in organic matter [28]. For example, 6 species of sub-merged plants grew 2 to 7 times faster in a mixture of sand, horticultural soil and leaf mould (equal parts) than in pure sand [28]. And one investigator [33] used a 3 parts soil and 1 part leaf mould to successfully grow 'difficult' *Cryptocoryne*.

The soil supporting optimal growth of an aquatic plant species may sometimes be different than the soil of the plant's natural habitat. Thus, *Isoetes lacustris* in its natural habitat was found in mud containing 8% organic matter. However, the plant actually grew better in sediment con-taining 24% organic matter [31]. Perhaps *Isoetes lacustris* is restricted to bare and sometimes unfavorable habitats, because this slow-growing plant can't compete with faster-growing plants under more favorable conditions.

In general, aquatic plants seem to do well in a variety of soils– clays or loam soils with some organic matter [34]. Indeed, I haven't been able to find any major or consistent difference in plant growth in various ordinary soils. In an experiment where I grew plants in separate bot-tles, *Vallisneria spiralis* grew just as well in an alkaline desert soil (pH 8.0) as topsoil from my yard (a Southeastern red clay that I had limed).

In a separate study where I grew *Alternanthera* in separate pots in the same aquarium, I found that plants grew well in potting soil and in the clay topsoil from my yard [35]. However, plants grew poorly in the corresponding clay subsoil with metal toxicity from manganese the probable cause. In most instances, substrate fertilization appeared to be either detrimental or not helpful. Best plant growth (under aquarium conditions) often appears to be not in the most fertile soil, but in the one that is the least toxic.

E.   Problems of Sediments and Submerged Soils

Anaerobic, water-saturated sediments present several problems to aquatic plants, such as toxicity from heavy metals, hydrogen sulfide, low Redox, and organic acids.

1. Metal Toxicity

I had a first-hand experience with iron toxicity when I mixed potting soil with laterite, which is sold as an iron-rich clay. (At the time, I mistakenly thought I needed to add iron to the substrate.) Although I added only about a cup of laterite to the potting soil underlayer, within two weeks the roots of all floating plants died. Java fern turned brown and died. Plants rooted in the substrate didn't die right away, but eventually they detached from the substrate and floated to the surface. I measured high iron levels in the water. (Generally, my tanks show no measurable water iron.) Also, I had a persistent problem with algae in this tank. Eventually, I gave up and tore the tank down. I believe that the strong acidity and high humus content of the potting soil solubilized massive amounts of iron from the laterite causing iron toxicity to plants.

Metal toxicity is common in acidic soils, especially in subsoils, which contain little of the protective humus. Acidity and the soil's initial submergence induce the release of plentiful metals like aluminum, manganese, and iron from their metal oxide precipitates into the soil solution. Investigators have shown that iron toxicity may develop when iron levels reach 1 mM (~56 ppm) in the soil water [21].

Metal toxicity may be lessened by oxygen diffusion from plant roots (see page 152). Ironically, the very toxic hydrogen sulfide may reduce metal toxicity by precipitating metals out of the soil solution. For example, the seagrass *Halodule wrightii* appears to grow better in sediments where the H_2S concentration is high enough to reduce levels of soluble iron [21]. [Soluble iron reacts with H_2S to form precipitates of FeS_2 (iron pyrite)].

2. Hydrogen Sulfide (H₂S) Toxicity

Hydrogen sulfide (H_2S) inhibits root growth or function at a very low concentration (0.034 ppm) [21]. Symptoms of H_2S toxicity are blackened and stunted roots. In aquariums, H_2S toxicity may result in poor plant growth or plants actually dislodging from the substrate and floating to the water surface.

The mechanism of H_2S's toxicity is poorly understood, but since H_2S is quite toxic to many organisms including mammals [37], it probably affects a basic cellular function like enzyme activity. (Many important enzymes contain metals like iron and zinc, which could react with H_2S thereby inactivating the enzyme.) For example, a study on H_2S 's effect on wetland plants showed that sulfide inactivated the enzyme alcohol dehydrogenase, thereby inhibiting fermentation and plant growth [38].

All sediments seem to contain some sulfides [31], and those with high concentrations of organic matter and sulfates inevitably produce more. I became acutely aware of H_2S toxicity after adding a sulfate-containing fertilizer to a potting soil substrate [35]. Roots were stunted and blackened; plants grew poorly. The same fertilizer added to garden soil showed no toxicity.

Despite H_2S's toxicity, aquatic plants apparently have learned to cope with some H_2S in their natural environment. Root oxygen release gives plants some protection, because it encourages H_2S-oxidation by bacteria (see pages 152-153). Plant roots are also protected from H_2S toxicity by soluble iron (Fe^{2+}) in the soil solution [21].

H_2S would probably not harm fish, because it is almost immediately oxidized to harmless sulfates in the presence of oxygen. H_2S diffusing upwards from sediments would be quickly converted to sulfates by H_2S-oxidizing bacteria (see page 67). Thus, H_2S was found to be negligible in oxygenated swamp water, even though sediment levels were high [39].

3. Organic Matter

Sediment organic matter has been implicated as a problem for aquatic plants. However, the results and opinions of botanists are mixed. For example, when investigators [27] added either leaves or algae or pine needles (5% additions) to fertile lake sediment, *Hydrilla* growth was considerably reduced. However, other investigators [32] showed increased *Hydrilla* growth on terrestrial soils amended with either barley straw or river peat (5-20% additions).

Finally, the aquatic plant species used for studies showing growth inhibition by organic sediments are often temperate species from hardwater lakes. For example, the plants Barko and Smart [27] used in their classic study showing plant inhibition by sediment organic matter were *Hydrilla verticillata*, *Myriophyllum spicatum*, and *Elodea canadensis*, all 'hardwater' species.

Emergent plants and softwater plant species from forest habitats inundated with leaf litter might be less inhibited (or actually stimulated) by sediment organic matter.

Ethanol and organic acids are products of bacterial decomposition of sediment organic matter under anaerobic conditions (see page 68). Although ethanol has been cited as a problem for aquatic plants, it is rarely found in inhibitory concentrations in substrates [40]. Rather, organic acids like acetic, butyric, propionic and formic acids may present greater potential problems to aquatic plants [21], especially in freshly submerged soils where concentrations of organic acids may reach 15 to 45 mM [18]. Indeed, one common organic acid (acetic acid) has been shown to inhibit the sprouting of *Hydrilla* propagules within this concentration range [41].

4. Low Redox

Roots require oxygen for normal (aerobic) metabolism and energy production. When the substrate has a very low Redox and roots cannot get enough oxygen, roots are forced to ferment to obtain energy (see page 147). Although aquatic plants, especially emergent plants, can survive for awhile by fermenting stored carbohydrates, fermentation slowly drains energy from the plant. Thus, fermentation in aquatic plants is often associated with lower energy, reduced nitrogen up-take, and slower growth [38,42].

5. Acid Sulfate Soils

Coastal soils often contain large amounts of iron pyrite (FeS_2) and are called 'acid sulfate soils', because they become acidic when dried and wetted. For example, soil from South Carolina tidal marshes containing over 5% sulfur showed a pH of 2-3 when it was resubmerged [43]. When this soil was submerged and anaerobic, there was no acidity problem. However, when it was exposed to oxygen, sulfuric acid (H_2SO_4) was generated by the following reaction:

$$FeS_2 + H_2O + 3\frac{1}{2}O_2 \Rightarrow FeSO_4 + H_2SO_4$$

Acid sulfate soils can cause major problems in managing aquaculture ponds. When the ponds are drained to catch the fish and the bottom soil exposed to air, sulfuric acid forms. When the ponds are refilled, acid leaches into the water and may bring the pH down to as low at 2 or 3.

6. Turbidity

Water turbidity is not simply a function of soil particle size. Thus, even sediments containing the smallest clay particles may cause no water cloudiness. This is because bacteria and multivalent cations (e.g, Ca^{2+} and Fe^{3+}) can aggregate the smallest soil particles.

Bacteria in nature like to attach to surfaces and live within a protective environment called a 'biofilm' (see page 69). They produce polysaccharide 'gums' that aggregate soil particles, even the smallest humic substances and clay particles [44]. Bacterial biofilms probably keep small sediment particles from entering the overlying water and creating turbidity problems.

Figure VIII-7 is of two bacteria that have colonized a plastic disk suspended in an alpine stream. Surrounding the bacteria are polysaccharide fibers that have trapped several dense clay particles.

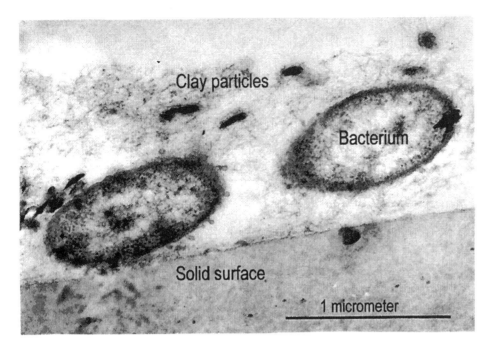

Fig. VIII-7. Clay Particles Trapped within a Bacterial Biofilm. Fig. 12.13 from Costerton [45] modified slightly. Copyright © 1980 John Wiley & Sons. Reprinted by permission of Wiley-Liss, Inc., a subsidiary of John Wiley & Sons, Inc.

Turbidity may also be caused by excess electro-negativity of soil particles. This happens when too many monovalent cations are bound to the soil particles. For example, sodium (Na^+), with it single positive charge, is not very effective in neutralizing the inherent negative charge of soil particles. Thus, saline soils with much bound sodium, may become very turbid when submerged. (Because the clay particles are more negatively charged than usual, the particles repel each other and stay in suspension.)

Soils tend to cause less turbidity if the clay's negatively charged binding sites are neutralized by ions with multiple positive charges (e.g., Al^{3+}, Ca^{2+}, and Mg^{2+}). Because the total electro-negativity of the soil particles is less, the particles tend to aggregate and precipitate out of the water. Thus, for aquaculture ponds in regions with saline soils, lime or $Al_2(SO_4)_3$ (alum) may be added to decrease water turbidity [46].

Comment. I sometimes use pottery clay in my planted aquariums, and there's lots of turbidity that seems to take weeks to settle. If there is any disturbance from fish, or even convection currents from sunlight, then the clay doesn't settle out for a long time.

However, when I've used the clay along with soil, the clay has not shown this kind of problem. The water will be a little cloudy at first, but if I let it be it will clear up. Even if I stir the soil-clay up a lot, it settles out in a few hours.

Reply. Bacterial biofilms probably explain the difference. Apparently, the soil you added contained enough organic matter and soil bacteria to form biofilms. Once established, these 'sticky' biofilms would aggregate clay particles and reduce the water's turbidity.

F.   Effect of Aquatic Plants on Substrates

All plant roots release considerable oxygen and organic compounds as part of their normal functioning (see pages 148-149 and 153). This release encourages bacterial activity in the

136

rhizosphere, the sediment area immediately (within about 1-2 mm) surrounding the roots. Thus, the bacteria responsible for ammonification, acid production, and nitrate reduction were found to be more numerous in the rhizosphere of the aquatic plant *Myriophyllum heterophyllum* than in the surrounding unplanted sediment [47]. Other investigators found a higher Redox under sites planted with rooted plants *Isoetes braunii* and *Myriophyllum tenellum* than under bare sites or those covered with an aquatic moss [48].

Root oxygen release by one submerged plant (*Potamogeton perfoliatus*) was calculated to be 3.8 mg O_2/h/mg plant dry wt [49]. This oxygen release was found to greatly enhance denitrification in the deeper sediment layers [50]. Another investigator [51] showed that intact roots of *Pontederia cordata* (but not *Sparganium eurycarpum*) greatly stimulated methane oxidizing bacteria (see page 68).

Thus, the evidence suggests that plant roots have a major impact on sediment ecology, stimulating the processing and recycling of sediment nutrients and toxins. Without the normal root release of oxygen and organic compounds by aquatic plants, the substrate could become a mulm-ridden 'dead zone'.

Aquaculture ponds illustrate the problems of having a substrate without rooted plants. These ponds, which are designed for raising fish and shrimp commercially, have the soil bottom and suspended algae, but usually they have no rooted aquatic plants. One of the major problems of aquaculture ponds is that the soil substrates deteriorate over time and large mulm accumulations must be removed. Apparently, the sediment surface becomes increasingly anaerobic after a few years and loses its critical oxidized microzone. Aquaculture scientists noted that even if the overlying water

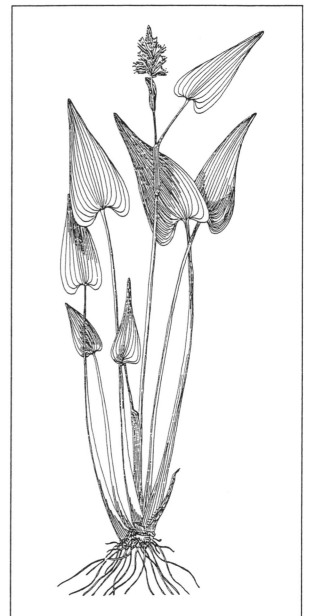

Pickerelweed *Pontederia cordata*. *P. cordata* inhabits shallow waters throughout the eastern USA. Investigators showed that methane oxidation was greatly stimulated by its roots. (Aquatic plants influence the substrate by releasing oxygen and organic compounds from their roots.) Drawing from Muenscher [52].

was satisfactorily oxygenated, when the surface of the pond soil became anaerobic, fish growth declined [53]. Fish would not eat food on these old anaerobic sediments as readily as they would on newer, more aerobic sediments. Perhaps the water is purified and oxygenated by the algae, but the substrate is not? Without rooted aquatic plants, substrate deterioration is likely.

G.   Substrates in Aquariums

In my experience, tanks with pure gravel substrates are hopeless for growing aquarium plants. Then, because the plants don't grow well, the gravel needs to be vacuumed and algae becomes a problem.

I use soil underlayers for all of my aquarium substrates, because they work well for me and fit with my ideal of the aquarium as approximating– at least to some degree– the natural environment. Soil is especially helpful for plants in the beginning when the tank is first set up and low in nutrients. Soil provides rooted plants with a concentrated nutrient supply on 'day one'. This gets them off to the good start they will need to compete with algae. Also, the decomposition of soil organic matter releases CO_2, which plants may badly need in a new tank. Potting soil with its plentiful organic matter would be expected to provide substantial CO_2.

1.   Selecting Soils

I use either pure potting soil or pure garden soil in my aquariums. (They should not be mixed together.) Both seem to work about equally well for plants. Over the years, though, my tanks with potting soil do seem to have had less problems with algae than those with garden soil. I believe this is because the iron-rich clay I use inevitably leaches more iron into the water than potting soil. [Iron in the water can stimulate algae (see pages 167-170).]

On the other hand, potting soil may not be ideal for plants in softwater tanks. (My tanks all have hard water.) This is because both softwater and potting soil would be expected to be deficient in 'hardwater nutrients'. The hobbyist might be required to periodically fertilize the tank with Ca, Mg, and K. Thus, for softwater tanks, garden soil might work better than potting soil.

> **Q.**   I set up my new 20 gal tank with a potting soil underlayer. During the first week, the plants weren't doing well; the floating plants actually died. pH was less than 5 and water hardness was only 3, so I added some baking soda to bring the pH up. Is there anything else I should do?
>
> **A.**   It's good that you monitored your new tank so carefully. Water this acidic will definitely kill plants [54]. Apparently, your soft tapwater doesn't have much alkalinity. The alkalinity wasn't strong enough to buffer any acidity the potting soil might have released into the water. (Potting soil is invariably acidic.)
>
> In addition to increasing the alkalinity, I would also increase your tank's water hardness (see methods on page 87). Both softwater and potting soil are often deficient in several important macronutrients. Unless you add these nutrients, your tank may only support the slow growth of softwater plants.
>
> **Reply.**   I added enough K, Ca, and Mg to approximate hardwater. GH is now 8, pH has stabilized, and plants/fish are doing fine.

> **Q.**   There are so many regional differences in soils. Could you give me some guidelines for using soils in the aquarium?

A.   I would consider potting soil or any local topsoil, preferably the kind you would want to use for a garden. I would not use subsoils or clay soils from coastal areas near brackish water (see page 134).

Many ordinary potting soils have worked well for me and other hobbyists with hardwater tanks.[4] I would caution hobbyists to avoid brands containing the small styrofoam balls that float to the surface every time the substrate is disturbed.

For acidic clay soils of the Southeastern U.S., I would add dolomite lime to stimulate bacterial activity and reduce turbidity. Thus, when I set up tanks with my acidic garden soil (pH 5.5), I mixed a half cup of powdered dolomite lime to each gallon of soil before adding the soil to the tank.

2. Setting Up Tanks with Soils

I've set up tanks with soils several ways. Probably the easiest way is as follows:

I layer the tank bottom with dry soil to a depth of 1 to 1½". Next, I cover the soil with about 1" of gravel so that the substrate is about 2 ½" deep. (I don't bother to wash the gravel beforehand.)

I add water to the tank so that the substrate is covered with about 3" of water. The next day the tank can be planted, more gravel added to cover the soil, the cloudy water drained off, and the tank filled with new water.

I usually let the tank run overnight with the heater, lights, and filter all hooked up. The next day I'll add a water conditioner and then add the fish. Any initial water cloudiness is gone within a day or two.

Q.   I'd like to add soil to my tank, but I don't want to have to tear it down. Is there a way I can get soil into the tank without making a mess?

A.   Yes, there is. I've wrapped chunks of soil in wax paper, taped them with scotch tape, and then inserted these packages of soil under the gravel. Gradually, the paper decomposes and the soil infiltrates the gravel along the bottom of the tank. [If you punch holes in the wax paper with a knife (**after** the package is inserted under the gravel), the process can be speeded up.]

3. Fertilization

Well-decayed organic matter (e.g. kitchen compost) is a good soil amendment, because unlike peat moss, it has a relatively neutral pH. The compost can be mixed with the soil when the tank is first set up. I would not add fresh organic matter, such as manure, to the substrate. I would probably not mix peat moss– because of its strong acidity– with soil. (The acidity may bring toxic levels of heavy metals into the soil solution.) Nor, would I add inorganic fertilizers to soils. Inorganic fertilizers can easily become toxic in submerged soils. For example, many house-

---

[4]Potting soil may not work well in a large pot where there would be little exchange of oxygenated water. (Potting soil with its high concentration of organic matter would become severely anaerobic within a large mass.) Thus, pond hobbyists are justifiably cautioned not to use potting soil in their large 1 to 3 gal planting containers. However, as a thin (1-1½") underlayer for aquarium substrates, potting soils work fine.

plant sticks and water lily fertilizers contain large amounts of sulfates [as $(NH_4)_2SO_4$ and/or K_2SO_4]. These fertilizers work fine for terrestrial plants or emergent aquatic plants but not for submerged aquatic plants in anaerobic substrates. (Bacteria convert sulfates to toxic H_2S, which can kill plant roots.)

Adding fertilizers containing nitrates to soil substrates can also cause problems, because bacteria readily convert nitrates to nitrites, which are toxic to fish. Because nitrites do not bind well to soil particles, they quickly enter the water where they can harm the fish. Thus, when I was setting up one aquarium and had not yet learned to respect the bacterial process of nitrate respiration (see page 65), I added nitrate fertilizer to the dry soil beforehand. Within a week I measured very toxic levels of nitrite (1-2 ppm of NO_2-N) in the water.

The bottom line is that I wouldn't be overly concerned about soil fertility in aquariums. Submerged aquatic plants without CO_2 injection really don't grow fast enough to warrant the nutrient levels that a lawn or a vegetable garden might require. Moreover, the nutrients that plants remove from the soil will gradually be replaced by the continuous fishfood nutrient input and the buildup of fish mulm. In aquariums, fishfood is the fertilizer.

4. Gravel Additives

Many hobbyists with 'High-tech' aquariums grow plants effectively using commercial gravel additives. (A small portion of these substances is mixed with the bottom layer of gravel when the tank is set up.)

One difference between my soil method and using commercial gravel additives is the much greater soil volume used, about 50 times more. For example, I used about 3 gallons of garden soil in setting up my 45 gal tank. If I had set up this same tank with laterite (sold as a gravel additive), I would have only used about a cup of the laterite soil; the rest would have been gravel.

Because of the greater soil volume used, the soil method provides a much greater reservoir of plant nutrients than tanks with gravel additives. Also, decomposition of the soil's organic matter adds CO_2 to the water, which greatly benefits plants in aquariums without CO_2 injection.

Gravel additives such as laterite were designed for tanks with CO_2 injection, substrate circulation, and macronutrient/trace element fertilization. Under these conditions, laterite supports excellent plant growth. Generally, hobbyists with 'High-tech' tanks use laterite; those with 'Low-tech' tanks like mine use soil.

The idea that a commercial gravel additive is more dependable and entails less risk than potting soil or garden soil is an attractive one. However, several hobbyists using various gravel additives have reported problems, such as uncontrolled water clouding, substrate deterioration, and death of bottom-feeding fish. So, in my opinion, there is no guarantee that a gravel additive, just because it comes in an expensive package rather than a shovel, entails less risk than ordinary soil.

5. Substrate Degradation over Time?

Substrates without rooted plants and without undergravel filters will degrade with time. As they collect organic matter and become increasingly anaerobic, they will release toxins that kill fish. However, aquariums with soil substrates and rooted plants seem to do well indefinitely without any maintenance (e.g., gravel vacuuming).

A. I just noticed that my fish seem to have lost their appetite this morning when I tried to feed them. Maybe there's nothing wrong, because the tank looks fine; the water's crystal clear, and the fish seem healthy otherwise.

I keep some plants in pots with soil and others like Hornwort and Elodea are just floating. They're all doing well. I'm also trying to grow some plants in the gravel (no soil). Curiously, one of these, an Amazon Swordplant just won't take root. I've tried weighing it down with rocks, but it keeps floating to the surface. Maybe I need to vacuum the gravel?

Q. I would vacuum the gravel immediately. Long-term solution is to either use an under-gravel filter with plastic plants or to set up the tank with a soil underlayer for growing live plants. Pure gravel substrates without undergravel filters quickly become toxic. Even though the gravel looks clean, organic matter inevitably accumulates and decomposes anaerobically. Anaerobic toxins like H_2S and organic acids are released. Plants won't take root and the fish lose their appetites. The irony here is that good growth of rooted plants could prevent this inevitable substrate degradation, but plants don't grow well enough in pure gravel to 'do the job' (i.e., prevent toxin accumulation).

Q. If you have a 75 gal tank and put in 1" of top soil and cover it with gravel, does the soil have to be removed and replaced with new soil after 1 yr? 2 yrs?

A. How long a soil substrate lasts may depend upon whether or not you use CO_2 injection. For example, 'High-tech' aquariums with CO_2 injection and artificial fertilization, but without the recommended heating cables, often show spectacular plant growth for about a year before the substrate begins to give out. (Plant growth slows such that algae becomes a problem.) This happens despite the fact that the plants are well fertilized with all nutrients. I believe that allelochemicals and other inhibitors build up faster in the substrate than they can be decomposed (see page 48). Heating cables, which in essence, continuously 'wash' the substrate, may prevent this substrate poisoning.

In aquariums like mine (without CO_2 injection), allelochemicals accumulate at a slower rate whereby bacteria can decompose them before they cause major problems. Nutrient depletion should also not cause the substrate to give out. If you allow mulm to accumulate and replenish the nutrients removed by the plants, the soil should continue to support good plant growth for many years. I have three tanks that have the same potting soil underlayers they started with 6 or 8 years ago, and the plants continue to do very well. Other tanks with garden soil underlayers have been doing well for the last 4 to 5 years. (However, plants in pots with the same soil I use for the tank substrates do seem to go bad after a couple of years.)

REFERENCES

1. Nortcliff S. 1988. Soil formation and characteristics of soil profiles. In: Wild A (ed.). Russell's Soil Conditions and Plant Growth (11th Edition). John Wiley (NY), pp. 168-212.
2. Mott CJB. 1988. The inorganic components of the soil. In: Wild A (ed.). Russell's Soil Conditions and Plant Growth (11th Edition). John Wiley (NY), pp. 213-238.

3. Thurman EM. 1985. Organic Geochemistry of Natural Waters. Martinus Nijhoff/Dr W. Junk (Boston), p. 367.

4. Boyd, CE. 1995. Bottom Soils, Sediment, and Pond Aquaculture. Chapman & Hall (NY), p. 40.

5. Boyd 1995, p. 22.

6. Barko JW and Smart RM. 1986. Sediment-related mechanisms of growth limitation in submersed macrophytes. Ecology 67: 1328-1340.

7. Wetzel RG. 1983. Limnology (Second Ed.). Saunders College Publishing (Philadelphia, PA), p. 595.

8. Spotte S. 1979. Fish and Invertebrate Culture. Second Ed. Wiley-Interscience Publications (NY), p. 8.

9. Rheinheimer G. 1985. Aquatic Microbiology (3rd ed.). John Wiley (NY).

10. Meadows PS and Anderson JG. 1966. Micro-organisms attached to marine and freshwater sand grains. Nature 212: 1059-1060.

11. Marshall KC. 1976. Interfaces in Microbial Ecology. Harvard University Press, Cambridge, MA, p. 87.

12. Glass ADM. 1989. Plant Nutrition: An Introduction to Current Concepts. Jones & Bartlett Publishers (Boston MA), p. 26.

13. Boyd 1995, p. 143.

14. Wetzel 1983, Ch. 13, 14.

15. Boyd.1995, p. 92.

16. Tyler G and Strom L. 1995. Differing organic acid exudation pattern explains calcifuge and acidifuge behaviour of plants. Ann. Bot. 75: 75-78.

17. Hopkins WG. 1995. Introduction to Plant Physiology. John Wiley (NY), p. 76.

18. Ponnamperuma FN. 1981. Some aspects of the physical chemistry of paddy soils. In: Proceedings of Symposium on Paddy Soil. Institute of Soil Science, Academia Sinica (ed.), Springer-Verlag (NY), pp. 59-94.

19. Boyd 1995, p. 94.

20. Boyd 1995, p. 132.

21. Rowell DL. 1988. Flooded and poorly drained soils. In: Wild A (ed.). Russell's Soil Conditions and Plant Growth (11th Edition). John Wiley (NY), pp. 899-926.

22. Roelofs JGM, Brandrud TE, and Smolders AJP. 1994. Massive expansion of *Juncus bulbosus* L. after liming of acidified SW Norwegian lakes. Aquat. Bot. 48: 187-202.

23. Wetzel 1983, p. 261.

24. Jensen HS, Mortensen PB, Andersen FO, Rasmussen E, and Jensen A. 1995. Phosphorus cycling in a coastal marine sediment, Aarhus Bay, Denmark. Limnol. Oceanogr. 40: 908-917.

25. Grise D, Titus JE, and Wagner DJ. 1986. Environmental pH influences growth and tissue chemistry of the submersed macrophyte *Vallisneria americana*. Can. J. Bot. 64: 306-310.

26. Drew MC and Lynch JM. 1980. Soil anaerobiosis, microorganisms, and root function. Annu. Rev. Phytopathol. 18: 37-66.

27. Barko JW and Smart RM. 1983. Effects of organic matter additions to sediment on the growth of aquatic plants. J. Ecol. 71: 161-175.

28. Denny P. 1972. Sites of nutrient absorption in aquatic macrophytes. J. Ecol. 60: 819-829.

29. Bowen HJM. 1979. Environmental Chemistry of the Elements. Academic Press (NY), pp. 36-37, 42-43.

30. Donahue RL, Miller RW, and Shickluna JC. 1983. Soils. An Introduction to Soils and Plant Growth (Fifth Ed.). Prentice-Hall (Englewood Cliffs, NJ), p. 140.

31. Misra RD. 1938. Edaphic factors in the distribution of aquatic plants in the English lakes. J. Ecol. 26: 411-451.

32. Spencer DF, Ksander GG, and Bissell SR. 1992. Growth of monoecious Hydrilla on different soils amended with peat or barley straw. J. Aquat. Plant Manage. 30: 9-15.

142

33. Jacobsen N. 1992. Cultivation of some difficult *Cryptocoryne* species in humus-rich beech leaf-mould. The Aquatic Gardener 5(5): 133-137.

34. Gopal B and Sharma KP. 1990. Ecology of Plant Populations I: Growth. In: Gopal B (ed.), Ecology and Management of Aquatic Vegetation in the Indian Subcontinent, Kluwer Academic Publishers (Boston MA), pp 79-106.

35. Walstad DL. 1994. Soil Substrate Experiment. The Aquatic Gardener 7(5): 171-183.

36. Pulich WM Jr. 1982. Edaphic factors related to shoalgrass (*Halodule wrightii* Aschers.) production. Bot. Mar. 25: 467-475.

37. Bowen 1979, p. 149.

38. Koch MS, Mendelssohn IA, and McKee KL. 1990. Mechanism for the hydrogen sulfide-induced growth limitation in wetland macrophytes. Limnol. Oceanogr. 35: 399-408.

39. Westermann P. 1993. Wetland and swamp microbiology. In: Ford TE (ed.). Aquatic Microbiology. An Ecological Approach, pp 205-238.

40. Smits AJM, Laan P, Thier RH, and van der Velde G. 1990. Root aerenchyma, oxygen leakage patterns and alcoholic fermentation ability of the roots of some nymphaeid and isoetid macrophytes in relation to the sediment type of their habitat. Aquat. Bot. 38: 3-17.

41. Spencer DF and Ksander GG. 1995. Differential effects of the microbial metabolite, acetic acid, on sprouting of aquatic plant propagules. Aquat. Bot. 52: 107-119.

42. Yamasaki S, Kimura M, and Yoneyama T. 1992. Early withering of lower leaves of *Phragmites australis* (Cav.) Trin. ex Steud. in a eutrophic stand: Role of oxygen concentration, fate of nitrogen and nitrogen uptake by the plants. Aquat. Bot. 42: 143-157.

43. Boyd 1995, p. 49.

44. Payne D. 1988. Soil structure, tilth and mechanical behavior. In: Wild A (ed.). Russell's Soil Conditions and Plant Growth (11th Edition). John Wiley (NY), pp. 378-411.

45. Costerton JW. 1980. Some techniques involved in study of adsorption of microorganisms to surfaces. In: Bitton G and Marshall KC, Adsorption of Microorganisms to Surfaces, John Wiley (NY), pp 403-425.

46. Boyd 1995, p. 39, 237.

47. Blotnick JR, Rho J and Gunner HB. 1980. Ecological characteristics of the rhisosphere microflora of *Myriophyllum heterophyllum*. J. Environ. Qual. 9: 207-210.

48. Jaynes ML and Carpenter SR. 1986. Effects of vascular and nonvascular macrophytes on sediment redox and solute dynamics. Ecology 67: 875-882.

49. Caffrey JM and Kemp WM. 1991. Seasonal and spatial patterns of oxygen production, respiration and root-rhizome release in *Potamogeton perfoliatus* L. and *Zostera marina* L. Aquat. Bot. 40: 109-128.

50. Caffrey JM and Kemp WM. 1992. Influence of the submersed plant, *Potamogeton perfoliatus*, on nitrogen cycling in estuarine sediments. Limnol. Oceanogr. 37: 1483-1495.

51. Calhoun A and King GM. 1997. Regulation of root-associated methanotrophy by oxygen availability in the rhizosphere of two aquatic macrophytes. Appl. Environ. Microbiol. 63: 3051-3058.

52. Muenscher WC. 1944. Aquatic Plants of the United States. Comstock Publishing Inc., Cornell University (Ithaca NY).

53. Boyd 1995, p. 263.

54. Arts GHP, Roelofs JGM, and De Lyon MJH. 1990. Differential tolerances among soft-water macrophyte species to acidification. Can. J. Bot. 68: 2127-2134.

Chapter IX.

THE AERIAL ADVANTAGE

The 'aerial advantage' is bestowed on all aquatic plants growing partially in air. Plants that can or do grow in air are shown in **Table IX-1**.

Table IX-1. Aquatic Plants with the Aerial Advantage.	
Category	**Examples**
emergent plants	cattails, reeds, pickerelweed
amphibious plants	species of *Anubias, Bacopa, Cryptocoryne, Echinodorus, Hygrophila, Ludwidgia, Myriophyllum, Potamogeton*
floating plants	duckweed, waterhyacinth, water lettuce, *Salvinia, Azolla*
plants with emergent leaves	water lilies, lotus plants, 'banana' plants

In comparison to fully submerged plants, emergent plants are characterized by:

- Much faster growth
- More efficient use of CO_2 and light
- More efficient oxygenation of the root area
- Enhanced biological activity (in the root masses of floating plants)

The richness of an aquatic ecosystem is often based on the aerial advantage. Thus, lake areas containing emergent plants (wetlands and lake shallows) are characterized by enormous productivity; they support at least three times greater biological activity than the open water.[1] And invariably, plants used for wastewater treatment– waterhyacinth, duckweed, pennywort,

---

[1]Littoral and wetland zones, which contain emergent, amphibious, and floating plants and their associated bacteria and algae, are more productive than the pelagial zone (open water), which contains only submerged plants and phytoplankton (i.e. 'green-water' algae). The difference is enormous– 30-80 mT/ha/yr for the littoral and wetland zones versus a mere 0-10 mT/ha/yr for the pelagial zone [1]. (Also, see Table VI-1 on page 93)

water lettuce, pickerelweed, and cattail– are emergent or floating aquatic plants [2,3].   Faster growth means faster contaminant removal.

Although submerged plants may appear to grow quickly, much of that 'growth' may simply be water. Submerged plants have often been found to contain only 6.7% dry matter, whereas a terrestrial leaf usually contains 20% dry matter [5]. This means that a terrestrial plant might represent three times more actual photosynthetic output– real growth– than a submerged plant of similar size and fresh weight.

The aquatic environment presents plants with several problems: (1) not enough CO_2 (see page 93); (2) too much oxygen;[2] and (3) anaerobic substrates (see page 132). Submerged aquatic plants have apparently adapted to these constraints by becoming permanently handicapped. These handicaps are genetically fixed, so that no matter how much light or CO_2 is available, they will not grow as well as plants growing in air.

A.   Aerial Advantages

Submerged aquatic plants can greatly overcome the difficulties they have in obtaining sufficient CO_2 from water by producing emergent growth that can tap into air CO_2. Thus, the amphibious plant *Hygrophila polysperma* reportedly grew 4 times faster when it was grown in air than in water [10]. The stream plant *Callitriche cophocarpa* reportedly grew 4 - 9 times better when it sprouted aerial leaves than when it grew fully submerged [7]. For five *Potamogeton* species, the average photosynthesis was ten times faster for emergent leaves than submerged leaves [6]. Not surprisingly, floating and emergent plants obtain most of their CO_2 from the air, not the water [4,7]. Indeed, the floating plant *Spirodela polyrhiza* obtains only 5% of its CO_2 from the water; the rest is from the air [8].

1.   Aerial Growth Uses CO_2 More Efficiently

When aquatic plants break the water surface, they not only obtain more CO_2, but they appear to be released from their own internal handicaps. Perhaps submerged plants have permanently adjusted their physiology to limited CO_2? **Figure IX-1** compares the photosynthetic response of aerial leaves and submerged leaves of *Pomamogeton amplifolius* to increased CO_2 fertilization. The floating leaves responded much better to increased CO_2 than the submerged leaves. For example, at 0.12% CO_2, which is about 4 times more than air's CO_2 level of 0.035%, floating leaves were photosynthesizing 10 times faster than the submerged leaves (i.e., ~300 v. ~30 μm CO_2/mg Chl/h). Thus, even under ideal conditions and plenty of CO_2, submerged leaves still photosynthesized much more slowly than aerial leaves. This is because submerged leaves are internally handicapped.

---

[2]Oxygen (like CO_2) diffuses 10,000 times slower in water than in air. Because oxygen cannot readily escape from the plant, it inhibits photosynthesis by stimulating *photorespiration*, a wasteful process for the plant that releases fixed CO_2. The loss of fixed CO_2 may reduce photosynthetic efficiency by about 20-25% [9]. Submersed plants, most of which have a C_3-type photosynthetic metabolism, are particularly vulnerable.

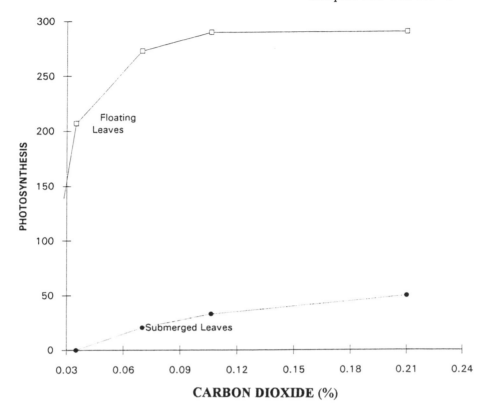

Figure IX-1. CO_2's Effect on Floating and Submerged Leaves of *Potamogeton amplifolius*. Photosynthesis was measured in water-saturated air (to prevent drying out of the more delicate submerged leaves). 'Photosynthesis' represents µmoles CO_2/mg chlorophyll/h of net photosynthesis. Fig. 4 from Lloyd [11] redrawn and used with the permission of the *Canadian Journal of Botany*.

Potamogeton amplifolius (Bigleaf pondweed). *P. amplifolius* is found throughout the eastern states north of Georgia. Investigators showed that its floating leaves responded to CO_2 fertilization much better than its submerged leaves. This is typical, because all submerged growth of aquatic plants are basically handicapped; they can only grow so fast even under optimal growing conditions. Drawing from Hellquist [12].

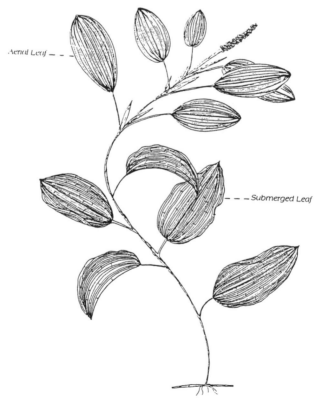

146

2.   Aerial Growth Uses Light More Efficiently

Submerged plants and leaves also cannot use light as effectively as aerial growth. **Figure IX-2** compares the effect of increasing light on the photosynthesis rate of the aerial leaves and submerged leaves of *Myriophyllum brasiliense*. In very low light (~45 μmol/m²/s), both leaves photosynthesized at the same rate. However, as the light intensity increased above 300 μmol/m²/s, the aerial leaves photosynthesized faster whereas the submerged leaves did not. That is, the submerged leaves became 'light saturated'.

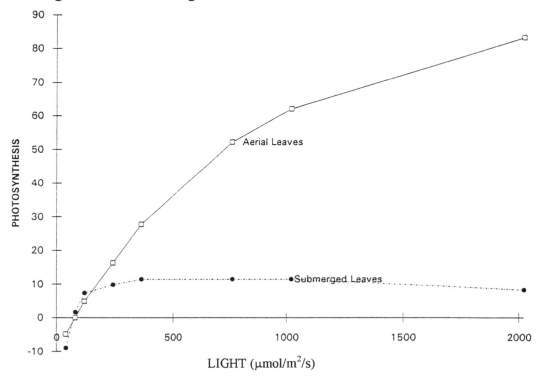

Figure IX-2. Effect of Light on the Aerial and Submerged Leaves of *Myriophyllum brasiliense*. Investigators collected both emergent and submerged forms of *M. brasiliense* from a Florida lake and measured net photosynthesis on 4" apical segments. Measurements were done on emergent plant segments while incubated in humidified air, while submerged plant segments were measured while incubated in solution. Plant segments were provided with equal amounts of CO_2. 'Photosynthesis' represents micromoles CO_2 fixed per mg chlorophyll per hour. Values obtained from the plant segments represent the mean of three separate experiments. (Figure from Salvucci [13] redrawn and used with permission of Elsevier Science Publishers.)

Big differences in response to light were also found between the aerial and submerged leaves of *Myriophyllum spicatum* and *Potamogeton amplifolius* [11]. The submerged leaves of both species were light saturated at 200 μmol/m²/s, whereas the aerial leaves showed light saturation at or above 1,200 μmol/m²/s. Indeed, *P. amplifolius* had a maximum photosynthesis rate 20 times greater for its floating leaves than its submerged leaves.

In general, submerged plants are considered to be shade plants, able to use only a fraction of full sunlight. In contrast, aerial growth can be adapted (gradually) to use full sunlight [5].

3.   Emergent Plants Ferment Better

In severely anaerobic sediments, aquatic plants may resort to fermentation to obtain energy. While fermentation yields only about 6% of the energy of aerobic metabolism (14.6 kcal v. 263 kcal per mole of glucose [15]), it may be essential for plant root survival. Several aquatic plants, both submerged and emergent, have been shown to contain the enzymes necessary for fermentation [16].

However, emergent plants, which often come from severely anaerobic substrates, ferment better. Thus, in an experimental study, 3 submerged species did very poorly in comparison to 3 emergent species under anaerobic conditions. For example, *Isoetes lacustris* (a submerged species) produced ethanol at a slow rate (0.041 mg/h/g dry wt) and showed poor viability. In contrast, *Nymphaea alba*, an emergent plant, released ethanol at a much faster rate (1.6 mg/h/g) and showed strong viability [17].

Thus, wetland plants have shown either moderate or no inhibition by low Redox [19]. For example, *Spartina alterniflora* showed no inhibiton of photosynthesis and N uptake when the Redox was maintained at -200 mV for 20 days [20]. (In this investigation, the Redox was lowered by bubbling nitrogen gas into the sealed culture chambers.)

Q. I'm confused by light quantitation. How do you convert μmol/m²/s to Lux, the term that most hobbyists are familiar with?

A. I'll not try to explain light quantitation, which confuses me as well. There is no way to precisely convert μmol/m²/s to Lux, so I've not done so in this book. While the term Lux is fine for hobbyists, most biologists use μmol/m²/s, which is more accurate for their purposes. This is because the light used in biological reactions like photosynthesis and human vision invariably involves pigment excitation (i.e., a 'photochemical reaction'.) Thus, photosynthesis is the photochemical reaction of the chlorophyll molecule. Biologists precisely measure only the light that induces photochemical reactions and they express that intensity as photon fluence rates or μmol/m²/s (micromoles per meter squared per second). (This term is equivalent to the earlier term of μEinsteins/m²/s.)

Don't be intimidated by μmol/m²/s. All you have to know (for reading this book) is that sunlight is about 2,000 μmol/m²/s and that normal light intensity (for many aquatic plants) would be about 120 μmol/m²/s.

White water lily *Nymphaea alba*. *N. alba*, like other emergent plants, can efficiently ferment stored carbohydrates into ethanol. Thus, its roots can obtain the energy they need to grow in severely anaerobic substrates. Submerged plants, which do not ferment efficiently, would be at a disadvantage in these substrates. Drawing from Preston [18].

4.   Aerial Growth Aerates the Root Area Better

a)   Root Release of Oxygen by Aquatic Plants

The roots of all aquatic plants release oxygen into their environment. This release may be small or considerable depending on the age and species of the plant. In an experimental study, oxygen release rates were measured for several aquatic plants (**Table IX-2**). The floating plant Pennywort released oxygen into the water faster than the other plants.

PLANT	Oxygen Release
Pennywort (*Hydrocotyle umbellata*)	3.5
Pickerelweed (*Pontederia cordata*)	1.5
Cattail (*Typha latifoia*)	1.4
Waterhyacinth (*Eichhornia crassipes*)	1.2
Water lettuce (*Pistia stratiotes*)	0.30

Table IX-2. Oxygen Release by the Roots of Aquatic Plants [2]. An airtight seal at the crown of the plant prevented air from entering the bottom chamber, which contained the roots in nutrient solution. Oxygen (mg O_2/h/g root dry wt.) released by the roots was measured with an oxygen electrode inserted into the bottom chamber. Values are for young plants, which produced the most O_2.

Root oxygen release is critical for aquatic plant survival in anaerobic substrates. All aquatic plants have massive internal gas channels (lacunae), often exceeding 70% of the plant's total volume [24] that conduct oxygen to the roots. Indeed, in comparison to terrestrial plants, most aquatic plants are simply a hollow, gas-filled tube.

b)   Root O_2 Release is More Efficient in Emergent Plants

Although all aquatic plants must bring oxygen to the root area, emergent plants do it better. **Figure IX-3** shows the Redox profiles of three sediment samples. (See page 128 for how oxygen relates to Redox.) Some samples were not planted; others were planted with either an emergent plant (*Sagittaria latifolia*) or a submerged plant (*Hydrilla verticillata*). The Redox of all three sediments decreased with depth (i.e., sediments became increasingly anaerobic). However, sediments with no plants or submerged plants showed a very low Redox potential of

> **Q.**   If the floating plants in my pond release so much oxygen into the water, why do I need to add 'oxygenating' plants like *Elodea*?
>
> **A.**   Ponds with only floating plants often have decreased oxygen levels.[3] This is because the plant cover keeps oxygen from entering the water. Also, oxygen is consumed by bacteria and protozoa as dead plant matter decays within the plant cover. Thus, while floating plants are great for removing nutrients from the water, they provide little oxygen to fish. (This is why most pond keepers include submerged plants along with floating plants.)

---

[3]For example, experimental ponds with a waterhyacinth cover but no submerged plants were shown to have very little dissolved oxygen (DO) in the water (0.2 to 3.0 mg/l) [22]. In contrast, ponds with algae or *Elodea* had 5 to 20 mg/l of DO during midday and 2 to 8 mg/l at night. (Fish require a minimum of 2 mg/l DO for survival [23].)

-200 mV at only 2.5 cm below the sediment surface. In contrast, the Redox potential of sediments with emergent plants was still positive (about +100 mV), even at a 4.5-cm sediment depth.[4]

Figure IX-3. Redox of Sediments Containing Either Emergent Plants, Submerged Plants, or No Plants. Plants were grown in separate 1.5 liter containers containing lake sediment. 'No Plants' represents a container with the same sediment but no plants. 'Redox Potential' was measured after 6 weeks of growth. Fig. 2 from Chen [25] redrawn and used with permission from the *Journal of Freshwater Ecology*.

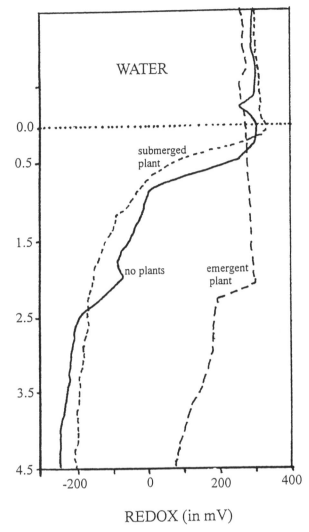

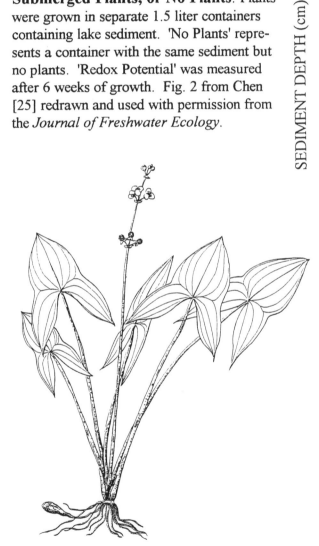

Sagittaria latifolia, an 'Arrowhead'. Investigators showed that *S. latifolia*, an emergent plant, released enough oxygen into the sediment to keep the sediment Redox positive. The Redox of its sediment was much higher than unplanted sediments or those planted with *Hydrilla*, a submerged plant. (In general, emergent plants can oxygenate the root area much better than submerged plants.) Drawing from Hellquist [26].

---

[4] Hobbyists should not conclude that because submerged plants did not affect sediment Redox in this experiment that they do not release oxygen. Submerged plants not only release oxygen but often have a profound effect on substrate ecology (see page 135). However, in sediments the root released oxygen is consumed so rapidly by rhizosphere bacteria and chemical processes that a Redox probe placed into the bulk soil will often detect no effect. Here my point was simply to show that emergent plants have a greater capacity to oxygenate their substrates than submerged plants.

150

The first reason emergent plants can oxygenate the root area more effectively than submerged plants is simply because they have a direct pipeline to air oxygen. (Air contains a bountiful 21% oxygen.) Indeed, all emergent plants use air oxygen to supply the root area [24,27]. In contrast, submerged plants cannot use air oxygen; they depend on photosynthetic oxygen to aerate their roots. Thus, root oxygen release by the submerged plant *Potamogeton perfoliatus* dropped off within 2 min following the cessation of photosynthesis (investigators turned the lights off) [28].

Second, many emergent plants have ventilating systems where outside air enters the plant's lacunae and actually moves within the plant (see page 151). In contrast, submerged plants depend on oxygen diffusion within a stagnant gas, a relatively slow process. (Although one investigator [29] found gas pressure build-up in the submerged plant *Egeria densa*, it lasted less than an hour and there was no sustained gas movement.)

Third, emergent plants seem to release oxygen more efficiently into the root area than submerged plants. Investigators compared the pattern of root oxygen release of an emergent plant (*Nuphar lutea*) and a submerged plant (*Isoetes lacustris*). They found that the emergent plant supplied considerable oxygen to the root tip where it would do the most good. (Because the root tip is the growing region and the site of most nutrient uptake [30], it needs more oxygen than the rest of the root.) In contrast, the investigators found that the submerged plant released oxygen wastefully all along the root length, such that the root tip got no more than the root shaft.

Because emergent plants oxygenate their roots more efficiently, they are better adapted than submerged plants to grow in highly anaerobic sediments containing lots of organic matter. Thus, in a study where 5 different types of organic matter was added to identical sediment samples, submerged plants (*Elodea canadensis, Hydrilla verticillata*, and *Myriophyllum spicatum*) were severely inhibited whereas emergent plants (*Myriophyllum aquaticum, Potamogeton nodosus*, and *Sagittaria latifolia*) were either stimulated or much less inhibited [31].

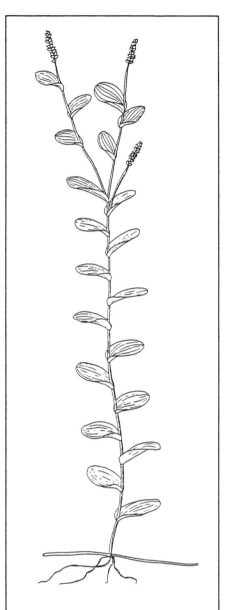

Potamogeton perfoliatus. *P. perfoliatus*, because it is a submerged plant, depends on photosynthesis to aerate its roots. Thus, investigators showed that root aeration stopped abruptly when there was no light for photosynthesis. Drawing from Muenscher [21].

c)   How Emergent Plants Aerate the Root Area

Emergent plants bring air oxygen to the root area efficiently. For example, the common yellow water lily brings several liters of air each day down to its roots and rhizomes (**Fig. IX-4**).

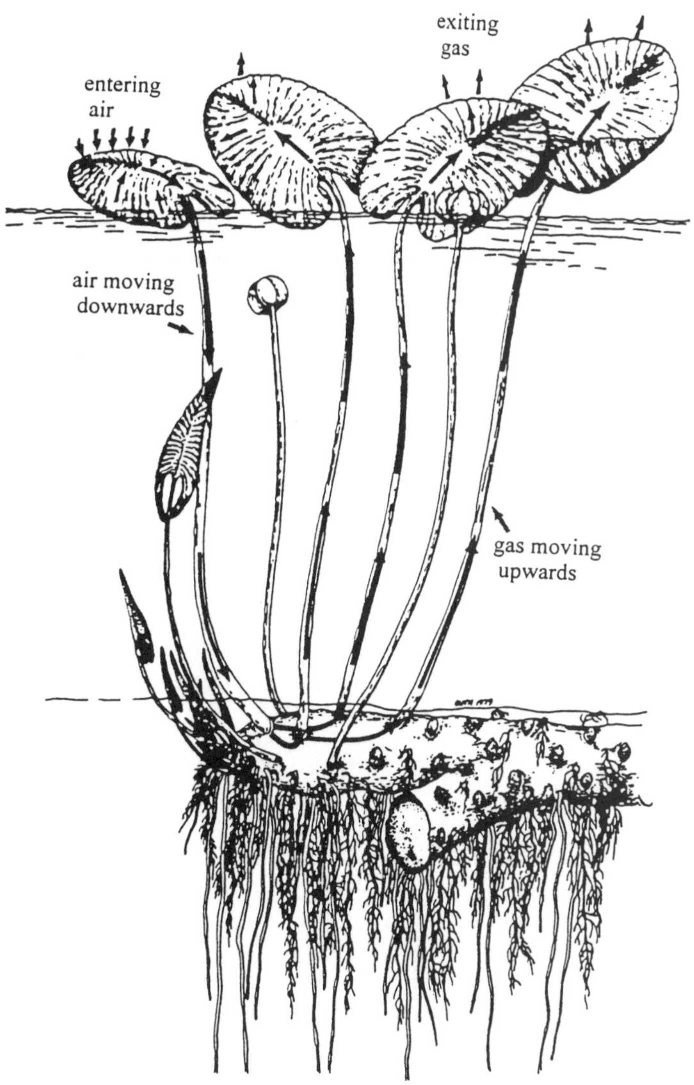

Air enters the younger emergent leaves of the waterlily and flows internally down the petioles to the roots and rhizomes bringing oxygen to the underground tissues. The gas picks up CO_2 from the sediment and underground plant tissue and continues flowing up the petioles of the older emergent leaves and finally exits to the atmosphere. Gas flows through the plant at an impressive rate, up to 50 cm/min. The CO_2 concentration of the exiting air sometimes exceeds 3%, which is almost 100 times air CO_2 levels. The investigator showed that 85% of this CO_2 was used for photosynthesis. Thus, the gas flow system of the water lily not only aerates the root area but also provides the leaves with a rich carbon source.

Many other emergent plants have been found to have ventilating systems similar to the yellow water lily. Thus, several species of water lily and water lotus [32], reed [33], and cattail [34,35] were found to use atmospheric air for rhizosphere ventilation. Heat build-up within the plant from absorbed sunlight increases gas efflux from the older leaves of the plant in exchange for an air influx into the younger leaves. Deepwater rice uses a unique external ventilating system, which depends on a thin air layer on the surface of its leaves [36]. (Gas flow between the atmosphere and the sediment is conducted externally along the leaf surface, rather than internally as in the water lily.) All of these strategies allow emergent plants to survive and prosper in severely anaerobic sediments.

Figure IX-4. Flow-through Ventilation in the Yellow Waterlily *Nuphar luteum*. Investigators used a tracer gas (ethane) to show flow-through ventilation in *Nuphar luteum*. Figure from Dacey [27] modified slightly and used with permission of *Physiologia Plantarum*.

Without their gas ventilating systems, emergent plants could probably not survive in anaerobic sediments. Manual pruning or animal grazing of emergent plants below the water surface often kills the plants [37]. For example, investigators [38] showed what happened to reeds that were cut below the water and thus denied access to air. Reeds growing in an aerobic sediment (coarse sand) were relatively unaffected, but those growing in an anaerobic sediment (mud containing 50% organic matter) died. (Reeds cut above the water were unaffected or only slightly inhibited.)

d)   How Oxygen Benefits Rooted Aquatic Plants

Oxygenation of the root and root area (rhizosphere) benefits aquatic plants in three ways.

First, roots need respiratory oxygen for growth, maintenance, and nutrient uptake. Plants that can best meet their oxygen demands, grow better.

Second, root oxygenation of the rhizosphere counteracts substrate toxins. For example, excessive soluble iron is potentially toxic to plant roots. But root oxygen release causes iron to precipitate as iron oxides on the outside of the root, thus preventing excessive iron from entering the roots [39]. Iron precipitation can be seen as brown stains or precipitates on the roots [40,21].

Rhizosphere oxygen also protects the plant from hydrogen sulfide (H_2S), which is a major substrate toxin (see page 133). Specific bacteria use the oxygen to oxidize H_2S to non-toxic sulfates (see page 67). This oxidation is a common bacterial process and provides considerable protection for aquatic plants against H_2S [42]. **Table IX-3** shows how bacteria and plants together control H_2S in two different soils. Thus, the H_2S concentration in the Bernard clay soil was reduced from 0.46 to 0.25 µg/g. Although H_2S is not completely removed, total removal from the soil mass may not be necessary. For as long as there is a oxygenated zone around the roots where H_2S-oxidizing bacteria can destroy the toxic H_2S, the plant will be protected, even if the bulk of the soil still contains toxic levels of H_2S (**Figure IX-5**).

Treatment	H₂S Concentration (µg/g of soil)	
	Bernard Clay	Crowley Loam
Soil only	0.46	0.33
Soil + Bacteria	0.32	0.31
Soil + Plants	0.35	0.30
Soil + Bacteria + Plants	0.25	0.27

Table IX-3. Effect of Plants and H₂S-oxidizing Bacteria on H₂S in Two Soils [43]. Soils were inoculated with a purified soil culture of *Beggiatoa*, a common soil bacterium that oxidizes H_2S to SO_4^{2-}. Each treatment was done in triplicate and in jars containing 300 g moist soil. H_2S was measured 2 weeks after planting rice seedlings. Numbers were significantly different from each other.

In a manner similar to the oxidation (and destruction) of H_2S, many ordinary bacteria might use oxygen released into the root area to degrade inhibitory organic acids.

Third, root oxygen release can acidify the rhizosphere by oxidizing iron ($Fe^{2+} + 3 H_2O \Rightarrow Fe(OH)_3 + 3H^+ + e^-$). This acidification dissolves metal oxides thereby bringing nutrients into the soil solution. Thus, investigators working with rice showed that root oxygen release coupled with Fe^{2+} oxidation could increase plant uptake of zinc and phosphate [44,45].

Q.   When I transplanted one of my water lilies, it bothered me that the soil in the pots smelled bad, like H_2S. Should I be planting my water lilies in something that might be more aerobic, like sand? I'm also concerned that the H_2S might poison the fish.

A.   I wouldn't worry about the foul odor in the soil unless the roots are blackened and stunted at the tips. Water lilies, which have the aerial advantage, are very efficient at protecting their roots against hydrogen sulfide and other substrate toxins. If your water lilies and fish are healthy, I wouldn't be concerned.

Finally, oxygen also provides the required aerobic environment for various symbiotic fungi (mycorrhizae), which assist plants by greatly increasing nutrient absorption.[5]

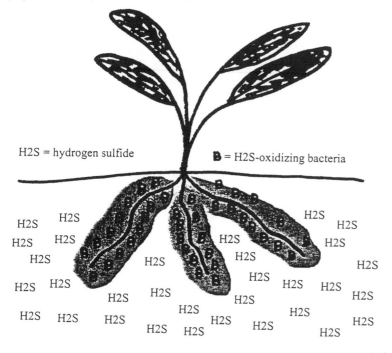

H2S = hydrogen sulfide   B = H2S-oxidizing bacteria

Figure IX-5. How Rhizosphere Ecology Protects Plant Roots from Toxic H₂S. Oxygen is released from the plant's roots into the rhizosphere (shaded area surrounding roots). Within this oxygenated zone, various H₂S -oxidizing bacteria proliferate and remove H₂S. Thus, while the bulk of a soil or sediment may contain toxic levels of H₂S, the rhizosphere may be free of H₂S.

B.   Floating Plants Increase Biological Activity

Many bacteria and zooplankton, including most rotifers, are sessile by nature, in that they require surfaces for attachment [49,50]. Also, nutrients tend to accumulate at surfaces, thereby attracting microorganisms (see page 69). Thus, for studying aquatic microorganisms, investigators often suspend glass slides in the water to which organisms readily attach and colonize.

Floating plant roots function in a similar way to glass slides– only better. For example, one investigator [52] showed that over 100 times more bacteria and other microorganisms colonized duckweed roots than glass slides. Floating plants encourage biological activity in the water, because the roots release both oxygen and organic matter.[6]

Just as lake areas of plant growth are enormously more active biologically than the open water, so too are the roots of floating plants. We cannot see root-associated microorganisms without a microscope, but we should not discount their importance to the aquarium ecology.

---

[5]Beneficial mycorrhizal associations are well documented in the terrestrial literature [46] and have only recently been shown in several aquatic plants, especially those with the Isoetid life-form in nutrient-depleted environments [47]. Thus, Sharma [48] depicts the ultrastructural association of a fungus with the roots of *Isoetes tuberculata*, a fully submerged aquatic.

[6]Oxygen release by aquatic plant roots is discussed on page 148. Organic matter released by floating plants would include root excretions, cell lysates, and whole cells sloughed off from growing root tips. Aquatic plants often release 1-10% of the their photosynthetic carbon as DOC [53]. Terrestrial plant roots also give off a great deal of DOC, up to 40% of the plant's dry matter as a wide variety of sugars, amino acids, organic acids, nucleotides, and enzymes [54]. Not all of these compounds represent the passive release of dead cells; some may be actively released and play a role in allelopathy or nutrient uptake.

154

Attached microorganisms may be critical to nutrient cycling, nitrification, denitrification, decomposition, and the consumption of algae.

C.   Aerial Growth in the Aquarium

I keep some floating plants in all my tanks and encourage the aerial growth of amphibious aquarium plants such as *Ludwigia*, *Hygrophila*, and *Bacopa*. Sometimes just a small adjustment will help. For example, I removed the top plastic strip on the back of one tank, which allowed *Bacopa monnieri* to grow out. Because the tank was next to a sunny window, eventually the *Bacopa* formed a large mat on the back of the tank. In another tank, I decreased the water level by about an inch, so that *Cryptocoryne* would have room to sprout aerial leaves. Indian Fern (*Ceratopteris thalictroides*) seems to grow best in shallow (12" high) tanks when its roots can mine soil nutrients and its aerial branches can get air CO_2 and the stronger lighting at the surface.

When I do my routine plant pruning, I am very careful not to prune or damage aerial growth. Thus, for Indian Fern, I carefully remove the submerged (but never aerial) branches. I cut the stems of amphibious plants like *Bacopa caroliniana* above the water line. As for duckweed and water lettuce, I thin it out regularly, such that new growth is continuously encouraged.

Admittedly, in some of my tanks floating plants die out over time. (It may be that they don't get enough iron or light.) If the tank is otherwise stable, I accept the loss and leave well enough alone.

Also, I suspect that aerial growth is less important in tanks with CO_2 fertilization. CO_2 fertilization probably provides enough CO_2 so that amphibious plants don't need to resort to aerial strategies to increase their carbon uptake. In aquariums without CO_2 fertilization (such as mine), using aerial growth and/or just allowing amphibious plants some emergent growth becomes much more critical.

Just as floating plants are used to remove nutrients efficiently from wastewater, aerial growth can be used in aquariums to efficiently remove excess nutrients from the water. By combining aerial growth with submerged plants, the hobbyist greatly increases total plant growth in the same volume of water. Not only does enhanced plant growth contribute to fish health by removing nutrients and pollutants from the water, but it also discourages algal growth. Aerial growth enhances the health and functioning of aquarium ecosystems.

REFERENCES

1. Wetzel RG. 1983. Limnology (Second Ed.). Saunders College Publishing (Philadelphia, PA), p. 135.
2. Moorhead KK and Reddy KR. 1988. Oxygen transport through selected aquatic macrophytes. J. Environ. Qual. 17: 138-142.
3. Reddy KR. 1983. Fate of nitrogen and phosphorus in a waste-water retention reservoir containing aquatic macrophytes. J. Environ. Qual. 12: 137-141.
4. Wetzel RG. 1990. Land-water interfaces: Metabolic and limnological regulators. Verh. Int. Ver. Limnol. 24: 6-24.
5. Bowes G. 1987. Aquatic plant photosynthesis: Strategies that enhance carbon gain. In: Crawford RMM (ed), Plant Life in Aquatic and Amphibious Habitats. Blackwell Scientific Publications (Boston, MA), pp. 79-98.

6. Frost-Christensen H and Sand-Jensen K. 1995. Comparative kinetics of photosynthesis in floating and submerged *Potamogeton* leaves. Aquat. Bot. 51: 121-134.

7. Madsen TV and Sand-Jensen K. 1991. Photosynthetic carbon assimilation in aquatic macrophytes. Aquat. Bot. 41: 5-40.

8. Boston HL, Adams MS, and Madsen JD. 1989. Photosynthetic strategies and productivity in aquatic systems. Aquat. Bot. 34: 27-57.

9. Bowes G. 1991. Growth at elevated CO_2: photosynthetic responses mediated through Rubisco. Plant Cell Environ. 14: 795-806.

10. Botts PS, Lawrence JM, Witz BW, and Kovach CW. 1990. Plasticity in morphology, proximate composition, and energy content of *Hygrophila polysperma* (Roxb.) Anders. Aquat. Bot. 36: 207-214.

11. Lloyd NDH, Canvin DT, and Bristow JM. 1977. Photosynthesis and photorespiration in submerged aquatic vascular plants. Can. J. Bot. 55: 3001-3005.

12. Hellquist CB and Crow GE. 1980. Aquatic Vascular Plants of New England. Part 1. Zosteraceae, Potamogetonaceae, Zannichelliaceae, Najadaceae. NH Agric. Exp. Sta. Bull No. 515.

13. Salvucci ME and Bowes G. 1982. Photosynthetic and photorespiratory responses of the aerial and submerged leaves of *Myriophyllum brasiliense*. Aquat. Bot. 13: 147-164.

14. Aquatic plant line drawings are the copyright property of the University of Florida Center for Aquatic Plants (Gainesville). Used with permission.

15. Raven PH, Evert RF, and Eichhorn SE. 1992. Biology of Plants (5th ed.), Worth Publishers (NY), p. 97.

16. Smits AJM, Kleukers RMJC, Kok CJ, and van der Velde G. 1990. Alcohol dehydrogenase isozymes in the roots of some nymphaeid and isoetid macrophytes. Adaptations to hypoxic sediment conditions? Aquat. Bot. 38: 19-27.

17. Smits AJM, Laan P, Thier RH, and van der Velde G. 1990. Root aerenchyma, oxygen leakage patterns and alcoholic fermentation ability of the roots of some nymphaeid and isoetid macrophytes in relation to the sediment type of their habitat. Aquat. Bot. 38: 3-17.

18. Preston CD and Croft JM. 1997. Aquatic Plants in Britain and Ireland. B.H. & A. Harley Ltd (Essex, England).

19. Koch MS, Mendelssohn IA, and McKee KL. 1990. Mechanism for the hydrogen sulfide-induced growth limitation in wetland macrophytes. Limnol. Oceanogr. 35: 399-408.

20. DeLaune RD, Smith CJ, and Tolley MD. 1984. The effect of sediment redox potential on nitrogen uptake, anaerobic root respiration and growth of *Spartina alterniflora* Loisel. Aquat. Bot. 18: 223-230.

21. Muenscher WC. 1944. Aquatic Plants of the United States. Comstock Publishing Inc., Cornell University (Ithaca NY).

22. Reddy KR. 1981. Diel variations of certain physico-chemical parameters of water in selected aquatic systems. Hydrobiologia 85: 201-207.

23. Wetzel 1983, p. 170.

24. Wetzel 1983, p. 530.

25. Chen RL and Barko JW. 1988. Effects of freshwater macrophytes on sediment chemistry. J. Freshwater Ecol. 4: 279-289.

26. Hellquist CB and Crow GE. 1980. Aquatic Vascular Plants of New England. Part 3. Alismataceae. NH Agric. Exp. Sta. Bull No. 518.

27. Dacey JWH and Klug MJ. 1982. Tracer studies of gas circulation in *Nuphar*: $^{18}O_2$ and $^{14}CO_2$ transport. Physiol. Plant. 56: 361-366.

28. Caffrey JM and Kemp WM. 1991. Seasonal and spatial patterns of oxygen production, respiration and root-rhizome release in *Potamogeton perfoliatus* L. and *Zostera marina* L. Aquat. Bot. 40: 109-128.

29. Sorrell BK. 1991. Transient pressure gradients in the lacunar system of the submerged macrophyte *Egeria densa* Planch. Aquat. Bot. 39: 99-108.

30. Gregory PJ. 1988. Growth and functioning of plant roots. In: Wild A (ed.). Russell's Soil Conditions and Plant Growth (11th Edition). John Wiley (NY), pp. 113-167.

31. Barko JW and Smart RM. 1983. Effects of organic matter additions to sediment on the growth of aquatic plants. J. Ecol. 71: 161-175.

32. Grosse W, Buchel HB, and Tiebel H. 1991. Pressurized ventilation in wetland plants. Aquat. Bot. 39: 89-98.

33. Armstrong J and Armstrong W. 1991. A convective through-flow of gases in *Phragmites australis* (Cav.) Trin. ex Steud. Aquat. Bot. 39: 75-88.

34. Bendix M, Tornbjerg T, and Brix H. 1994. Internal gas transport in *Typha latifolia* L. and *Typha angustifolia* L. 1. Humidity-induced pressurization and convective throughflow. Aquat. Bot. 49: 75-89.

35. Tornbjerg T, Bendix M, and Brix H. 1994. Internal gas transport in *Typha latifolia* L. and *Typha angustifolia* L. 2. Convective throughflow pathways and ecological significance. Aquat. Bot. 49: 91-105.

36. Raskin I and Kende H. 1983. How does deep water rice solve its aeration problem. Plant Physiol. 72: 447-454.

37. Gopal B and Sharma KP. 1990. Ecology of Plant Populations I: Growth. In: Gopal B (ed.), Ecology and Management of Aquatic Vegetation in the Indian Subcontinent, Kluwer Academic Publishers (Boston MA), pp 79-106.

38. Weisner SEB and Graneli W. 1989. Influence of substrate conditions on the growth of *Phragmites australis* after a reduction in oxygen transport to below-ground parts. Aquat. Bot. 35: 71-80.

39. Armstrong W. 1979. Aeration in higher plants. Adv. Bot. Res. 7: 225-332.

40. Horst K and Kipper HE. 1986. The Optimum Aquarium. AD aquadocumenta Verlag GmbH (Bielefeld, West-Germany), p. 54.

41. Rowell DL. 1988. Flooded and poorly drained soils. In: Wild A (ed.). Russell's Soil Conditions and Plant Growth (11th Edition). John Wiley (NY), pp. 899-926.

42. Barko JW, Adams MS, and Clesceri NL. 1986. Environmental factors and their consideration in the management of submersed aquatic vegetation: A review. J. Aquat. Plant Manage. 24: 1-10.

43. Joshi MM and Hollis JP. 1977. Interaction of *Beggiatoa* and rice plant: Detoxification of hydrogen sulfide in the rice rhizosphere. Science 195: 179-180.

44. Kirk GJD and Bajita JB. 1995. Root-induced iron oxidation, pH changes and zinc solubilization in the rhizosphere of lowland rice. New Phytol. 131: 129-137.

45. Saleque MA and Kirk GJD. 1995. Root-induced solubilization of phophate in the rhizosphere of lowland rice. New Phytol. 129: 325-336

46. Raven 1992, p. 238-241.

47. Raven JA, Handley LL, MacFarlane JJ, McInroy S, McKenzie L, Richard JH, and Samuelsson G. 1988. The role of CO_2 uptake by roots and CAM in acquisition of inorganic C by plants of the isoetid life-form: A review, with new data on *Eriocaulon decangulare* L. New Phytol. 108: 125-148.

48. Sharma BD. 1998. Fungal associations in the roots of three species of *Isoetes* L. Aquat. Bot. 61: 33-37.

49. Fairchild GW. 1981. Movement and microdistribution of *Sida crystallina* and other littoral microcrustacea. Ecology 62: 1341-1352.

50. Wetzel 1983, p. 587.

51. Wetzel 1983, p. 563.

52. Coler RA and Gunner HB. 1969. The rhizosphere of an aquatic plant (*Lemna minor*). Can. J. Microbiol. 15: 964-966.

53. Wetzel 1983, p. 534.

54. Lynch JM and Wood M. 1988. Interactions between plant roots and micro-organisms. In: Wild A (ed.). Russell's Soil Conditions and Plant Growth (11th Edition). John Wiley (NY), pp. 526-563.

Chapter X.

ALGAE CONTROL

Undesirable algal growth is probably the number one problem that hobbyists have in maintaining planted aquariums (or any aquarium for that matter). I suspect that many aquarists ultimately give up on keeping planted aquariums because of their frustration in trying to combat uninhibited algal growth.

Unfortunately, most hobbyists see plants only as decoration; they have not learned to use plants to control algae.

A.   Common Methods for Controlling Algae

1. Algaecides, Chlorox, and Antibiotics

Algaecides, which are chemicals that kill algae, often cause more problems than they solve in planted aquariums. The active ingredient of almost all common algaecides is either copper or simazine. Both are toxic to fish and plants [1,2]. The dose that will kill algae in an aquarium without harming fish or plants is often hard– if not impossible– to determine. Even if the algaecide doesn't kill the fish, the dead algae sometimes will. Dying algae may release toxins into the water or its decomposition may remove oxygen from the water. Thus, it is not uncommon for fish to die when algae is abruptly killed.

Chlorox is a sterilizing agent that is sometimes used by botanists to remove

Q.   My 55 gal tank is plagued with an algae that is black and velvety, like black fur. It is very tenacious. About every other month, I have to scrub the algae off of the bogwood. I have been keeping fish since 1956 and have picked up this very difficult algae only in the past 5 years. (The substrate is a small gravel.)

A.   I've had few problems with algae in my planted tanks since I started (in 1987) using soil substrates, adequate lighting, and lots of different plant species. I've asked fellow hobbyists to give me their worst algae to test my theory that good plant growth will control **any** algae. These test algae usually spread a little and grow for awhile. After a year or so, though, they seem to just disappear or hang on at manageable levels. It doesn't matter whether the algae is 'black fur', 'blue-green', 'green water', or 'green mat' algae.

I would focus on increasing total plant growth in your tank. First, gravel is a very poor substrate for rooted aquatic plants. Second, I would make sure the lighting is adequate. Third, I would also consider adding emergent plants, even if it is only duckweed, to your tank. Once the tank has the combination of good growing conditions and many fast-growing plants, plants should prevent algal takeovers.

filamentous algae from plants that will be used in short-term experiments. A few experienced hobbyists routinely dip the stem tops of new plants in a 1:20 dilution of ordinary household bleach for a few minutes to kill attached algae. This method should be used with great care as it can easily kill delicate plants or endanger fish if the chlorox gets into the aquarium itself.

Some hobbyists, desperate to control 'green water' algae, have tried flocculents such as alum, which are sold by some aquarium manufacturers as 'water clearing' agents. These products should never be added to home aquariums, or at least those containing fish. For flocculents are positively charged compounds that non-specifically bind negatively charged particles, so that they clump and precipitate out of solution, thereby, resulting in the clearing. Because the membranes of algal cells have a negative charge, flocculents will indeed remove 'green water' algae from the water. [The mechanism of flocculation is the same as that for chemically removing soil particles from water (see page 135).] The problem is that the gill surfaces of fish also carry a negative charge; flocculents readily bind the delicate gill filaments together, destroying gill structure and function [3,4].

Less objectionable are antibiotics. Erythromycin and kanamycin can sometimes be effective in the specific killing of blue-green algae. (Blue-green algae, which are actually cyanobacteria, share enough characteristics with gram-positive bacteria to make them sensitive to antibiotics.) However, some hobbyists report that their tank's blue-green algae become antibiotic-resistant after the first treatment, and when they tried higher doses, all the plants died.

The home aquarium is an ecosystem. It does not react well to toxins and antibiotics. Even if the initial treatment is successful, re-infestation is more than likely.

2. Light Reduction

Algae are similar to submerged plants in that they can use only a fraction of full sunlight

---

Q. I am having a major problem with algae in my tank. Do you think I should add copper sulfate?

A. No, because copper is toxic to plants and fish as well as algae. What's more, it is virtually impossible to predict what is a safe copper level. There are just too many variables that affect copper toxicity (see page 14). Thus, you can't safely predict if you add X amount of copper to X amount of water that the copper will kill algae but not harm the plants or fish. Even if the copper doesn't kill the fish immediately, it may prevent them from spawning, inhibit their growth rate, or harm them in other insidious ways.

Q: I am having a battle with 'green water' algae in my 40 gal tank. After I change water or use a diatom filter, the water looks clear for a day or two. By the second day, though, the green water algae comes back.

I have also tried several times at least two different aquarium brands of flocculents. They seem to work better than the diatom filter. The problem, though, is that the flocculents seem to stress the fish, especially the tetras. (I have lost about 10 green neons, among other fish.) Are the flocculents clogging their gills?

A: Yes. If flocculation is effective enough to remove green water algae, then it would be potent enough to clog fish gills and possibly kill the fish.

and are harmed by high light intensities; most algae are basically 'shade organisms' [5,6]. Furthermore, many species can adapt to very low light levels (see page 162).

Most algae cannot use strong light (**Table X-1**). (While they may survive at higher levels, they aren't growing any faster.) Although green algae (Chlorophyta) can use moderately intense light (211 $\mu mol/m^2/s$), none of the algae listed come even close to using full sunlight (2,000 $\mu mol/m^2/s$).[1]

Moreover, algae are inhibited by intense light, both ultraviolet and visible light. 'Photoinhibition' by ordinary light generally begins at about 200 $\mu mol/m^2/s$, but ranges from 86 $\mu mol/m^2/s$ for the Dinophyceae to 233 $\mu mol/m^2/s$ for the Bacillariophyceae [7].

Table X-1. Light Levels Required for Saturating Algal Growth [7]. 's.e.' is standard error of the mean.

Algal Class:	Saturating Light (± s.e.) ($\mu mol/m^2/s$)
Bacillariophyceae (22 species)	84 (± 8.1)
Chlorophyta (9 species)	211 (±58)
Cyanophyceae (14 species)	39 (±6.2)
Dinophyceae (17 species)	47 (±6.6)
Rhodophyceae (3 species)	79 (±20)

3. Water Changes

Many hobbyists report that they have been unable to combat an entrenched algae with water changes. Indeed, I see little connection between water changes and algal growth. Well-established tanks with plants usually have few algae problems. Even though I only change the water every few months or so, there is little algae. And when algae problems occasionally arise, water changes seem quite ineffective.

Q.   If algae doesn't need much light, why do many algae seem to grow so much better in sunlight?

A.   Intense light makes iron more available for algae in a process called 'iron photoreduction' (see page 169). Iron's increased availability, not the intense light per se, may be what stimulates the algae.

4. Algae-Eating Fish, Shrimp, and Snails

Algae-eating fish and shrimp can be useful, especially in a new tank set-up where algae problems are common. Snails also help by cleaning plant leaves of attached microorganisms and debris, thereby preventing algae from gaining a foothold [10,11].

However, depending on fish (and other organisms) to control algae may be self-defeating in the long run. This is because algae-eating fish will often rid the tank of algae they like to eat. If the tank remains out of balance, though, it is only a matter of time before less tasty algae enter the tank. No aquarium fish will eat blue-green algae and only the Siameses algae eater

---

[1]The exceptions are various marine turf algae associated with tropical coral reefs that can maintain rapid growth with no apparent photoinhibition under the full tropical sun [8]. Turf algae have been used by some marine aquarists to filter their large salt-water tanks [9]. (Rapid growth of these unique algae can often reduce both nitrates and ammonia to undetectable levels.)

(*Crossocheilus siamensis*) will eat the black fur algae. These algae can rapidly gain a foothold when the more palatable algae are no longer in the tank to compete with them.

For example, I was able to eliminate a slimy, brown algae in one of my tanks by adding several Chinese algae-eaters. The algae-eaters devoured the algae within a week. But a few months later the tank was overtaken by the potentially devastating blue-green algae, which the Chinese algae-eaters would not touch.

Although I have no objection to algae-eating fish, I no longer bother keeping them for algae control.

5. Phosphate Removal

In natural waters, nutrient increases from pollution often lead to undesirable algal growth and the destruction of aquatic plants. After years of controversy between biologists and the detergent industry, it is now commonly accepted that phosphate limits algal growth in many freshwaters. The phosphate concentration in unpolluted natural waters is indeed very low, between 0.003 and 0.02 mg/l P, which limits algal growth since only a few algal species can use less than 0.02 mg/l P [12].

However, home aquariums typically have much higher phosphate levels. My own aquariums contain about 1-5 mg/l P, which is more than sufficent for almost any algal species. Because of the continuous addition of phosphate via fishfood, it is highly unlikely that phosphate deficiency would ever limit algal growth in the typical aquarium.

Q. I have a 300 gallon 'High-tech' tank. I fertilize the plants with plant tablets and liquid fertilizers every other day or so. Substrate is iron-rich laterite mixed with 2-3 mm gravel.

Weekly, I change about 40 gal of water and replace it with de-ionized water. Gravel is cleaned here and there, wherever there is room. There are relatively few fish in the tank and they are fed very sparingly. Nitrite level is zero, and Fe is 0.1 mg/l. Nitrates are less than 0.2 mg/l and the phosphates are 0.15 mg/l, at the most.

What is really driving me up the wall is the fact that I have had the little tuffs of the red algae and a green thread algae on rocks and older leaves. I also have a number of so-called algae-eating fish, but they have never shown me anything.

All the literature points to poor maintenance, overfeeding, high nitrates and phosphates, but as I have already pointed out, the tank is maintained religiously and both nitrates and phosphates are almost non-existent. I also understand that there will always be algae in a healthy tank, but I have seen too many plant tanks, especially in Europe that have none at all.

A. Although your phosphate levels are indeed very low (lower than for most aquariums), they are quite sufficient for many algae. As you have seen, trying to reduce P levels in the aquarium to levels that will eliminate algal growth is almost impossible. I would be more concerned about Fe than P (or nitrates). That 0.1 ppm Fe level may be more than the plants need, and the excess may just be encouraging algae.

B. Competition between Algae and Plants

Algae is almost always more adept than plants at using light and nutrients. It is surprising then that ponds, aquariums, and lakes containing dense plant growth often seem to have little algal growth. Investigators [13] tested this field observation experimentally by monitoring algal growth in fish ponds when they contained no plants or when they contained *Elodea canadensis* (**Table X-2**). Algae didn't grow as well when the ponds contained *Elodea*. For example, in Pond A, the number of alga cells was 6,600 cells/ml without plants in the pond. When plants were added to the pond, the number of alga cells was reduced to only 430 cells/ml.

Table X-2. Effect of *Elodea canadensis* on 'Green-water' Algae in Fish Ponds [13].

Pond	No Plants (algae cells/ml)	With Plants (algae cells/ml)
A	6,600	430
B	13,000	1,300
C	1,700	460
D	3,900	1,000

Q.   I am having a terrible time with 'green water' in my large Koi pond. The problem is that the Koi will eat any plants I put into the pond. Another problem is that the pond is in direct sun, so the algae is very thick. How can I get rid of the algae? (As it is, I can't even see the fish except when I feed them.)

A.   Ponds with Koi are a problem, because these fish eat just about any plant. However, you can get around this by somehow creating a place where the plants are protected. If you establish a protected area for plants, the plants will prevent the algal growth.

Hobbyist's Follow-up Letter. I built a 'mini-pond' for plants slightly above the main pond. Water from the main pond is pumped into the 'mini-pond' and then flows via a waterfall into the main pond with the Koi. I keep water lilies, emergent plants, and *Vallisneria* in this small pond. During the winter, a mat type of algae grows on the waterfall. I keep this algae, which I don't mind, and the plants pruned regularly. The main pond is now crystal clear even during the hottest and brightest summer months; it has stayed that way for several years. My fish are doing well, and best of all I can now see them!

Hobbyist Observation. Since there has been so much discussion about algae lately, I thought I'd throw in this recent experience. One of my swordplants was rapidly being covered by a short, brushy, fur-like alga. I tried all sorts of treatments—lots of water changes (1/3 volume per week), did not feed the fish, dark periods, hydrogen peroxide. The swordplant was doing OK but not **great**. I finally had a period where I was too busy to do proper maintenance, and during that time one of the faster growing weeds just took over the tank, shading the sword and other undergrowth. After this happened, the sword started to grow much better! There are a lot of new leaves, none of which has algae. I know this is telling me that light was the problem, but my reducing light levels and subjecting the tank to darkouts just wasn't getting the job done. The undergrowth is obviously getting enough light, so I'm leaving well enough alone.

My Comment: I couldn't have said it better. The bottom line is: 'Let the plants do the work for you.'

1. Advantages Algae have over Plants

a) Better Adaptation to Low Light

In some instances, reducing light levels in a planted tank would hurt plants more than algae. This is because the light requirements of aquatic plants are often greater than those of many algae, especially 'green-water' algae (**Table X-3**). The median light required by 7 plant species for growth was 6.1 μmol/m^2/s while algae required about one-third less (1.8 μmol/m^2/s). Also, the efficiency with which algae used light was found to be 7 times greater than for the plants (7.5 v. 1.1). (This greater efficiency is apparently linked to algae's higher chlorophyll concentration and smaller cell size.)[2]

Table X-3. Minimum Light Required by Several Algae and Aquatic Plants [14]. Plants and algae were exposed to fluorescent light at different light intensities for 16 hr per day. Plant species were 7 submerged species including *Elodea canadensis* and *Ceratophyllum demersum*. Algae were 8-16 species of phytoplankton. 'Low Light Growth Efficiency' was calculated from the slope (b) of growth versus light intensity.

Organism	Minimum Light Requirements (μmol/m^2/s)		Low-Light Growth Efficiency (b)	
	Median	Range	Median	Range
Algae	1.8	0.8 - 9	7.5	0.4 - 44
Plants	6.1	3 - 12	1.1	0.2 - 1.8

b) Algal Adaptation to the Light Spectrum

Although both green algae and plants have chlorophyll, which absorbs mainly red and blue light, many algae have accessory photosynthetic pigments that allow them to better use the full light spectrum. Thus, certain siphonaceous green algae have special carotenoids that absorb green and blue-green light and contribute to photosynthesis [6]. Many red and blue-green algae readily adapt (*chromatic adaptation*) to light spectral changes by changing the proportions of their specialized photosynthetic pigments. For example, when *Synechocystis* (a blue-green alga) is grown in green light, it

Q. I was told that there is a certain type of fluorescent light that is better for plants than algae. Is there any evidence for algae requiring a different light spectrum than plants?

A. No. Many algae readily adapt to light spectral changes, probably more so than plants. However, full-spectrum light, which usually has a fair amount of blue light, may stimulate algal growth more than light sources with less blue light (e.g., 'Cool-white' fluorescent, incandescent light, and high pressure sodium lamps). This is because blue light makes iron in the water more available to algae, thereby stimulating its growth (see page 168).

---

[2] The light requirements of plants for proper development were found to be even greater. Apparently, *Elodea canadensis* could grow at 11 μmol/m^2/s, but it required 24 μmol/m^2/s for branching and more than 54 μmol/m^2/s for root development. (Light required for maximum growth of *E. canadensis* is 290 μmol/m^2/s [15].)

produces non-chlorophyll photosynthetic pigments in a 2:2:1 ratio of red, blue, and blue-gray, respectively. When the same algae is grown in red light, it produces much less red pigment, and the ratio of pigments changes to 0.4:2:1 [16].

Because aquatic plants don't have these specialized pigments (e.g., phycoerythrin, phycocyanin, and siphonoxanthin), they exhibit little (if any) chromatic adaptation [17].

Chromatic adaptation probably takes only a few days. For example, when investigators suddenly changed the lighting of one algae culture (filtered out the shorter wavelengths below 520 nm from 'Cool-white' fluorescent light), algal growth lagged for 3 days [18]. However, the culture apparently adjusted to the restricted light spectrum, because it was eventually able to grow at almost the same rate as algae growing in normal light.

c) Better Adaptation to High pH and Alkaline Water

Algae appear to be better adapted to alkaline water than aquatic plants [21]. For example, in a certain canal in Lancashire (U.K.), filamentous algae (*Cladophora glomerata* and various *Spirogyra* species) have replaced *Elodea canadensis*. In trying to explain how this happened, investigators compared the photosynthesis rates of the algae with *E. canadensis* at 4 different pHs (**Table X-4**). At pH 6, *Elodea* was actually able to photosynthesize better than both algal species, producing 45 µg O_2/mg chl/min. However, with increasing pH, *Elodea* was inhibited much more than the algae, producing only 10 µg O_2/mg Chl/min at pH 8. Apparently, the algae could extract bicarbonates from alkaline water better than *Elodea*.

In a competitive situation, algae could easily enhance their initial advantage by driving the pH of the water up (by their own photosynthesis) such that aquatic plants would be even less able to obtain photosynthetic carbon.

Table X-4. pH's Effect on the Photosynthesis of Algae and an Aquatic Plant [15].

Algae or Plant	Maximum Photosynthesis Rate (µg O_2/mg Chl/min)			
	pH 6	pH 7	pH 8	pH 9
Cladophora glomerata	18	27	27	25
Spirogyra sp.	35	43	41	26
Elodea canadensis	45	40	10	1

Red algae may not have the alkaline advantage. Marine scientists report that certain species of red and brown macroalgae from the Division Rhodophyta depend primarily upon free CO_2; they cannot use bicarbonates [6].

Q. I used to see black fur and brush algae (red algae) in my softwater South American cichlid tanks, but never in the Tanganyikan tanks with their crushed coral substrate and high pH. Perhaps red algae are among those algae and water plants that can only use free CO_2?

A. I would agree. In my own tanks, which contain alkaline hardwater, the black fur and brush algae that I've purposely added to the tanks eventually die out. These same algae have plagued other hobbyist tanks, but usually their tanks had softwater and low light.

The green mat and green water algae have been much more difficult for me to get rid of. These same green algae, which have plagued other hobbyists tanks with hardwater and intense light, probably have the 'alkaline advantage'.

> **Q.** I seem to have a persistent problem with a 'green mat' algae in my tanks where I'm trying to grow Java Fern, Amazon Swordplants, Water Sprite, and *Cryptocoryne*. They just don't seem to grow faster than the algae. So many times I'll end up losing the plants when algae covers their leaves. What can I do? (Hobbyist from AZ.)
>
> **A.** Arizona water has a high pH (>8), so many aquarium plants, especially those that can't use bicarbonates, are going to have a tough time competing with algae for their carbon.
>   I would make sure you have plenty of plants like *Vallisneria*, Hornwort, and *Elodea* that can use bicarbonates. (I have seen *Vallisneria spiralis* splendidly outcompete algae in hardwater tanks with a fertile substrate and plenty of light.) Also, I would try to include emergent plants in the tank, since they can use air CO_2.

d) More Efficient Uptake of Nutrients from the Water

Another advantage is that some algae may be more adept than plants at taking up nutrients from the water. For example, the filamentous alga *Draparnaldia plumosa* was shown to be more efficient than the aquatic plant *Elodea occidentalis* in taking up major nutrients N, P, Ca, and Mg (but not K) [19]. Thus, when the algae and the plant were grown together with low phosphates (0.075 mg/l P), algal growth was not affected, but plant growth was cut in half. Furthermore, P uptake was much faster for *Draparnaldia* than for *Elodea*.

Also, blue-green algae secrete a wide assortment of iron chelators (siderophores) that help them take up iron from the water [20]. Active secretion of iron chelators might give blue-green algae an advantage over plants in iron-limited environments.

e) Greater Species Distribution

One overlooked advantage that algae have over plants is simply that they have a greater species distribution. An aquarium only contains the plant species that a hobbyist adds to it. Those plants may or may not adapt well to tank conditions. In contrast, any algal species could be brought in initially with plants, fish, and soil or could drop in later as an airborne spore.

Some algae produce spores that are extremely tough and long lasting. For example, spores from one blue-green algae (*Anabaena*) were still able to germinate after 64 years [22]. Thus, a hobbyist may have great success with aquariums– often for years– until just one little spore from a new, more resilient species of algae lands in the tank.

> **Q.** Why don't you use scientific names for the aquarium algae you are discussing? For example, the red algae in softwater aquariums is usually an *Audouinella* species.
>
> **A.** I gave up on algal taxonomy after I had some 'green mat' algae from my tanks examined by a biologist. Under the microscope, the algae turned out to be a conglomerate of many separate species. The two dominant genera identified by their filamentous branching pattern and characteristic spores, were *Oedogonium* and *Pithophora* (both green algae from the Division Chlorophyta). The *Oedogonium* appeared to be a mixture of not one, but several species. In addition, blue-green algae *Chamaesiphon* and *Chroococcus* species appeared as small blue-green bulbs attached to the green algae filaments. Finally, there were small populations of diatoms (Division Chrysophyta) and other miscellaneous algal species within the green mat. Thus, I decided to use common, descriptive names for algae found in aquariums.

2. Advantages Plants have over Algae

Aquatic plants have several advantages over algae. First, rooted plants can get their nutrients from the substrate, so they do not depend on water nutrients. Even in aquariums, where the water may have excessive N and P, some of the trace elements, especially iron, may only be in the substrate. Second, emergent aquatic plants can use full sun, whereas most algal species can only use a fraction of full sunlight (see page 158). Third, emergent plants can use air CO_2, whereas algae must use water CO_2. Thus, algae have the same carbon limitations that inhibit submerged plant growth [23].

Finally, aquatic plants have much larger stores of food reserves. For example, *Myriophyllum spicatum* and *Vallisneria americana* were found to contain between 2 and 20% carbohydrate reserves during different times of the year [24]. Generally, these food reserves confer a seasonal advantage to temperate plants. For example, water lilies emerging in the early spring use energy from rhizomal stores of carbohydrates to cover the water surface with their floating leaves before the temperature and light are sufficient for algal growth [25].

C.   Factors in Controlling Algae

1. Emergent Plants

Emergent and floating plants, which have the 'aerial advantage', are much faster growers than fully submerged plants (see page 93). Faster growth means faster removal of nutrients that can stimulate algae in aquariums. They also reduce excessive light that submerged plants don't need and which may only be encouraging algae. Emergent plants can protect submerged plants from algae.

Thus, I have always encouraged emergent plants in my aquariums. Rather than dimming lights to control algae, I prefer to keep the lighting moderately high but add floating plants and encourage emergent growth. Thus, I can increase total plant growth and the uptake of light and nutrients by aquatic plants– rather than algae– in the same volume of water. For example, when I set up an outdoor pond (50 guppies in 25 gal) in a sunny location, there was lots of 'green-water' algae. However, once the floating plants (mostly Indian Fern and duckweed) began to grow, the water cleared within a week or two.

Q.   I have a 125 gal 'High-tech' tank with plenty of light and CO_2 fertilization. The substrate contains laterite clay. Lately, I have noticed a brown slimy coating on the leaves of the plants, and the plants don't seem to be growing as well. Is there a way to stop this algae? The only thing that I have changed lately is to remove some swordplants. Also, a few months ago, I removed all of the duckweed, because it was overrunning the tank.

A.   I would have left the duckweed in. Far better that the tank be overrun by duckweed than algae. I would recommend that you add floating plants back to this tank and thin them out periodically. (I've found that water lettuce is a little easier to manage than duckweed.)

All submerged plants are basically shade plants; the strong lighting in this tank is basically wasted on them. But duckweed can efficiently use your high light levels.

Q.   About a month ago I redid my 65 gal 'High-tech' show tank from scratch partly because of a dark brown/black coating that was covering everything in the tank.

Now another algae problem has arisen. The fastest growing plants are two thickets of *Rotala indica*, and I have had to repeatedly prune them back below the water line. After the most recent cutting, a blue-green film began coating the upper portion of the thickets that were pruned and is impeding new growth. The blue-green film is now spreading to the neighboring plants.

This form of algae does not appeal to my *Ottocinclus* or *Siamensis* algae-eaters. What can I do to get rid of this algae, which I read somewhere is actually a bacteria?

A.   Encourage aerial growth in your tank. Plants that have access to air have an incredible advantage over both submerged plants and algae. It was not a good idea to cut your *Rotala indica* thickets below the water line. Cutting off your plant's access to air injured your plants and probably contributed to your algae problem. If you can lower the water level a little to encourage renewed aerial growth of your *Rotala indica*, I would do so.

Q.   Algae is taking over my 45 gal tank. It grows as a film in small circles on the glass, which can only be removed with a razor blade. The algae is spreading to the *Anubias*.

I add CO_2 and change the water weekly. This tank contains 12 one-inch fish and is planted with 12 various *Anubias* that are doing very well. I am not using floating plants, because I don't feel I have excess nutrients. I don't know where I'm deficient?

A.   Even though you don't think you have excess nutrients in the water, if there's algae, then you have excess nutrients– period. (Otherwise the algae could not grow.)

Tanks containing only *Anubias*, which are slow growers, are subject to being overridden with algae. These plants need protection– protection that only faster-growing plants, especially emergent plants, can provide. Thus, I keep *Anubias* with swordplants in one tank and with partially emergent Indian Fern in another tank. Floating duckweed is in both tanks. Other hobbyists have had good luck with Water Lettuce and Water Sprite.

Q.   I have a 'Tiny tank' set-up (5 gal) with 1 *Anubias barterii*, 3 *Anubias nana* and 3 small *Cryptocoryne* in which I cannot get the 'fur algae' under control. The substrate consists of 1- 1.5 inches of sifted backyard soil under 1-1.5 inches of gravel (sandblasting grit). I have 15 watts of cool-white fluorescent light over the tank. I have about 8 Ramshorn snails and 6 Malaysian Trumpet Snails, 1 *Siamensis* algae-eater and 5 Mollies– all for algae control. However, these measures aren't doing the job. Any suggestions?

A.   Your 'Tiny tank' sounds just about perfect, one that I would highly recommend for a beginner's first tank. I like the tank size, the lighting, and the soil underlayer. There's only one problem– the slow-growing plants. This tank desperately needs some fast-growing plants, especially emergent plants. (Your letter supports my contention that you can't depend on fish and invertebrates to control algae.)

2. Iron

Iron may be the limiting nutrient for algal growth in aquariums, if only because so many other nutrients (e.g., N and P) are so plentiful. Also, iron is the one nutrient that is required in fairly large quantities while being the least available in oxygenated water. Thus, I sometimes have problems with algae after setting up a tank with garden soil, because considerable iron is released into the water during the first two months (see page 131). Only after the soil has 'settled down', does the iron release stop and algal problems dimminish.

a) Iron as the Limiting Nutrient for Algae

Iron's limited availability in oxygenated water sets iron apart from all other plant nutrients.[3] This is because free iron (Fe^{2+} and Fe^{3+}), which is the only form that algae can use [28], doesn't ordinarily accumulate in the water. It either forms various iron precipitates (FeOOH, $FeCO_3$, etc) or binds to dissolved organic carbon (DOC).

It is not surprising that most natural freshwaters contain only small amounts of iron, most of it bound to DOC. Indeed, the iron concentration of most oxygenated surface waters is less than 0.2 mg/l, and almost none is in the free form that algae (or plants) can use [26]. Hardwater lakes, in particular, may have little available iron. Thus, one investigator [29] found algal growth to be limited by iron in several natural lakes. For example, phytoplankton cultures from Lake Tahoe (U.S.) were greatly stimulated by adding as little as 0.005 ppm Fe.

Enormous areas of open ocean have limited algal growth despite relatively high nitrate and phosphate levels. Because these areas are far removed from terrestrial sources of iron (e.g., soil dust), iron is present in exceedingly small amounts, less than 0.000056 ppm. Thus, when investigators added iron to experimental bottles containing these algae and their natural ocean water, algal growth was stimulated [30].

My point is that because iron doesn't stay around very long in oxygenated water, it can limit algal growth—in aquariums as well as oceans. Unlike phosphate and other plant nutrients, which can and often do accumulate in aquarium water, the reservoir of free iron in aquarium water is limited.

b) How Algae Gets Iron

Plants can get their iron from the substrate, but algae depend on free iron (Fe^{2+} and Fe^{3+}) in the water. Although iron in the water is indeed bound up, often to dissolved organic carbon, it is made transiently available by a common process called the 'photoreduction of iron'. The reaction for the photoreduction of DOC-bound iron is:

$$DOC\text{-}Fe^{3+} + light \Rightarrow Fe^{2+} + oxidized\ DOC$$

---

[3]Manganese (Mn) is the only other plant nutrient that might not accumulate in aquarium water, because like Fe, it forms insoluble oxides. However, Mn is a little more soluble than Fe, and algae and plants require considerably less Mn than Fe [26,27]. Therefore, Mn has less potential to limit algal growth than Fe.

168

This light-requiring reaction, which also applies to manganese and copper, is greatly accelerated by DOC [31,32,33]. The photoreduction of DOC-bound iron is invariably accompanied by the decomposition of DOC (see page 59).[4] The Fe^{2+} released may be taken up by algae or quickly oxidized to Fe^{3+}, which can also be taken up by algae or bind to fresh DOC, whereby the process repeats itself.

Different investigators demonstrated iron photoreduction using a variety of light sources ('Cool-white', 'Daylight', and Vita-Lite™ fluorescent bulbs as well as sunlight). However, UV and blue light induce the most photoreduction, because only wavelengths below about 500 nm are energetic enough to break the chemical bonds [31].[5] Thus, investigators showed that only wavelengths below 520 nm released free iron from one DOC-chelated iron (**Figure X-1**). Algae grew well under normal light with chelated iron as the only iron source, but when light wavelengths below 520 nm were filtered out, the same algae became iron deficient and would not grow.

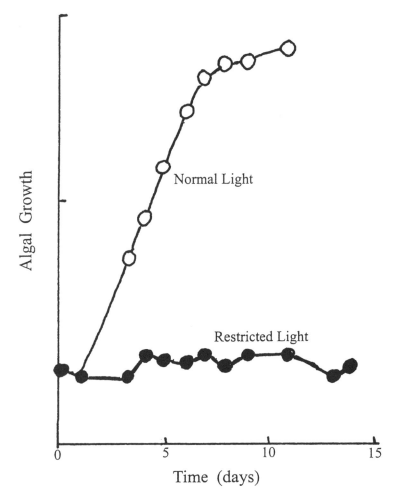

Figure X-1. Algal Growth and the Photoreduction of Iron. 'Normal light' cultures of algae were grown in nutrient media under continuous 'Cool-white' lighting at 120 μmol/m²/s. The only iron source was 'HN', a hexanuclear iron and sorbitol complex, which is a type of DOC-bound iron. 'Restricted light' cultures were grown under identical conditions except light wavelengths below 520 nm were filtered out. As a control, investigators showed that the algae could grow with restricted light if adequate Fe was present. Thus, the non-growth of the 'Restricted light' culture in Fig. X-1 was due to Fe limitation, not light limitation. 'Growth' was determined from chlorophyll *a* fluorescence. Figure from Rich [18] redrawn and used with the permission of the American Society of Limnology and Oceanography.

---

[4]The reaction also applies to chelated iron such as FeEDTA, where EDTA is oxidized and decomposed as it releases Fe^{2+}.

[5] The 280 to 400 nm portion of the light energy spectrum encompasses UV (ultraviolet) light, while the 400 to 500 nm range consists of violet and blue light (see light spectrum on page 181).

Iron is bound to a variety of chemicals and different types of DOC. These iron complexes all have their own peculiar 'iron-binding tightness' and susceptibility to both photoreduction and chemical reduction [34]. Thus, algae may, indeed, have access to some iron even in the dark. However, algae will get a far larger supply in the presence of light and DOC. Thus, Fe^{2+} levels in one lake were found to be almost 5 fold higher at midday when light intensity was greatest than at night [31]. In natural systems (and aquariums) the photoreduction of DOC-bound iron is probably essential to supplying algae with iron.[6]

c) Iron and Algae Control

Aquatic plants readily take up iron directly from the water [35], even when planted in iron-containing substrates [36,37]. For example, iron uptake by *Hydrilla* planted in a peat substrate was shown to actually equal iron precipitation as a means of removing iron from oxygenated water [36]. Plants would continuously drain free iron (Fe^{2+} and Fe^{3+}) from aquarium water, thereby depriving algae of a much-needed nutrient.

In aquariums containing soil underlayers, fertilization with chelated iron is almost surely unnecessary. Soils have enormous quantities of iron (see page 83). Not only do they contain plentiful iron, but also the anaerobic conditions that keep some iron in the free, unbound form that plants can use.

In my opinion, the substrate– not the water– is the primary place to provide plants with iron. Recommendations to maintain a certain water level of iron may be based on work that doesn't apply to the home aquarium. For example, aquatic botanists and hydroponic growers routinely add EDTA-chelated iron, but their plants may be

Q.   My tank has a soil underlayer, CO_2 injection and intense light. After I added iron, Fe went from 0.25 ppm to 0.03 ppm in 48 hr. Is 0.03 ppm Fe enough to make algae starve?

A.   No. Algal growth can be stimulated by as little as 0.005 ppm, which you probably can't measure.

The fact that iron is being rapidly removed from the water in your tank does not mean that you need to add iron. Plants quickly take up iron from the water, even though the substrate can provide the iron they need. Therefore, I would not feed your plants iron based on what you measure in the water.

High-tech tanks and those with CO_2 injection may indeed require some iron and/or micronutrient fertilization of the water, but I would use these fertilizers sparingly and only if the plants were showing severe symptoms of iron deficiency (interveinal chlorosis of younger leaves).

sterilized beforehand or grown emergent. Under these circumstances, chelated iron is essential and won't promote algae. But what is appropriate for aquatic botanists and hydroponic growers is not always appropriate for the home aquarist.

---

[6] Iron is also released by acidity and anaerobic conditions, which don't require light and would occur mainly in aquarium substrates. However, in the aquarium water where there is light, oxygen, and DOC, photoreduction would be the main mechanism for releasing iron.

> **Hobbyist's Comment.** I thought you might be interested in my experience with controlling algae by limiting iron in the water. The tank is a 55 gal with 32 Tetra-size fish, heavily planted, CO_2 injection, KH of 4, phosphates = 0, nitrate = 10 or less, 110 watts of light, and gravel over a no longer used Undergravel Filter.
>
> I was having severe problems with thread algae as well as some red algae. At the same time, my large Amazon swordplant almost died. My aquarium dealer suggested fertilizing with chelated iron, so that water Fe levels never falls below 0.1 ppm. Soon I had a beautiful Amazon sword, but the thread algae increased greatly. I could no longer control the algae by hand removal.
>
> Eventually, I realized that the fact that the substrate was not iron-enriched might be the problem. So, I limited iron additions at water changes to once every two weeks. At the end of the week, water Fe was at or near zero, so half the time my plants had no free water iron. I added some laterite balls around plants and potted a couple of Crypts in laterite and potting soil.
>
> The results were amazing. I noticed less algae almost immediately. Two months later thread algae is zero, algae on glass is 5-10% of former infestation, and I can find only two leaves on all my plants with a couple of tufts of red algae.

3. Allelopathy

If iron limitation was the only force controlling algal growth in my aquariums, then the iron-rich lava rocks in my tanks should be covered with algae. They are not. Allelopathy may be the 'wild-card' in the formula for controlling algae. Different species of aquatic plants produce different allelochemicals. Ditto for algae. Thus, the possiblities for unpredictable interactions in the home aquarium are truly enormous.

However, all aquatic plants contain chemicals that are mildly inhibitory to algae (see page 41). Allelopathy may explain the unexplainable, why algae, which has so many advantages, is unable to take over heavily planted aquaria– even when nutrients and light are abundant.

Conversely, some algae secrete allelochemicals that inhibit plants (see page 49). Thus, the hobbyists should be aware that if algal growth becomes excessive in the aquarium, these allelochemicals may inhibit plant growth. The hobbyist can easily remove the algal allelochemicals by water changes and adding charcoal to the filter.[7]

D.   Intensive Care for Algal Takeovers

In every home aquarium, there's a delicate balance between plants and algae. Occasionally, even in aquariums that are set up for ideal plant growth and that have never had problems, algae may seemingly arise from nowhere and take over the tank. These takeovers may defy explanation or standard treatments.

---

[7] Activated carbon (e.g. aquarium 'charcoal') is used by municipal treatment plants to remove organic chemicals from water by the non-specific process of adsorption. Although virtually any organic chemical would be removed, specific compounds on a list of 56 organics reported to be absorbed are: aldrin, diquat, gasoline, lindane, malathion, paraquat, phenols, PCB, rotenone, and simazine [38]. In aquariums it would remove almost all allelochemicals, humic substances, artificial chelators, antibiotics, and dyes.

For years I had no problems with algae, even though I had added other hobbyist's most troublesome algae to my tanks. Eventually, though, two types of algae ('green water' and 'green mat' algae) became troublesome in some of my tanks. I found that these algae weren't going to go away no matter how many water changes or how much hand removal I did. Thus, I devised a plan to rid the tanks of this algae using a combination of measures that would shift the balance towards the plants rather than algae.

I'll start with the 45 gal that suddenly developed a bad case of green water algae. The tank was not only unsightly, but the fish and plants were not doing well in this tank. I measured a very high pH during the day (~8) confirming my suspicion that algal photosynthesis was driving the pH so high that the plants were being inhibited by a lack of carbon.

First, I did a complete water change to remove the majority of the algae. (Although I knew the algae would grow right back, I didn't want a mass of dying algae to pollute the tank or to clog up the charcoal in the filter.) Second, I added fresh charcoal to the filter. (This would remove DOC along with its propensity to provide iron to algae much as artificial chelators do. Also, charcoal would remove any allelochemicals or toxins released by the algae that might be inhibiting the plants or hurting the fish.)

Third, I taped duct tape across the bottom 3" of glass at the tank's back to keep all strong light off the soil underlayer. (Soil contains so much iron that exposure to intense light generates soluble iron, some of which will escape into the overlying water.) Fourth, I reduced light levels by taping cloth across the entire back of the tank, so that the sunlight was diffused more. Then I removed one of the two 40 watt fluorescent lights overhead. In deciding which light to remove, I chose to remove the Sylvania Gro-Lux™, which has a large blue peak in its spectrum. This blue light would stimulate iron release more than the 'Cool-white', which has mostly green-yellow light. Now the light source for the tank was one 40 watt 'Cool-white' bulb and some diffuse window light entering through the cloth. [The lighting changes were not just to deprive algae of light, but to deprive the algae of water iron by slowing the iron photoreduction process (see page 167).]

Fifth, I kept the pH down to my tank's normal range (~7 to 7.5). I did this by adding either vinegar or phosphate salts whenever the algae started to grow and the pH started to climb. This would deprive algae of their 'alkaline advantage' (see page 163). Finally, I realized that this tank really needed some serious floating plants not just the few straggly duckweed that were in the tank, so I started a colony of water lettuce (*Pistia stratiotes*) in this tank. The water lettuce immediately started growing, forming long (6-10") bushy roots quite suited for pulling nutrients out of the water. Although the small starting colony would probably not have a major impact on algae until later, I wanted to use these floating plants for the long-term protection that this tank seemed to need.

For the first week, the green water algae held on, visible now only as a slight cloudiness. So I changed the charcoal one more time and continued to keep the pH down. During the second week the tank water started to clear. At the end of two weeks the tank cleared completely, the plants were growing again and the fish looked much healthier than I had seen them in a long time. This tank has continued to do well.

I used a similar combination of measures for an infestation of green-mat algae in a 29 gal tank. However, instead of a 100% water change, I removed the algal mats by hand and did a small water change sucking up as much of the algae as I could. All the other measures were

172

identical to what I used for the 45 gal. It's hard to say which measure was responsible for tipping the balance in favor of the plants. Each one is designed to give plants a slight 'edge'.

Hobbyists should keep in mind that the 'combination strategy' I used was designed for two green algaes that typically thrive in nutrient-rich water with fairly intense light. The strategy would probably need to be altered somewhat for infestations of red and brown algaes in softwater tanks. In softwater situations, I would try to increase water hardness and add fast-growing hardwater plants to the tank. pH reduction might not be necessary for red/brown algae infestations, but I would definitely keep fresh charcoal in the filter and avoid blue light.

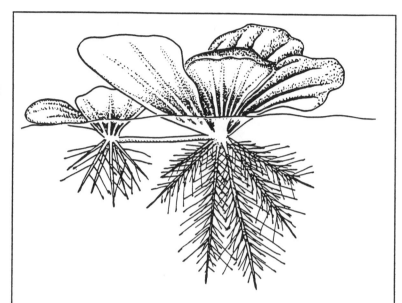

Pistia stratiotes **(water lettuce).** This floating plant, which has been used in waste water treatment, is a good tool for combatting algal takeovers. It doesn't have to compete with algae for CO_2, and like all emergent plants, it has the 'aerial advantage'—the capacity to grow much, much faster than submerged plants. Drawing from IFAS [39].

Q. I've set up a 20 gal trial tank. The substrate has 1 ½" of topsoil covered with about 1" of 2-3 mm gravel. Lighting is from three 20 watt full-spectrum bulbs. The tank also gets some direct sunlight. Tank is stocked with *Vallisneria, Sagittaria, Aponogeton crispus,* and *Saururus cernus,* which are doing fairly well. The problem is that there is an algal bloom/green water that I can't get rid of. I've tried everything I could find in the literature and over the Internet. Nothing has worked. Do you have any suggestions?

A. Yes. Here are four simple measures you can try that will limit iron availability to algae. If this works, the algae should clear up within two weeks.

1. Run duct tape along the entire bottom/back 3" of the tank so that the soil underlayer is never exposed to sunlight
2. Tape a piece of diffusive paper or cloth to the back of the tank to reduce the light
3. Replace your 3 full spectrum lights with one Cool-white light
4. Add fresh charcoal to the filter

Reply. I followed the four steps you prescribed. After about a week and a half, I observed a great improvement in the water's clarity. After about 2 weeks, I now have a very clear aquarium. The plants also seem to be doing much better. Thanks so much!

REFERENCES

1. Frank N. 1991. Chemicals to control algae. The use of simazine. The Aquatic Gardener 4(6): 185-189.
2. Frank N. 1991. Chemicals to control algae. The use of copper. The Aquatic Gardener 4(5): 150-155.
3. Biesinger KE and Stokes GN. 1986. Effects of synthetic polyelectrolytes on selected aquatic organisms. Water Pollut. Control Fed. 58: 207-213.
4. Lacroix GL, Peterson RH, Belfry CS, and Martin-Robichaud DJ. 1993. Aluminum dynamics on gills of Atlantic salmon fry in the presence of citrate and effects on intergrity of gill structures. Aquat. Toxicol. 27: 373-402.
5. Wetzel RG. 1983. Limnology (Second Ed.). Saunders College Publishing (Philadelphia, PA), p. 355.
6. Reiskind JB, Beer S, and Bowes G. 1989. Photosynthesis, photorespiration and ecophysiological interactions in marine macroalgae. Aquat. Bot. 34: 131-152.
7. Richardson K, Beardall J, and Raven JA. 1983. Adaptation of unicellular algae to irradiance: an analysis of strategies. New Phytol. 93: 157-191.
8. Carpenter RC. 1985. Relationships between primary production and irradiance in coral reef algal communities. Limnol. Oceanogr. 30: 784-793.
9. Adey WH and Loveland K. 1991. Dynamic Aquaria. Building Living Ecosystems. Academic Press (NY).
10. Jernakoff P and J Nielsen. 1997. The relative importance of amphipod and gastropod grazers in *Posidonia sinuosa* meadows. Aquat. Bot. 56: 183-202
11. Rogers KKH and Breen CM. 1983. An investigation of macrophyte, epiphyte and grazer interactions. In: Wetzel RG (ed). Periphyton of Freshwater Ecosystems. Dr. W. Junk Publishers (Boston), pp 217-226.
12. Wetzel 1983, pp. 255-297 (The Phosphorus Cycle).
13. Hasler AD and Jones E. 1949. Demonstration of the antagonistic action of large aquatic plants on algae and rotifers. Ecology 30: 359-364.
14. Sand-Jensen K and Madsen TV. 1991. Minimum light requirements of submerged freshwater macrophytes in laboratory growth experiments. J. Ecol. 79: 749-764.
15. Simpson PS and Eaton JW. 1986. Comparative studies of the photosynthesis of the submerged macrophyte *Elodea canadensis* and filamentous algae *Cladophora glomerata* and *Spirogyra* sp. Aquat. Bot. 24: 1-12.
16. Lee RE. 1989. Phycology (Second Edition). Cambridge University Press (NY), p. 21.
17. Kirk JTO. 1994. Light and Photosynthesis in Aquatic Ecosystems. 2nd Edition. Cambridge Univ. Press (Cambridge MA), pp. 406-407.
18. Rich HW and Morel FMM. 1990. Availability of well-defined iron colloids to the marine diatom *Thalassiosira weissflogii*. Limnol. Oceanogr. 35: 652-662.
19. Gerloff GC. 1975. Nutritional Ecology of Nuisance Aquatic Plants. National Environmental Research Center (Corvallis OR), 78 pp.
20. Wilhelm SW and Trick CG. 1994. Iron-limited growth of cyanobacteria: multiple siderophore production is a common response. Limnol. Oceanogr. 39: 1979-1984.
21. Allen ED and Spence DHN. 1981. The differential ability of aquatic plants to utilize the inorganic carbon supply in fresh waters. New Phytol. 87: 269-283.
22. Lee 1989, p. 65.
23. Raven JA. 1993. Phytoplankton: limits on growth rates. Nature 361: 209-210.
24. Titus JE and Adams MS. 1977. Comparative carbohydrate storage and utilization patterns in the submersed macrophytes, *Myriophyllum spicatum* and *Vallisneria americana*. Am. Mid. Nat. 102: 263-272.

25. Brinson MM and Davis GJ. 1976. Primary Productivity and Mineral Cycling in Aquatic Macrophyte Communities of the Chowan River, NC. Water Resources Research Institute. University of North Carolina (Chapel Hill, NC).

26. Wetzel 1983, pp. 298-341 (Iron, Sulfur and Silica Cycles).

27. Brand LE, Sunda WG, and Guillard RRL. 1983. Limitation of marine phytoplankton reproductive rates by zinc, managanese, and iron. Limnol. Oceanogr. 28: 1182-1198.

28. Anderson MA and Morel FMM. 1982. The influence of aqueous iron chemistry on the uptake of iron by the coastal diatom *Thalassiosira weissflogii*. Limnol. Oceanogr. 27: 789-813.

29. Goldman CR. 1972. The role of minor nutrients in limiting the productivity of aquatic systems. In: Likens GE (ed.), Nutrients and Eutrophication: The Limiting Nutrient Controversy. Special Symposium, Am. Sol. Limnol. Oceanogr. 1: 21-38.

30. Martin JH, Gordon RM, and Fitzwater SE. 1991. The case for iron. Limnol. Oceanogr. 36: 1793-1802.

31. Morel FMM. 1983. Principles of Aquatic Chemistry. John Wiley & Sons (NY), p. 371.

32. Sunda WG, Huntsman SA, and Harvey GR. Photoreduction of manganese oxides in seawater and its geochemical and biological implications. Nature 301: 234-236.

33. Brezonik PL. 1994. Chemical Kinetics and Process Dynamics in Aquatic Systems. Lewis Publishers (Ann Arbon MI), pp 688-697.

34. Finden DAS, Tipping E, Jaworski GHM, and Reynolds CS. Light-induced reduction of natural iron(III) oxide and its relevance to phytoplankton. Nature 309: 783-784.

35. Basiouny FM, Garrard LA and Haller WT. 1977. Absorption of iron and growth of *Hydrilla verticillata* (L.F.) Royle. Aquat. Bot. 3: 349-356.

36. Cooley TN, Dooris PM, and Martin DF. 1980. Aeration as a tool to improve water quality and reduce the growth of *Hydrilla*. Water Res. 14: 485-489.

37. DeMarte JA and Hartman RT. 1974. Studies on absorption of ^{32}P, ^{59}Fe, and ^{45}Ca by Water-Milfoil (*Myriophyllum exalbescens* fernald). Ecology 55: 188-194.

38. Symons JM. 1978. Interim Treatment Guide for Controlling Organic Contaminants in Drinking Water Using Granular Activated Carbon. Water Supply Research Division (Cincinnati OH), p. 14.

39. Aquatic plant line drawings are the copyright property of the University of Florida Center for Aquatic Plants (Gainesville). Used with permission.

Chapter XI.

PRACTICAL AQUARIUM SETUP AND MAINTENANCE

My goal in writing this book was to explain ecological principles (allelopathy, biofilms, sediment chemistry, etc) behind keeping attractive, low-maintenance planted tanks. (For want of a better term, I'll call them 'Low-tech' aquariums.)

Maintaining any aquarium is difficult. Pitfalls abound. There are just too many variables in aquarium keeping for one single book to address every possible pitfall. So I caution beginning hobbyists that there are no guarantees that even if they diligently follow the methods I use that they will be pleased with the results.

The well-established home aquarium is a complex ecosystem. Even when one tank is set up identically to another, it will surely– over time– take on 'a life of its own'. You cannot purchase an ecosystem. All you can do it set it up the aquarium as best you can and hope that it will develop in a way that pleases you.

A.   Typical Pathways for Beginning Hobbyists

Countless beginners set up their first tank with great enthusiasm. The plants, fresh from Florida nurseries, are lush and algae-free. The fish, chosen carefully, are healthy and active. The water is crystal clear, sparkling, and bubbling. The gravel, having been thoroughly washed, is 'clean as a whistle'. The tank looks exactly like the display tanks in aquarium stores and magazine photos.

It is not long, though, before this pretty picture turns sour. The plants don't grow well or start dying and algae begins to grow everywhere. Unless the owner changes the water and vacuums the gravel frequently, the fish start to sicken, too. Beginning hobbyists are instructed to use algaecides, do more water changes, do more gravel cleaning, buy bigger filters, and feed their fish less. Hobbyists may try to cultivate plants again, but this time they are careful to add fertilizers. ('Maybe fertilizer will keep the plants alive.') Unfortunately, this usually doesn't help; the algae only grows better and the plants grow worse.

At this point, many beginners understandably give up on plants altogether. ('After all, plants aren't that important, anyway.') And so, in defeat, they switch to plastic plants, and to keep their fish healthy, they laboriously continue to change the water, clean the filters, and vacuum the gravel. Not much fun... Such discouragement, especially with keeping plants, is the norm within the aquarium hobby. But it shouldn't be that way.

A few energetic beginners, not so easily defeated, decide to take the plunge and set up 'High-tech' tanks. These aquariums are generally successful and quite beautiful. The problem is that High-tech aquariums require a tremendous commitment in time and money.

B.   Setting up a Basic, 'Low-Tech' Aquarium

I set up my first **true** planted aquarium about 10 years ago as an experiment. I had always kept fish successfully, but plants were another matter. I had tried many times to grow plants in my fish aquariums and had consistently failed; the plants didn't grow and the tanks were taken over by algae. This time, I decided to ignore all the many warnings from the hobbyist literature not to use sun and soil. (After all, plants and fish in natural habitats were doing well enough with sun and murky sediments?)

I placed the tank next to a large window with a Southern exposure so that the sun shone through the back of the tank for a few hours on most days. The 29 gal I used was a nice size (12" wide X 30" long X 18")– high enough that taller plants could reach their full height. The artificial light was only a single 20-watt fluorescent bulb. I layered the tank bottom with 1½" of ordinary potting soil and covered the soil layer with a 1½" layer of small, natural gravel.

At the time, I had no idea which plants would grow well in this untested setup. Therefore, I bought a wide assortment of plants– various species of swordplants, *Vallisneria*, *Bacopa*, *Ludwigia*, *Cryptocoryne*, *Aponogeton*, *Sagittaria*, etc. Many species I was unfamiliar with and some plants were not in very good condition, but I used them anyway.

I chose fish that would stay small and would not dig– neon tetras, guppies, mollies, platies, dwarf gouramis, and a male Betta. The fish seemed right at home.

Within a week the response of the plants was phenomenal. I had never seen plants in an aquarium grow like this. Plants that had been so weak and unhealthy at planting that I thought would die, slowly recovered and began to grow. The Amazon sword quickly got so big that I had to remove it. Over the years, the Crypts took over the tank and many of the other plant species gradually disappeared. Now the tank contains a massive grove of tall, red Crypts, some of the feathery stem plant *Ambulia*, and a little duckweed. It is still an attractive, easy-to-keep tank.

Since the success of that first tank, I have watched other beginners set up similar tanks with ordinary soil, lots of plants, and a little sunlight. They've been thrilled with the results.

C.   Major Factors

1.   Fish

I choose fish that will fit the tank and avoid fish that get too large as adults for their tank. (It's distressing and hard to find a home for a huge pet Oscar or a *Plecostomas*.) For 10 and 20 gal tanks, Dwarf gouramis, small tetras, dwarf cichlids, White Clouds, and Zebra danios are nice. Angelfish, Clown Loaches, the larger gouramis, Congo tetras, and Rainbows fit well in larger tanks of 50 gal or more. All of these fish are easily kept with plants.

I avoid popular but problem fish such as large cichlids. Large cichlids are exciting and exotic fish, but they do enjoy tearing up a planted tank and killing each other. For a long time, I kept a breeding colony of *Tropheus duboisi* in a planted aquarium and enjoyed them, but it was a challenge– not a project recommended for a first planted tank.

Dedicated herbivores like Silver Dollars will also cause problems by eating plants. Less obvious are problems from highly bred fish like fancy guppies and Discus. I've had problems trying to raise some (but not all) show guppies in my planted aquariums. (I believe that some strains of these fish have been bred for so many generations in sterilized surroundings that they have lost much of their natural immunity.)

Advice on fish selection in books usually tends to be sound. At specialty aquarium stores, the sales personnel are often knowledgeable and have a good idea of which fish species in the store will present the least problems. The other potential source of sound information (and good fish) is aquarium societies.

I don't like to add new fish to an established tank. Often the new fish, no matter how healthy they appear, can introduce disease into the tank or they may get picked on by the earlier inhabitants. I'd rather just enjoy the fish I have. The other alternative is to set up a quarantine tank for newly purchased fish.

Q. How do you catch fish in a heavily planted tank? (I don't like to keep plants, because it's almost impossible to catch the fish.)

A. I keep bricks or rocks at one end of my tanks in order to easily catch the fish. I herd the fish to the rock end of the tank and quickly insert a tank-divider between the fish and the rest of the tank. After removing the rocks, I can easily catch the fish without disturbing the plants and the rest of the tank.

Mosses and ferns can soften the effect of the rocks and increase total plant growth in the tank. I especially like to use lava rocks covered with Java fern or *Bolbitis* fern. Getting these plants to grow on the rocks is easy. I just secure their rhizome to the rock with string. The plants will eventually attach and cover the rock.

For breeding guppies, I keep the bottom bare except for a thin layer of gravel but add Hornwort, floating plants, and potted plants. The plants are easily removed when I need to catch the fish.

(Recommended quarantine time is at least 2 weeks.) Hobbyists that compulsively buy fish and put them directly into their large, established tanks sometimes end up with no fish.

Finally, euthanizing fish is unfortunately a reality of aquarium keeping. Fish can get incurable diseases and tumors. Healthy fish, especially livebearers and dwarf cichlids, will multiply to the point where they cannot be sold or given away. I dispose of excess fry and sick or mortally injured fish with a quick dip in ice water or carbonated water. (They are never flushed down the toilet to a cruel, lingering death in a sewer line or dark septic tank.)

Treating fish for disease, especially in established tanks, can be problematic. Although aquarium stores carry a dizzying selection of antibiotics, I have not found them to be that useful. Without a proper diagnosis, antibiotic treatment for fish is often unhelpful for the fish while potentially disastrous for the tank's ecosystem. If antibiotics are warranted, and that is a big if, fish should probably be removed from the tank and treated elsewhere.

However, there are some common diseases, usually parasitic, that are easily treated in the tank itself. New fish sometimes get 'ich', so I watch them closely and at the first sign of white spots on the fish, I'll raise the temperature to 82° for about a week until the spots clear up. And if I see fish scraping their gill covers, I'll treat the tank for external parasites (e.g., gill flukes). In one instance where my guppies were dying inexplicably, I sought help from a fish veterinarian at the local vet school. I learned that the guppies had fish nematodes (*Camallanus*) and was able to cure the problem with the appropriate 'wormer'.

2. Light

Providing adequate lighting for the planted aquarium can easily degenerate into a confusing muddle of technical terms about light intensity and wavelengths. It shouldn't be that hard. For my own tanks, I follow a few simple rules that make plant keeping easier and less expensive:

1. Use about 1-2 watts of fluorescent light per gal of tank water. (I use less if the tank is near a window or if it's a shallow tank like the 10 gal, which is only 10" deep.).
2. For tanks without window light, I use glass covers and dual strip lights with one Cool-white and one fluorescent light designed for growing plants (e.g., Sylvania 'Gro-Lux').
3. Avoid buying tall tanks (> 18 inches high) unless they will be getting window light.
4. Purchase tanks that use the more common lengths of fluorescent light (i.e., 2 ft and 4 ft bulbs), which are cheaper and often available at hardware stores.
5. Use a light-timer to automatically keep lights on 10 to 14 hours per day
6. Take full advantage of available window light.
7. Expect to replace the bulbs every year. (A typical fluorescent bulb under aquarium conditions may lose 50% of its original light intensity within 6 months [1].)

Q. I used the double lighting that you suggested, because the plants weren't growing well. That is, I used two 30 watt bulbs over my 26 gal, 3 ft long tank. As a consequence, I had a lot of trouble with algae.

So I put back the old lighting, which is an old 15 watt bulb. I'm much happier with the tank now. There is no algae on the glass, and the plants grow slowly, so I don't have to be continuously cleaning the glass and removing dead or excess plants. I think my tank contradicts all these recommendations for high lighting (2 watts/gal) to grow plants.

A. In some instances it is indeed necessary to reduce light intensity to control algae (see page 171). I would make sure, though, that some plant growth continues under your new light regime. (If rooted plants don't grow well enough to keep the root area oxygenated, the substrate and water may become increasingly contaminated over time.)

Your letter brings up an important point. That is, submerged plants don't need much light and they can adapt to very low light levels.

---

a) Window Light and Sunlight

Why sunlight, the ultimate light source, is so often disparaged in the aquarium literature is difficult for me to understand. In my opinion, window light is perfect for planted aquariums. (I actually added a window to my house, so that I could set up tanks next to it.)

Three of my tanks are positioned in front of windows with a Southern exposure. During the summer, the oak trees outside partially shade the windows. As the trees outside shed their leaves, the sunlight angles into the house more during the winter, and the plants really take off. It is at this time the swordplants and *Aponogeton* species send up their blossoms. Plants in tanks facing a Western window that receive several hours of late afternoon sun all year around do very well.

I use some fluorescent lighting in tanks that are supplemented with sunlight, but the wattage is about a third of what I need for tanks without window light. Plus, the plants seem to thrive regardless of the bulb I use; there is no need to use two different fluorescent bulbs to get a fuller spectrum.

Another reason I position my tanks near windows is to get light through the backside of the tank where sunlight reaches the shorter plants. For example, my Red Tiger Lotus tends to cover the entire surface of the 29 gal with lily pads, but the sword plants below and finally the tiny *Anubias nana* hugging the bottom thrive as well. Why? Because for a half-hour or so on most days, the shorter plants are drenched in sunlight streaming in from the tank's backside. And the plants do grow normally and not tilted sideways.

> **Q.** When I put some duckweed and *Salvinia* outside in a bucket of pondwater, they turned brown and started dying. (I was hoping to grow plants for the Goldfish in my pond.)
>
> **A.** Sunlight is at least 20 times more intense than ordinary fluorescent light. Although floating plants *Salvinia* and duckweed will thrive in sunlight, sunlight can be deadly to them if they aren't prepared for it. Your plants need a little time to synthesize protective pigments to counteract photoinhibition (mostly from UV light). I'd gradually acclimate the plants by keeping them outside in partial shade for a few days before exposing them to full sun.

It is unfortunate that sunlight has often been criticized for promoting algal growth and generating heat. A little sunlight often stimulates plant growth so there is **less** algae. During the summer, heaters can be turned off completely and the covers opened to prevent excessive heat buildup during the day. (The temperature in my tanks stays between 80 and 85° F all summer long without obvious problems.)

> **Q.** I'm having a big problem with 'green water' algae in my new planted tank, which contains soil and is near a window. The tank gets about an hour of sunlight on most days. Maybe I should move the tank away from the window?
>
> **A.** I wouldn't. One hour of sunlight is not that much. Your new tank is going through a typical adjustment period. The paradox is that the plants that can help your tank the most– fast-growers and those with the 'aerial advantage'– will need good light to grow well. Once these plants adjust and the soil 'settles down', the green water should go away. Rather than move the tank, you can always tape a light-diffusing cloth or paper temporarily to the backside of the tank. I also would make sure that the soil underlayer isn't exposed to strong window light. If the 'green-water' problem persists, you can get rid of it (see page 170). There's no need to move the tank away from a good light source.

180

b) Fluorescent Light

Fluorescent light is generally satisfactory for growing plants in most aquariums.

One investigative hobbyist [2] used the experimental method to determine the best fluorescent lights for growing 5 freshwater plants and marine macroalgae. The starting hypothesis was that Vita-Lite™, a full-spectrum fluorescent bulb, was better than other fluorescent lights. However, the experiment proved otherwise (**Fig. XI-1**). Thus, *Elodea* produced the most oxygen (>45 ml) when exposed to a combination of Cool-white and Vita-Lite. Pure Cool-white gave the next best results (>35 ml) and out-perfomed pure Vita-Lite (25 ml). Results for the other plants and algae were similar to those for *Elodea*, with all organisms producing the most photosynthetic oxygen with Cool-white combined with Vita-Lite. Again, second best for all was not pure Vita-Lite but pure Cool-white.

The fact that plants did very well with Cool-white, which produces mostly green-yellow light was an unexpected result of this study. One would have expected the plants to do better with Vita-Lite. This is because Vita-Lite was designed for growing plants; its spectrum, which is rich in red and blue light, matches the light absorption of plant chlorophyll much better than Cool-white and many other fluorescent bulbs.

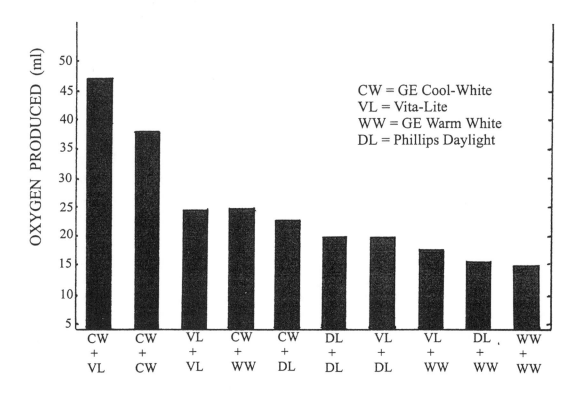

Figure XI-1. Effect of Fluorescent Lighting on *Elodea* Photosynthesis. *Elodea* was placed in sealed testtubes. 'Oxygen Produced (ml)' is the water volume displaced by the photosynthetic oxygen produced after 24 hours of continuous light from two 40 watt fluorescent lights. Figure from Richards [2] redrawn and used with permission of *Freshwater and Marine Aquarium*.

Cool-white was found to gives off 13% more photosynthetic light than Vita-Lite [3]. Perhaps Cool-white's slightly higher light intensity explains its better performance? However, I would also argue that green-yellow light is what many submerged aquatic plants encounter in their natural environment. Aquatic light is not like terrestrial light where the blue and red wavelengths predominate (**Fig. XI-2**). Aquatic light is unique. This is because the water itself (H_2O) absorbs red light, while DOC absorbs blue light. What's leftover for plant photosynthesis is mainly green-yellow light. Aquatic plants may have adapted their photosynthetic machinery (over the course of evolution) to use green-yellow light fairly efficiently. Thus, the assumption that aquatic plants grow best with full-spectrum light may not be valid.

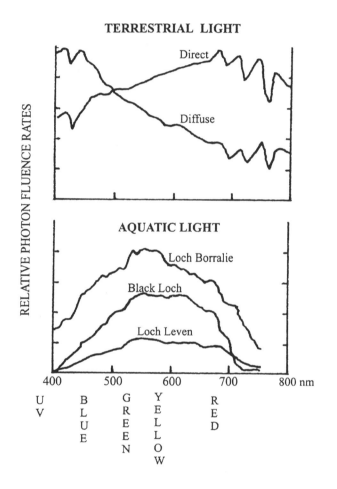

Figure XI-2. Aquatic Light versus Terrestrial Light. These spectra are from actual measurements [4]. 'Terrestrial Light' includes direct sunlight (no clouds) and diffuse light (light on an overcast day). 'Aquatic Light' was taken at a 1 meter (~ 3 ft) depth at 3 lakes in Scotland. Light intensity (μmol/m^2/s) was about 2,000 for direct light, 500 for diffuse light, 1,200 for Loch Borralie, 700 for Black Loch, and 300 for Loch Leven. [Figures modified slightly and used with permission from the *Annual Review of Plant Physiology*, Volume 33, © 1982, by Annual Reviews, www.annualreviews.org]

3. Plant Selection

Finding plants that will grow well is essential to having a natural, low-maintenance tank. Only healthy, growing plants can purify the water, protect the fish, and control algae.

Consulting other hobbyists may be helpful, but some advice on plant selection is based on generalities and misconceptions as to what constitutes good growth. For example, Amazon swordplants are sometimes mistakenly combined with Angelfish in acidic, softwater tanks, but they do much better in hardwater.

One approach to finding plants that will do well in an aquarium is just to plant as many species as possible and let the plants sort it out. This is what I do. I probably have planted over 50 different species at one time or the other. Plants that didn't grow well were lost and those that did grow well took over. I found that I could always count on the Amazon Sword-plant (*Echinodorus bleheri*), Ruffled Swordplant (*Echinodorus major*), Hornwort (*Ceratophyllum demersum*), *Limnophila*, and the Indian Fern (*Ceratopteris thalictroides*) for fast, quick growth. *Cryptocoryne wendtii*, *C. balansaea*, and Java Fern (*Microsorium ptero-pus*) take longer to establish, but once established, they grow well.

The sources of these plants were aquarium society auctions, stores, mail orders, garden pond suppliers, or other hobbyists. In addition, I've used native plants from local ponds and swamps.

In general, I would caution beginners to avoid expensive, 'showcase' plants like *Apo-nogeton madagascariensis* and the *Anubias*. Generally, expensive plants are expensive because they're hard to grow. The cheaper plants are better growers. Although cheap plants may look ragged and unattractive in the store, under the right conditions they will quickly turn a barren tank into a beautiful (and healthy) garden.

However, in the final analysis, the beginning hobbyist is best off selecting as many species as possible and finding the ones that work best for him (or her). Here is where I would focus my time, money, and energy.

D.   Guidelines in Aquarium Keeping

Tanks- I've always avoided tall, narrow tanks, because they are difficult to light. For example, the standard 55 gal is only 12" wide. There's really only room for two 48" bulbs, yet the tank is a full 22" deep. Unless this tank gets window light, plants at the bottom won't get enough light.

Small 2-5 gal tanks ('Tiny tanks') are perfect for first-time hobbyists for finding the right plant species, learning to deal with algae problems, etc. Small tanks are also easy to light with one hobbyist reporting excellent plant growth using a 'swing-arm' desk lamp containing a 13 watt fluorescent bulb over his 5 gal tank.

Tank Stands- I place a cushioning piece of wood or pressed fiber-board between the stand and the tank bottom, especially for large, heavy tanks (>20 gal). The board piece, which can be covered with a decorative adhesive paper, insulates the bottom of the tank from cold air and prevents point stresses that can cause the tank to leak or break later on.

Adequate Lighting- I prefer a combination of window light and mixed fluorescent light (see above).

Substrate- For growing plants, the bottom of the tank should be layered with something other than clean gravel or sand. I use a 1 to 1½" layer of garden soil or potting soil covered with 1 to 1½" of gravel.

Gravel- I think that the gravel used to cover the soil should be fairly small (2-3 mm), have a dull texture, and should be made out of an inert material such as silica (as opposed to calcium carbonates). Natural gravels that have a dull color and rough, porous texture are probably better than shiny, epoxy-coated gravels. Shiny gravels lack the desired cracks and crevices of natural gravel that encourage bacterial colonization (see page 125). Stones or pebble-sized gravel should **never** be used. Not only is the larger gravel inhospitable for plant roots, it can endanger the fish. (Uneaten fishfood trapped between the pebbles can rot anaerobically and pollute the entire tank, possibly killing the fish.)

Plants- I always set up my tanks with a large mass of various plant species, so that the plants can establish themselves before algae does. Emergent plant growth should be encouraged (see page 154). Because emergent plants grow so much faster than submerged plants, they can only enhance all the many benefits that plants provide.

Fish feeding- Despite warnings in the hobbyist literature, I always feed my fish well plus a little extra for the plants (see page 73). True overfeeding is evidenced by cloudy, smelly water or fishfood found rotting on the bottom the next day. (In my tanks, there are never any traces of leftover food or water cloudiness.)

Fishfoods- I buy dried foods in larger quantities, store most of it in the freezer, and keep some in a small can for everyday feeding. This way, the food is cheaper, yet doesn't lose all of its vitamin potency. I like to give my fish special treats once a week. 'Treats' include raw chicken liver, boiled egg yolk, and frozen Brine Shrimp. The treats are all stored in the freezer and chopped up before feeding.

Medications and chemicals- I avoid salts, antibiotics, copper, and dyes, which often harm the tank's ecosystem without curing the original problem. A little table salt (½ tsp/gal?), though, may be warranted in softwater aquariums; it is often prevents disease in 'hardwater fish' (e.g., mollies and Rainbows) and shouldn't hurt plants.

Moderate fish load- Tanks with a moderate fish load are healthier, easier to take care of and less vulnerable to unforeseen problems (malfunctioning filters, power outages, etc). A tank 'overstocked' with plants will be a lot less trouble than one overstocked with fish.

Catching fish- Reserve a small area at one end of the tank for portable plants. (See Q & A on page 177)

Water changes- Frequent water changes should be unnecessary in well-established tanks. (I change about 25 to 50% of the water every 6 months unless there is a problem.)

Gravel cleaning- Gravel cleaning is detrimental in planted aquariums, because it prevents nutrient replenishment of the substrate. In tanks with healthy rooted plants and a soil underlayer, gravel cleaning should be unnecessary.

Filters and water movement- Moderate water movement from filters brings nutrients to plants, oxygenates the water for both fish and bacteria, and distributes heat. But intense filtration (trickle filters, multiple filters in one tank) is unnecessary and may be detrimental in a well-planted tank (see page 111). I use 'hang-on-the-back' filters for tanks of 29 gal or less. For tanks longer than 30 inches, I use canister filters, because they efficiently (and quietly) move water from one end of the tank to the other.

To reduce tank maintenance (as well as promote plant growth), I remove the finer filtering media from the canister filters. That way I don't have to clean the filters as often and there is less chance that the filters will cause problems should they malfunction. (If the power goes off and a large mass of filter bacteria suffocates in a canister filter, their toxic remains will flood the tank when the filter starts up again.)

Charcoal filtration– Routine use may be detrimental, because it removes dissolved organic carbon (DOC), which not only helps counteract metal toxicity to fish (see page 14) but provides CO_2 and nutrients for plants (see page 58). However, under certain circumstances, such as combating a persistent algae, charcoal filtration is invaluable (see page 170). To test whether the charcoal is still 'working', I add a little food coloring to the tank in the evening; if the color doesn't disappear by morning, then its time to replace the old charcoal with fresh.

Airstones– Airstones and 'bubble wands' should only be used if the fish are showing clear signs of distress– gasping at the surface, especially in the early morning. (In this case, there's probably something very wrong with the tank.) Airstones quickly remove CO_2 from the tank and CO_2 is the one nutrient that submerged plants need more than any other nutrient. I don't use airstones in my tanks.

Pruning, thinning and transplanting– I remove excess plant growth to allow for fresh growth and the ongoing uptake of nutrients from the water. For Amazon swords and *Vallisneria*, I snip off the outer, older leaves. (*Vallisneria* shouldn't get a blunt 'haircut'.) I never cut amphibious plants like *Bacopa* or *Ludwigia* below the water line. Finally, because duckweed is such a wonderful water purifier, I don't begrudge the time I spend thinning it out.

pH– If the aquarium is balanced, the pH should be stable (see page 4). Tapwater used to fill the tanks should have a neutral or slightly acidic pH, but some municipal tapwater may have an artificially high pH, even if the water is soft. In this situation plants may not get enough free CO_2 to grow well, so it may be necessary to bring the pH down. On those rare occasions when I need to decrease the pH in my tanks, I use vinegar, which is a dilute and harmless solution of acetic acid. (In contrast to phosphate buffers, acetic acid doesn't add salts or phosphates to the tank; eventually, it simply decompose into CO_2.)

Plant fertilization– Artificial fertilization of plants with CO_2, trace elements, and macronutrients is unnecessary if the tank contains a fertile substrate, the fish are fed well, and the tank is not being constantly cleaned. I don't add fertilizers to my tanks.

Water hardness– Ideally, the water should not be too soft. (**Table XI-2** shows a classification of water based on water hardness.) Softwater is depleted of the hardwater nutrients (Ca, Mg, K, S, and Cl). In addition, it often has a low alkalinity that can mean rapid changes in pH. Softwater can't support good general plant growth. Floating plants, in particular, will need some water hardness. Hobbyists with softwater (0-60 ppm $CaCO_3$) may need to make some adjustments to their tanks (see page 87).

Table XI-2. Water Hardness Categories

Classification	ppm or mg/l $CaCO_3$	GH or °dH (German degrees of water hardness)
Soft	0-60 ppm	0-3
Slightly hard	61-121	4-7
Hard	121-180	7-10
Very hard	>180	>11

Note: Water hardness (combined Ca and Mg concentrations) is reported by water treatment plants as ppm $CaCO_3$. Hobbyist test kits, however, usually quantify water hardness as GH. (Each 17.8 ppm of $CaCO_3$ water hardness is equal to one GH.)

Chlorine and chloramine- If you are using municipal water, it is important to know if it contains chlorine or chloramine before ever setting up an aquarium; either one can quickly kill fish. Chlorine can be removed by degassing– letting the water stand overnight in a separate container before adding it to the tank. Chloramines need to be removed by using specific water conditioners.

Snails- Although snails are frequently disparaged by some aquarium hobbyists, they are actually quite useful in the aquarium. First, snails clean plant leaves of debris, algae, and bacteria (see page 44). Second, they greatly speed up the decomposition process, so that nutrients are recycled much more quickly to plants. Some snails, such as Malaysian Trumpet snails, dig into the gravel, thereby providing beneficial water circulation and aeration of the substrate. Many fish, including Clown loaches, Bettas, and cichlids, relish snails. (In fact, these fish can be added to the tank to control excessive snail populations.) I keep snails in all of my aquariums.

Temperature- I've given up on trying to keep my tanks at a constant and supposedly ideal 78° F. (The temperature in my tanks varies from 72 - 85° F degrees depending on the season, tank's heater, etc.) In the summer months, I turn the tank heaters off completely and open up the top covers to promote air circulation underneathe the lights. (On especially hot days, I keep a fan on nearby.) The fish and plants in my tanks seem to have adapted to seasonal temperature changes without evidencing obvious problems.

REFERENCES

1. Horst K and Kipper HE. 1986. The Optimum Aquarium. AD aquadocumenta Verlag GmbH (Bielefeld, West-Germany), p. 38.
2. Richards K. 1987. The effects of different spectrum fluorescent bulbs on the photosynthesis of aquatic plants. Freshwater and Marine Aquarium (July issue), pp. 16-20.
3. Mohan P. 1998. Converting foot-candles or Lux to PAR: Values for some common fluorescent lamps, and what to do with them. The Aquatic Gardener 11(6): 182-190.
4. Smith H. 1982. Light quality, photoperception, and plant strategy. Ann. Rev. Plant Physiol. 33: 481-518.

Abbreviations and Conversions

Abbreviation	Explanation
Chl	chlorophyll
cm	centimeter (0.01 m or 0.39 inch)
DIC	dissolved inorganic carbon ($CO_2 + HCO_3^- + CO_3^{2-}$)
DOC	dissolved organic carbon
e	electron
g	gram (0.001 kg)
gal	gallon (3.79 liters)
GH	General Hardness. See page 185
h, hr	hour
ha	hectare (2.47 acres)
HS	humic substances
IFAS	Institute of Food and Agricultural Sciences (Univ. of Florida, Gainesville)
Kcal	kilocalorie (unit of energy = 1,000 calories)
kg	kilogram (1,000 g or 2.2 lbs)
KH	carbonate hardness. See page 91
l	liter (0.26 gal)
μeq	microequivalent
μg	microgram (0.001 mg)
μm	micrometer (0.001 mm or 1 micron)
μM	micromolar (0.001 mM)
μmhos	measure of specific conductance [μmhos/cm = (R of 0.00702 N KCl $\div$ R of sample) X 1000] where R is the electrical resistance in ohms
μmol	micromole (molecular wt. of compound in μg); for example, a μmol of $CuSO_4$, which has a molecular wt. of 160, would by 160 μg
μmol/m^2/s	measure of light quantitation (see explanation on page 147)
M	molar (moles/liter) or (g/l divided by the compound's molecular wt)
m	meter (3.3 feet)
meq	milliequivalent = 1,000 μeq
mg	milligram (0.001 g)
min	minute

mM	millimolar (0.001 M) or 1 millimole/l
mm	millimeter (0.1 cm or 0.001 meter)
mmhos	measure of specific conductance = 1,000 μmhos (see μmhos above)
mo.	month
mT	metric ton (1,000 kg)
mV	millivolt
nm	nanometer (0.001 μm)
ppm	parts per million (can mean either mg/l or mg/kg)
RNA	ribonucleic acid
RUBISCO	ribulose bisphosphate carboxylase/oxygenase (major photosynthetic enzyme for 'fixing' carbon)
wt.	weight

mg/l v. molarity v. equivalents

Molarity defines the concentration of a compound in solution, **plus** adjusts for that compound's weight. In some instances, it is a better term than mg/l or ppm when comparing one compound with another. Table II-1 on page 9 compares the toxicities of several metals based on molarity– not identical mg/l. An investigator would probably not compare, for example, lead (Pb) and chromium (Cr) using a 1 mg/l solution of each. This is because Pb has an atomic wt. that is almost four times greater than Cr's (i.e., 207 v. 52). If an investigator used 1 mg/l solutions for toxicity testing, organisms would be exposed to almost 4 times more Cr atoms than Pb atoms. This is an 'unfair' comparison heavily biased to make Cr look more toxic than Pb. For Table II-1, however, the investigator compared toxicity on a molar basis. He/she probably used 1 mM solutions (i.e., 207 mg/l of Pb and 52 mg/l of Cr) to conclude– correctly– that Pb was more toxic to fish than Cr.

Related terms meq and μeq are further refinements. They not only adjust for the atom's weight, but its electrical charge. In instances where electrical charge influences something like binding or electrical conductivity, this term is most appropriate. For example, every mg of DOC is said to bind 1 μeq of metal (see page 15). We must assume that each mg of DOC has a fixed number of negative charges, so how much metal it binds will be influenced by the metal ion's electrical charge (i.e., valence). Thus, the copper ion (Cu^{2+}) will bind to two negative charges, whereas the aluminum ion (Al^{3+}) will instead bind to **three** negative charges. In this example, a μeq of Cu is 32 μg– copper's atomic wt (in μg) of 64 ÷ 2, while a μeq of Al is 9 μg– aluminum's atomic wt (in μg) of 27 ÷ 3. Thus, a mg of DOC will bind 32 μg of copper but only 9 μg of aluminum.

Examples of the overall relationship of mg/l to molar concentration to equivalents are:

Copper (Cu^{2+})	**Aluminum (Al^{3+})**
64 g/l = 1 M = 2 eq (equivalents)/l	27 g/l = 1 M = 3 eq (equivalents)/l
64 mg/l = 1 mM = 2 meq/l	27 mg/l = 1 mM = 3 meq/l
64 μg/l = 1 μM = 2 μeq/l	27 μg/l = 1 μM = 3 μeq/l

NOTES

Disclaimer Notice for Permissions

The publisher has made every effort to contact copyright holders prior to publication. However, in some instances, this has been impossible. If notified, the publisher will be pleased to rectify any omissions in future editions of this book.

Correspondence and Ordering Information

Correspondence:

Diana Walstad
Echinodorus Publishing
2303 Mt. Sinai Rd.
Chapel Hill, NC 27514 (U.S.A.)
Or:

dwalstad@bellsouth.net

For additional books, send personal check or money order to above address made out to Diana Walstad. Sorry, no credit cards. *Please* be sure to include your address with order.

Book Cost: $29.95 plus shipping (U.S. dollars)

Shipping: $3.50 for U.S.
$5 for Canada (please allow several weeks for delivery)
Europe, South America, Africa, and Pacific Rim (contact author for rates)

NC Sales Tax: North Carolina residents should include 6% sales tax (of book price only).

Shipping Schedule: Books will normally be shipped *within* one week of receiving order/payment.

Important: All prices guaranteed through the year 2002. After that (in the evident of printing or postage increases), costs may be subject to change without notice.